The Hospital on Seminary Ridge
at the Battle of Gettysburg

The Hospital on Seminary Ridge at the Battle of Gettysburg

by MICHAEL A. DREESE

WITH A FOREWORD BY FREDERICK K. WENTZ

McFarland & Company, Inc., Publishers
Jefferson, North Carolina, and London

In loving memory of my grandfather, Harvey Clay Dreese (1925–2001)
Corporal, World War II, 406th Signal Company, Aviation
You will be missed, but never forgotten.

Library of Congress Cataloging-in-Publication Data

Dreese, Michael A., 1963–
    The hospital on Seminary Ridge at the Battle of Gettysburg / by Michael A. Dreese;
with a foreword by Frederick K. Wentz.
        p.   cm.
    Includes bibliographical references and index.
    ISBN 0-7864-1224-0 (illustrated case binding : 50# alkaline paper) ∞
    1. Gettysburg (Pa.), Battle of, 1863.   2. United States— History — Civil War,
1861–1865 — Hospitals.   3. Military hospitals— Pennsylvania — Gettysburg — History —
19th century.   4. Theological seminaries— Pennsylvania — Gettysburg — History —
19th century.   5. Gettysburg (Pa.)—Church history — 19th century.   I. Title.
E475.53 .D764 2002
973.7'349 — dc21   2001052112

British Library cataloguing data are available

Manufactured in the United States of America

On the cover: A sketch of the campus in 1876
(Courtesy of the Lutheran Theological Seminary, Gettysburg)

McFarland & Company, Inc., Publishers
Box 611, Jefferson, North Carolina 28640
www.mcfarlandpub.com

Contents

Abbreviations in Photograph Credits

ACHS   Adams County Historical Society, Gettysburg, Pennsylvania
FM   Archives and Special Collections, Franklin and Marshall College, Lancaster,
         Pennsylvania
LC   Library of Congress, Washington D.C.
LTSG   Abdel Ross Wentz Library, Lutheran Theological Seminary at Gettysburg
NMHM   National Museum of Health and Medicine, Washington, D.C.
PSA   Pennsylvania State Archives, Harrisburg, Pennsylvania
USAMHI   United States Army Military History Institute, Carlisle Barracks, Pennsylvania

Acknowledgments

As the author of this work, I accept the blame for any errors or inaccuracies which appear on the pages before you. At the same time, I will not accept full credit for the book's positive features, because while this study might have been completed without the assistance of the following people, its quality and usefulness would have been diminished.

Frederick K. Wentz, Professor Emeritus of Church History, Lutheran Theological Seminary at Gettysburg, deserves first mention. Fred provided me with much-needed support and encouragement from the initial stages of this project until the very end. He also took the time to read through my entire manuscript, offered valuable suggestions for improvements, and shared his wealth of knowledge on the history of the Seminary.

I also owe a huge debt of gratitude to fellow author and historian Timothy Smith, who directed my attention to a number of sources that would have otherwise escaped my notice. When it comes to historical research, he has few equals. Tim also asked me a number of probing questions which helped me to better develop my subject matter. Thanks also to my good friend Peter Wilson for his diligent proofreading efforts.

Historians Seward Osborne, Olivebridge, New York; Keith Snipes, Willard, Ohio; and Gregory A. Coco, Bendersville, Pennsylvania, provided me with useful material from their research files. Mr. Coco's books on the Gettysburg field hospitals and the aftermath of the battle were invaluable reference tools and laid the foundation for this volume.

The Gettysburg Licensed Battlefield Guides (LBGs) are an excellent resource for those writing on any aspect of the Gettysburg Campaign. This book benefited from the previous research work of LBGs Timothy Smith, Jim Clouse, Fred Hawthorne, and Roy Frampton. I extend my heartfelt thanks to LBG Diana Loski, editor of *The Gettysburg Experience,* a monthly history and community events magazine. I have developed a close relationship with Diana and her husband, Leonard, as a contributing author to their fine publication. Diana has always been an ardent supporter of my work. As a fellow author, she truly understands the complexities of balancing a passion for writing with family and career.

Mr. Clair P. Lyons sent me valuable information and a rare photograph of his ancestor, Sarah Broadhead, and cleared up several popular misconceptions about her life.

Much of my research for this book was conducted at two facilities on the campus of the Lutheran Theological Seminary at Gettysburg. Old Dorm, the institution's first building, and the primary focus of this study, is now the home of the Adams County Historical Society. I wish to thank Dr. Charles Glatfelter and Elwood "Woody" Christ for their assistance during my frequent visits there.

Across the street at the Abdel Ross Wentz Library, Sara Mummert guided me through the archives of the Seminary and made me feel right at home. She courteously responded to my numerous requests for documents and located a number of photographic images for my use. The Reverend John R. Spangler, Director of Communications, provided useful statistics on the post-war development of the institution.

As in all my past research projects, I utilized the vast resources of the United States Army Military History Institute, Carlisle Barracks, Pennsylvania. The voluminous library of this facility contains many rare books, periodicals, and valuable reference volumes not readily found elsewhere, and the photo archives contain one of the most comprehensive collections of Civil War images in the United States. The assistance of Richard J. Sommers, Michael Winey, and Randy Hackenberg is duly noted.

A special thanks goes out to Alan Hawk, Historical Collections Manager, and Dr. Lenore Barbian, Assistant Curator of Anatomical Collections, at the Armed Forces Institute of Pathology, for their courtesy and professional guidance during my visit to the National Museum of Health and Medicine, Washington, D.C. I urge anyone with an interest in the field of Civil War medicine to visit this national treasure.

John Heiser, whose cartographic skills have been highlighted in *The Gettysburg Magazine*, provided the excellent maps for this book. It is always a pleasure to work with him.

Thanks also to the following individuals and organizations: Michael R. Lear, Archives and Special Collections Assistant, Shadek-Fackenthal Library, Franklin and Marshall College, Lancaster, Pennsylvania; Rod Clare, Reference Intern, Special Collections, Duke University, Durham, North Carolina; Caryl Gray, Librarian, Virginia Polytechnic Institute and State University, Blacksburg, Virginia; D. Scott Hartwig and John Heiser, Gettysburg National Military Park Library; Michael Musick, National Archives, Washington, D.C.; Karen Drickamer, Head of Special Collections, Musselman Library, Gettysburg College; Bonnie Weatherly, Assistant to the Archivist, Daughters of Charity, St. Joseph's Provincial House, Emmitsburg, Maryland; Beutonne McKean, Greenville, Illinois; and Chris Conti, Gettysburg, Pennsylvania.

I have saved the most important acknowledgment for last. Mere words could never express my full appreciation for the understanding of my wife, Heather, and our two children, Brooke and Shane, but these few lines will have to suffice. They have patiently indulged my love for history and the writing craft, while pretending to believe my oft made promise to "take a break" after the completion of my current project.

Foreword

Michael Dreese has pulled off an unusual feat. And he has done it well. He has combined careful and detailed history with attention-catching anecdote. But he has done more than that.

This volume combines church history and military history in an intriguing way. This in itself is rare, but the book also boasts an even more unusual achievement: it combines seminary history with Civil War medicine and hospital experience. This is brought off with flair by focusing upon one major hospital during and after the Battle of Gettysburg, namely, Schmucker Hall or "Old Dorm" at the Lutheran Theological Seminary at that battlefield.

Until recently, the Civil War events described in this book were little known by most historians. Why? Because they took place on the campus of a theological school.

The Seminary — intent for its 175 years upon training leaders for the Lutheran Church — has not cultivated the story of its involvement in the battle. There are no monuments on its 52 acres. Tourists have traditionally been considered a diversion from the task at hand. Yet, late on Day One of the battle, the seminary was the center of one of the fiercest attacks. Its building provided a signal tower and was the first used as a major refuge for casualties. Recent decades have brought so much research and writing on the Battle of Gettysburg that there has now emerged from the Seminary's life an independent Seminary Ridge Historic Preservation Foundation dedicated to the care and the best use for public education of the three historic buildings on campus.

I was born and raised in the Schmucker House, where Confederate soldiers ransacked and ravaged the papers of an abolitionist resident. I spent many hours playing Civil War in the fields nearby, and later gave informal tours for 50 cents. For three years, as a seminarian in the 1940s, I lived in Schmucker Hall, that former hospital. Returning in retirement I have been amazed at the outpouring of research and writing on the battle, especially during the past decade, with its intriguing bits and pieces about what happened at the Seminary. My father, whose history of the Seminary decades ago had a good chapter on the battle and the Seminary, would be astonished at the ever-growing interest in the battle and in the Seminary's role. Michael Dreese has pulled it all together in a readable volume, drawing on the best secondary sources and especially upon his own extensive, patient research.

It is interesting how much history one building can relate. It is equally engaging to see what threads of history and human ties bring people to that building's doors. But most compelling are the many stories, uncovering human nature in all its depth and variety, when crisis forces people out of their routines—women rising to levels of caring they hardly knew they were capable of, and men in great pain facing the loss of their dreamed future.

One of the encouraging features of contemporary research and writing on the Battle of Gettysburg is the movement beyond heroics and battle strategy into the life experience of soldiers and civilians, the wounded and those who served them. The heroic remains, but the harsh reality of the price of warfare is laid bare.

Michael Dreese has made a fine contribution to this endeavor, even as he provides an interesting story and many readable anecdotes.

Frederick K. Wentz
Professor Emeritus of Church
    History
Lutheran Theological Seminary,
    Gettysburg
Summer 2001

Introduction

"So many pathetic scenes took place during those days."

For nearly 170 years, westbound travelers departing Gettysburg have been treated to the sight of a stately four-story brick building with a prominent white cupola standing majestically atop Seminary Ridge. This impressive structure served as the first classroom and dormitory of the Gettysburg Lutheran Theological Seminary, which is recognized today as the oldest Lutheran school of theology in the Western Hemisphere.

Remarkably, "Old Dorm," as it came to be known, nearly disappeared from the Gettysburg skyline. In the late 1950s, serious consideration was given to razing the building since it was no longer suitable for its original purpose and had deteriorated to the point of condemnation following an extended period of vacancy. Fortunately, concerned citizens and preservation groups interceded and Old Dorm was spared the wrecking ball. Eventually, the historic edifice was restored to its original condition, and in 1974, it was placed on the National Register of Historic Places.

But this book is not merely a history of a building; it is more a study of the rich cast of characters who passed through its rooms and halls. Throughout its long history, the Gettysburg Seminary has been a progressive leader in social reform and equality. Samuel Simon Schmucker, the chief founder and first president of the institution, was an outspoken abolitionist, and there is evidence that his campus home functioned as a station on the Underground Railroad. One of the most distinguished early alumni of the school was Daniel Payne, a freeman from South Carolina. Later, it was the first Lutheran school of theology to admit females to a degree program and the first to elect a woman to its faculty as a full professor.

The institution has survived periods of internal discord, competition from rival schools, the Great Depression, and two world wars. But no event in its rich history has left a deeper mark than the American Civil War. From 1861 to 1865, American Lutherans and their fellow countrymen were deeply divided on political, economical, and ideological issues.

In the summer of 1863, the Seminary witnessed the horrors of war first-hand during Confederate general Robert E. Lee's invasion of Pennsylvania. On July 1, the opening day of the Battle of Gettysburg, advance elements of the two great armies

The Lutheran Theological Seminary, Gettysburg, viewed from the east. Courtesy of MOLLUS, USAMHI.

clashed just west and north of the town. Some of the bloodiest fighting of the three-day battle took place on the Seminary campus. The once peaceful and picturesque grounds of the school were littered with the dead and wounded of both armies.

From the very outset, Old Dorm, standing like a bastion in the midst of the terrible storm, offered a place of refuge for the wounded. Located close to the battle lines, it was first utilized by Federal surgeons as a large aid station. When the Confederates pushed the Union forces back through the town to Cemetery Hill during the late afternoon, several hundred wounded Union soldiers were trapped behind enemy lines. As the battle raged nearby, many of these captives died from a lack of medical attention and inadequate food and water.

Following the battle, the commodious building and campus housed between 600 and 700 wounded soldiers from both armies. With the notable exception of Camp Letterman, the large government hospital established along the York Pike, the Seminary Hospital was the largest and most important medical facility at Gettysburg, and it was among the last to close its doors. Within its sturdy walls, suffering and death did not discriminate. They struck Northerner and Southerner, the wealthy and the poor, the articulate and the illiterate, the young and old alike.

The hospital witnessed a timeless story of ordinary individuals struggling to adapt to a chaotic environment where life hangs precariously by a thread. This intense trauma triggered a variety of conflicting emotions and responses: joy and sorrow, bravery and cowardice, personal sacrifice and selfishness, humor and pathos.

For instance, an 18-year-old Union officer displayed tremendous courage and dignity in his darkest hour. After being informed of the mortal nature of his wounds, he stoically replied, "I am a very young man, but I am willing to die for my country."[1]

This kind of valiant behavior was not limited to soldiers. Gettysburg resident Sarah Broadhead overcame her initial repugnance upon viewing the horrid conditions inside the hospital and returned to nurse there at regular intervals. Her humanitarian efforts, together with those of other altruistic individuals and relief agencies, did much to alleviate the suffering of the wounded at a time when the few available medical personnel were severely overtaxed. The fortitude and skill of women like Sarah helped to erase many long-held stereotypes pertaining to the female sex.

The plight of the Ziegler family provides an illustrative example of how innocent civilians were caught up in the maelstrom of war. Emanuel and Mary Ziegler, the steward and matron of the Seminary, lived on the basement story of the building with their five children. The family was forced to flee their home when the fighting escalated on July 1st.

Following a five-day exile, they returned only to discover that nearly all of their possessions had been destroyed and the remainder converted to medical uses. But the family forgot their own losses and settled in to help take care of the wounded. Even after the passage of nearly four decades, Lydia Ziegler, a teenager at the time of the battle, found it difficult to dwell on the subject. "So many pathetic scenes took place during those days," she recalled painfully.[2]

Indeed, for the rich cast of characters assembled at the Seminary during and after the battle, life would never be the same. The dramatic events through which they lived would forever shape their personalities and perceptions.

There were a number of factors that led me to write about this compelling story. First, I am descended from a long line of Pennsylvania German Lutherans and am proud of my religious heritage. Secondly, I gathered a considerable amount of primary source material on the Seminary, particularly the hospital period, while conducting research for my first two books. I was thus gradually drawn towards the subject until it eventually took on a life of its own.

Thanks to the popularity of the motion picture *Gettysburg,* most history enthusiasts know that the cupola of Old Dorm served as an observation point and as a signal station for both armies. It is also well documented that General Lee's headquarters were established on Seminary Ridge. However, few visitors to the battlefield are aware of the important role played by the Seminary's buildings and campus as a hospital facility.

This oversight is understandable considering the fact that, of the thousands of books devoted to the Gettysburg campaign, relatively few have focused on the aftermath of the battle. In his landmark study of Gettysburg field hospitals, *A Vast Sea of Misery,* historian Gregory A. Coco notes in his section pertaining to the Lutheran Seminary: "There are several sites in this book which, alone, contain almost enough research material to warrant an individual study. This is one of them."[3]

I couldn't agree more. During my research, I compiled a number of excellent first-hand accounts concerning this hospital from soldiers, surgeons, relief agency personnel, and local civilians. Together these documents provide us with a compelling, and sometimes graphic, first-person view of a forgotten chapter in Gettysburg's rich history.

Although a considerable portion of this study is focused on the hospital period from July to September of 1863, I have also devoted sections to the pre-war and post-war history of the Seminary, including President Schmucker's role in the abolition movement. By presenting this material, much of it for the first time, I hope to reveal the full significance of one of Gettysburg's most familiar landmarks. The sight of that stately old building should serve as a reminder of the terrible price of war, as well as a beacon of hope for future generations.

Michael Dreese
Kreamer, Pennsylvania

Prologue

In the heavens a tent is set up for the sun.
It rises like a bridegroom
*   and gets ready like a hero eager to run a race.*
It travels all the way across the sky.
Nothing hides from its heat.

Psalm 19, verses 4–6[1]

At 8:45 on the morning of June 28, 1866, two colleagues in the Pennsylvania School Department boarded the cars at the railroad depot in the state capital of Harrisburg. Their destination: Gettysburg. One of the travelers, Professor Samuel P. Bates, had recently been appointed as State Historian. Bates' companion that morning was 32-year-old George F. McFarland, who three years earlier had led the 151st Pennsylvania Volunteers into combat at Gettysburg on the opening day of the battle.[2] His command fought gallantly, but was cut to ribbons, suffering the second highest number of casualties incurred by any Northern unit during the three days of fighting from July 1 to 3, 1863.[3]

George was among the regiment's numerous wounded. His severe injuries had necessitated the amputation of his right leg several inches below the knee joint and irreparably shattered his left ankle. As a result, he hobbled about on crutches and a wooden leg.[4] The physical scars were clearly visible. Would his first visit to the battlefield since that fateful day in July open new emotional scars, or would it help soothe the painful memories?

The train clattered out of the city along the tracks of the Northern Central Railroad. For a time the route paralleled the wide and picturesque Susquehanna River. The train continued on its southerly course, passing through the city of York, and then proceeded on to Hanover Junction. There, the pair embarked on the last leg of their journey aboard the Hanover, Hanover Junction, and Gettysburg Railroad. After a pleasant ride, the engine squealed into the station on Carlisle Street at 1 P.M.[5]

After partaking of dinner at a local hotel, the pair secured a carriage and spent the balance of the afternoon touring the field of the first day's fighting. At the outset, McFarland studied the terrain analytically, and he readily traced the various positions and movements of his regiment. Later, the tour turned more introspective when he stood among a fine grove of

7

hardwoods on the campus of the Lutheran Theological Seminary.[6]

Although the topography was largely unchanged, the debris of battle was no longer evident. The hastily prepared breastworks of earth and fence rails had been dismantled. The rotting corpses of man and beast no longer poisoned the fresh summer air. Gone, too, were the scattered muskets, canteens, bayonets, articles of clothing, and other accoutrements of battle. The restorative capacity of nature had covered the scars of war with a luxuriant growth of vegetation.

But evidence of the tragedy still remained. The western sides of the trees were thickly marked by bullet holes from the ground up to the height of a man.[7] For McFarland, this discovery might have triggered vivid images: the unearthly screams and shouted orders; the sickening thud of lead striking human flesh and bone; the deafening roar of thousands of muskets mingled with the deeper booming of the artillery; the fiendish look of the combatants, with black powder and blood smeared on their faces; the dense cloud of white, acrid smoke that hung over the ridge line, casting a surreal backdrop to the hellish scene.

In that terrible battle McFarland had fallen to the ground towards the enemy; then, an instant later, he had been lifted up by one of his men, who had dragged his limp body into the sanctuary of the large brick building a short distance to the rear, where surgeons manned a primary aid station. The severely wounded officer joined the masses of suffering humanity who occupied the bare floors and halls of this once peaceful religious institution — a strange juxtaposition! Trapped behind enemy lines, George lay helplessly in puddles of his own blood without food, drink, or medical attendance for three days.[8] A decidedly religious man, he must have believed in retrospect that providence had sustained him through the terrible ordeal.

Now the war was over — and through the invitation of Seminary professor Charles Hay, McFarland entered the building by the same door through which he had been carried moments after his wounding.[9] The Seminary was once again functioning in its intended purpose: to train young men for the ministry.

How different were the scenes in 1863: the pitiful groans of wounded soldiers and their desperate cries for water, the sickening rasp of the surgeon's saw as it sliced through bone, the constant buzzing of hordes of flies, and the overpowering smell of blood and decay. How much quieter and safer now than on July 3rd of that year, when a stray artillery shell had crashed through the wall, barely missing McFarland's head. Later on that same evening, he had been placed on an operating table, where his damaged limb was removed. Two and a half months had elapsed before his wounds mended sufficiently to permit his traveling home to McAlisterville, Pennsylvania. McFarland was the very last patient to leave the building.[10] During his protracted stay, he witnessed the intense suffering, and occasionally the deaths, of an untold number of comrades.

McFarland's 1866 tour of the Seminary culminated with him being carried up into the building's famous cupola to enjoy a bird's-eye view of the battlefield.[11] As he scanned the familiar killing ground, did the former officer pray that the terrible sacrifice of his men had not been in vain?

For McFarland it would be the first of several visits to Gettysburg. One of the most significant of these pilgrimages took place in June 1882, when government historian John B. Bachelder hosted a reunion principally of soldiers engaged in the first day's fighting. The grizzled veterans arrived from all parts of the country: from

Vermont and North Carolina, Wisconsin and Alabama, Indiana and Mississippi, Maine and South Carolina, Maryland, New York, and from all parts of Pennsylvania.

Unlike in 1863, the townspeople were prepared for this encounter between the Blue and the Gray, and a large public reception was held in the courthouse for the arriving guests. On behalf of the citizens of the community, Robert G. McCreary delivered a brief welcoming speech "bidding all of the gentlemen present a cordial welcome to the hospitality of the town."[12]

Much of the next day was spent verifying troop positions and movements during the opening day of the battle. Remarkably, the former combatants agreed on nearly all of the details.

Although nearly two decades had passed since the decisive struggle, at least one of the Southern delegates continued to lament the lost opportunities at Gettysburg. Isaac R. Trimble, now 80 years of age and feisty as ever, took center stage during the tour as he had so often done throughout his colorful life.

In rich detail, the old general delivered his commentary on how the entire battle was lost during the early evening of July 1st. The salient point of this argument was that his superior, General Richard S. Ewell, failed to seize Culp's Hill after the Confederates pushed the Northern troops back through the streets of Gettysburg. According to Trimble, he urgently pressed Ewell to occupy this strategic height as the position would command the entire area and make the Union position untenable. When his pleadings fell on deaf ears, Isaac stormed away in a rage.[13]

Two days later, he commanded a division during "Pickett's Charge." Shot from his horse during the assault, Trimble became a prisoner of war and was as much of a thorn in the side to his captors as he had been to Ewell. He was eventually placed in a room in the Seminary under an armed guard before being transferred to Fort McHenry. Like McFarland, Trimble's injuries required the amputation of a limb, his left leg.[14] Although far apart in ideology and in their views of the battle, the two men shared a mutual respect for one another due to their common suffering.

The reunion was no doubt an enlightening experience for all of the attendees. A newspaper correspondent reported that the contingent of visiting veterans departed the battlefield "apparently much pleased with their visit."[15]

The 1880s marked a period of intense interest in the battlefield, and by the end of the decade most of the Union regiments present at Gettysburg had erected a monument on the field to commemorate their deeds and to honor their fallen comrades. On July 1, 1888, George McFarland delivered the keynote address at the dedication of the 151st Pennsylvania's regimental monument on McPherson's Ridge. He concluded his speech with the following admonishment: "...let us not forget to impress upon all, especially the young, the great principles for which we fought and suffered."[16]

Twenty-five years earlier, nowhere had this suffering been more prevalent than within the walls of the Lutheran Theological Seminary, visible just over McFarland's shoulder as he spoke.

CHAPTER 1

The Seminary Comes to Gettysburg

LORD God All-Powerful, your temple is so lovely!
Deep in my heart I long for your temple,
and with all that I am I sing joyful songs to you.
Psalm 84, verses 1–2

On March 2, 1826, Professor Samuel Simon Schmucker and nine board members of the Theological Seminary of the Evangelical Lutheran Church met in Hagerstown, Maryland. A weighty decision hung in the balance — where to locate the permanent home of an institution dedicated to the training of English-speaking pastors for the growing congregations of Lutherans in America. The committee labored well into the night as it discussed the merits of the proposals that had been received from three potential sites: Carlisle and Gettysburg, in Pennsylvania, and Hagerstown. The latter location emerged as the front-runner, enjoying a homefield advantage and the endorsement of the influential Schmucker, who had been born there 27 years earlier.

Somehow, however, Gettysburg emerged victorious, receiving the near unanimous support of the delegates on the second ballot. Besides offering the largest financial inducement ($7,000 of subscrip-tions), the trustees of the Adams County Academy offered the use of their spacious building until the Seminary was able to construct a facility of its own. In addition, the Pennsylvania community was centrally located among the scattered congregations of Lutherans residing in the mid–Atlantic region and it was readily accessible from the large population centers of Baltimore, Washington, Philadelphia, and Harrisburg via a network of turnpikes which intersected at the town square. Furthermore, the prospects for growth were favorable since Gettysburg served as the county seat of Adams County.[1]

Besides these obvious qualities, there were intangibles that undoubtedly played a role in the selection process. The rural flavor and scenic surroundings of Gettysburg may have influenced the board, while one member cited "the healthiness of the place, and the morality of its inhabitants."[2]

Mary Cecilia Kendlehart, a 17-year-old student at the Female Institute in

Gettysburg, extolled the progressive spirit and the literary traditions of her hometown in a composition she wrote in the spring of 1860. Mary observed that "a refined, intelligent, and enterprising society" prevailed in the community, which from its first settlement during the colonial period had been "noted for the great exertions they have made for the advancement of education."[3]

Dr. Henry Eyster Jacobs, a renowned Lutheran theologian and professor, also noted the educational heritage of his hometown in his memoirs. "The intellectual standard of Gettysburg was high even before the founding of the college," he wrote.[4] Whatever the reasons for its ultimate selection, thenceforward the history of the Lutheran Theological Seminary would be inextricably linked to that of Gettysburg.

Following this historic decision, the board completed other business matters. A constitution was adopted, financial solicitors were appointed, and the first Wednesday of September was selected as the inauguration date of the new institution. Finally, after a laborious session, the meeting adjourned at 1 A.M. on March 3rd. After turning in for a few hours of much-needed sleep, the party set out at daybreak for a close-up inspection of Gettysburg. The 30-mile journey, by horseback over unimproved roads, took all day to complete. The travelers reached their destination an hour after sunset.

It did not take long for Professor Schmucker to form a favorable impression of the community. Late in the evening, although surely exhausted from the trip, he took the time to write his wife of the momentous events of the last two days. Optimism and exuberance pervaded his thoughts. "[I] am happy to tell you, my dear wife, that I believe the Seminary is located in the proper place, in the place which promotes the greatest happiness for us, but also the greatest usefulness for the church of our Redeemer ... & I believe that after I tell you all the circumstances, you would have chosen this place yourself."[5] The professor estimated the town's population at 1,100. It was duly noted that not only Lutherans, but the Presbyterian and Methodist congregations as well, were extremely anxious to have the Seminary located in their midst. A local newspaper verified Schmucker's observation, reporting that "many of the respectable citizens of this county expect considerable advantages to result from the location of the Seminary in our borough."[6]

But behind all of the euphoria there was a great deal of concern among the founders of the new institution. They had no way of knowing how many, indeed, if any, students would appear in Gettysburg for the first semester. Years later, a former student recalled the six months prior to the opening day as "a period of painful anxiety and apprehension."[7]

The founding of an educational facility was the culmination of three-quarters of a century of Lutheran settlement in the New World. The first Lutherans to arrive on American shores were part of the Dutch West India Company's trading posts along the Hudson River in the 1620s. A decade later, a contingent of Swedish Lutherans founded a colony in present-day Delaware.

The first substantial numbers of Americans practicing this faith hailed from Germany. Beginning in the late 17th century, these immigrants flooded into William Penn's new colony in pursuit of religious freedom and new opportunity. By 1750, at least 40,000 German Lutherans were living in Pennsylvania. Groups of these pioneers soon pushed westward across the Susquehanna River, spilling into Maryland and Virginia via the Cumberland and Shenandoah Valleys. Meanwhile, other Germans settled in the Carolinas and Georgia. Lutheran leaders in America now faced a difficult problem — how to provide pastors for their scattered and growing congregations.[8]

The popularity of Lutheranism in America was rooted in its growing influence throughout Europe. Martin Luther, a German Augustinian monk and theology professor at the University of Wittenberg in Saxony, sparked the Protestant Reformation in the early 1500s with his bold attacks on the Roman Catholic Church. Luther argued that the essence of Christianity lay not in an elaborate organization headed by the pope, but rather in each individual's personal relationship with God. He also attacked the sale of indulgences and other excesses of the religious hierarchy. Luther's protest weakened the dominance of Catholicism, and his widespread influence firmly ensconced the Protestant faith in Europe, and subsequently, in the New World.[9]

Not surprisingly, the ministerial needs of the early American Lutherans were first provided by temporary missionaries from the motherland. Later, as the numbers of Lutheran immigrants increased, church leaders such as Henry Melchior Muhlenberg privately tutored promising young men for pastoral leadership. But it soon became apparent that these disjointed efforts could not meet the needs of the church as a whole.

Following the War of Independence, the need for a permanent Lutheran seminary in the new nation increased due to the arrival of a fresh wave of immigrants, territorial expansion, and the severing of ties with Europe. In 1820, Samuel Schmucker proclaimed that an institution of higher learning was a necessary step in rescuing the Lutheran church from "her former lifeless and distracted condition."[10]

Several early attempts to organize a seminary had either failed or met with only limited success. Schmucker, himself, operated a fledgling school in his parsonage at New Market, Virginia. Although he attracted a number of gifted students, the young pastor realized that such an enterprise required the support of the entire church in order to succeed on a large scale.[11]

The first constitution of the General Synod of the Lutheran Church in the United States, drafted in 1820, empowered the organization to "devise plans for general seminaries of education."[12] A committee was appointed to draw up plans for a seminary, but it was later recommended that this action be deferred for several years.

Finally, on September 5, 1826, appropriate ceremonies in both English and German took place in Gettysburg, giving birth to the Lutheran Theological Seminary. A large crowd of citizens and clergyman looked on as Dr. Schmucker took the oath of office as "Professor of Christian Theology."[13] Classes began the next day with one professor, eight students, a small collection of books, and less than $1,700 in the treasury.[14]

The success or failure of the new venture rested largely on the shoulders of its chief founder and first professor, 27-year-old Samuel Schmucker. There was probably no one better qualified for the rigors and challenges of this position. At the time Schmucker was widely regarded as the most promising young theologian within the Lutheran Church in the United States. He was instrumental in the establishment of the Seminary and had helped to formulate its constitution.

Schmucker was born on February 28, 1799, in Hagerstown, Maryland, to the Reverend John George and Elizabeth (Gross) Schmucker. Ten years later, the family moved to York, Pennsylvania, where Reverend Schmucker accepted the pastorate at Christ Lutheran Church. Samuel received his early education at the York County Academy. At the tender age

Samuel Simon Schmucker. Courtesy of LTSG.

a Seminary to serve the Lutheran Church and for the foundation of a preparatory college.

These aspirations were not mere pipe dreams. In addition to his impressive intellect and credentials, Schmucker had the character needed to accomplish such a lofty goal. He was energetic, highly disciplined, methodical, and self-controlled. His deep piety and strict morality endeared him to his followers and won him the respect of his peers. During the first several years of the Seminary's existence, Schmucker served as its only faculty member as well as its chief financial solicitor.[15]

The professor's physical appearance belied the dynamo within. Samuel was thin, rather frail looking, with large ears, a hawk-like nose, long dark hair, and a distinctive forehead. In all of his extant portraits, he wears a serious countenance, his piercing gray eyes fixed on some distant point as if he is looking ahead to the future. One contemporary observed, "Dr. Schmucker was the most indefatigable man I ever knew — he never ceased work when at home and carried his work with him when he left … I never knew a man who needed and took less relaxation from severe mental toil than he."[16]

The cradle of the Seminary was the Adams County Academy, located on the southeast corner of Washington and High Streets. Two of the building's four large rooms housed the Seminary and its library.[17] The students obtained room and board from families in the town. A total of 15 young men enrolled at the school during

of 15, the promising youngster entered the University of Pennsylvania. After two years of study, he returned to York and took charge of the academy.

Samuel's life-long devotion to the ministry was cemented when he accompanied his older brother on a missionary trip to the frontier country of Ohio and Kentucky. Inspired by this experience, he entered Princeton Theological Seminary in the summer of 1818. Following a year and a half of instruction, the young man passed the examination required to be licensed as a minister. In the fall of 1820, he was assigned to a parish of four congregations in the vicinity of New Market, Virginia, in the heart of the Shenandoah Valley. From this rural location, the ambitious Schmucker tirelessly labored for the establishment of

The Adams County Academy, the first home of the Seminary. Author's collection.

the first year of operations. Six were college graduates, including four from Dickinson College in Carlisle. The first theologians hailed from Pennsylvania and Maryland, with the exception of one Virginian.

Schmucker believed the most important qualities of a theology student were piety and natural intelligence. The instructor placed a much greater emphasis on the former, and he repeatedly warned his pupils "never to prosecute study to the detriment of devotion."[18]

Benjamin Oehrle provided an intimate view of Schmucker in a letter to his parents near the close of 1826: "[H]e is a *true Christian and follower of Jesus,* as he proves in all his actions and conduct. The people of Gettysburg all love him sincerely and his students have an immense love for him, for to all of us he is just like a father — so gentle, so thoughtful, so faithful and loving in every respect."[19]

The young professor faced a number of unique challenges during his early years at the Seminary. While the curriculum offered a broad range of subjects, students often arrived with inadequate preliminary training. Schmucker's precious time was further diverted by trips to secure books and funds for the infant institution. Adding to his woes, he was frequently subjected to the widespread criticism leveled against theological seminaries from within his own denomination. Schmucker overcame these obstacles with his natural intellect, his thorough training, his imperturbability, and his boundless energy.

At times, the gifted teacher intimidated his pupils. John G. Morris, who studied under Schmucker at the York County Academy, at New Market, and as a member of the Seminary's inaugural class, wrote of his long-time mentor: "As a teacher he was not interesting, though he had complete mastery of his subject, yet he failed to awaken enthusiasm in his pupils ... he displayed an extent of reading and profundity of research that utterly astonished the raw youngsters, and would have called out the admiration of more intelligent men."[20]

Henry Eyster Jacobs, who attended the Seminary nearly 40 years later, recalled that "Dr. Schmucker had many qualities of a good teacher. He was clear, methodical, precise, decided, exacting, acute to a fault. He was never disconcerted, or excited; but cold and stern, keeping all students while in the class room at a distance, and dealing severely with even pardonable requests that did not meet the very letter of the rules."[21]

In May 1827, Seminary officials filed the necessary paperwork to become recognized as a legal corporation under Pennsylvania law. The official designation of the entity became "The Theological Seminary of the General Synod of the Evangelical Lutheran Church in the United States," a rather verbose title for the decidedly small enterprise.[22]

Professor Schmucker's charisma and various publicity campaigns continued to attract new students. After a year and a half of operations, the student body swelled to 23 from the original eight matriculated on opening day.[23] The increasing need for additional faculty and building space would have to be addressed before the institution could enter a new growth phase.

Meanwhile, the ambitious Schmucker continued to pursue his mission of establishing a classical school to provide adequate and uniform preparatory training for ministerial students. The groundwork for this venture was laid during the incorporation of the Seminary, and on June 25, 1827, the Gettysburg Academy commenced operations in the other half of the building. The first teacher chosen was David Jacobs, a prominent student in the Seminary. In 1829, a Scientific Department was added,

of which Michael Jacobs, David's brother, was placed in charge. The course of study was arranged for five years, the third year being roughly equivalent to the freshmen college level. The school was renamed the "Gettysburg Gymnasium." When David Jacobs died on November 4, 1830, Henry L. Baugher succeeded him at the head of the Classical Department.

Schmucker continued to play a leading role in the development of the school. In 1831, he called together the leading citizens of Gettysburg and Adams County to gain support for his plans to develop the Gymnasium into a college. In addition, he actively lobbied influential members of the Pennsylvania Legislature, and on one occasion, he addressed the House of Representatives on the advantages of the proposed college. These efforts proved successful and a charter was granted in April of 1832. The institution was named Pennsylvania College as an expression of gratitude to the lawmakers who had given it life. The forerunner of present-day Gettysburg College held its first semester of classes in the fall.[24]

With the advent of the College, finding a permanent site for the Seminary became a major priority. In the fall of 1829, a committee was formed to select a suitable building site. Eventually, a 20-acre tract owned by William McClellan and Samuel Buehler, situated on the western limits of the borough, was chosen as the new home of the Seminary. The property was located on a long, narrow ridge less than one mile from the center of town. Prior to the battle of Gettysburg, the entire length of this low elevation was referred to locally as "Oak Ridge." Today, all but the northern terminus of the ridge is popularly known as "Seminary Ridge." The northern boundary of the plot was formed by the Chambersburg Pike, while the Hagerstown or Fairfield Road represented the southern border.[25]

The Seminary's Board of Directors ratified the committee's choice at a meeting held during the following spring. The price to purchase the land and a well was $1,166.15. After building plans were drawn up by architect Nicholas Pearse of Chambersburg, notices appeared in local papers soliciting sealed proposals for the construction of the edifice.[26]

The August 10, 1830, issue of the Gettysburg *Compiler* listed the following specifications: "The whole building to be 100 feet, viz. the Centre building to be 50 feet square, two stories each 14 feet high — with two wings, 30 × 25 feet, three stories each 9 feet high. The wall of the first story of the Centre building is to be 18 inches thick — the second story and Wings to be 14 inches; to be covered with joint shingles, of white pine. The whole is to be of brick, and the exterior to be rough cast." The notice stipulated that the selected contractor was expected to complete the project within one year of acceptance.[27]

Four months later, the *Compiler* reported that the low bid of $7,750 had been submitted by the firm of Nicholas Pearse.[28] However, additions and alterations to the original plan greatly increased the final cost. The outer dimensions of the main edifice, which consisted of a basement story and three upper floors, were 100 by 40 feet. The prominent feature of the simple colonial style building was a distinctive white cupola that crowned the roof.

The cornerstone was laid with appropriate ceremonies on May 26, 1831. The edifice was ready for occupancy by the fall semester of 1832. At this time the basement story, reserved for the steward of the building, and two upper floors, consisting of lecture rooms, a main assembly area, a library, and dormitory space for the students, were completed. The building was located on the crest of the ridge equidistant from the Chambersburg Pike and the Hagerstown Road.[29]

The Seminary students delighted in their new home on "the Hill." Their enthusiasm was made manifest in an open letter to their constituents in Europe:

> It is a large, commodious and elegant structure, located on an elevated site, half a mile from the town, with a beautiful park of flourishing oaks in the rear, and commanding a noble prospect of the surrounding country to the distance of several miles. If there be any spot on earth where the human intellect can expand itself more nobly, where it can expatiate more freely through the almost illimitable extent of theological science, where it can rise more ardently and devoutly to the contemplation of the omnipresent Creator, than in any other place, surely it must be in such a delightful and hallowed retreat as this ... where the spirit of true devotion will be nursed in the lap of solitude, and where alone can be formed the necessary habits of elevated contemplation and profound thought, of close investigation and patient study, which are so necessary to every student of theology, and which too frequent an intercourse with the unthinking multitude is almost sure to destroy.[30]

Within two years of the completion of the initial construction project, brick homes for two professors were erected on either side (north and south) of the main building. Dr. Schmucker occupied the southernmost home, located a short distance from the Hagerstown Road. An additional tract of four acres was purchased to facilitate the construction of the second residence. These three structures were the only major buildings erected on the property until 1875.[31]

The work of landscaping and cultivating the grounds was begun almost immediately. Shade trees were planted throughout the campus, an acre of ground was laid out for a garden on the eastern slope of the ridge, and neat white picket fences

An early lithograph of the Seminary campus. Courtesy of LTSG.

enclosed the garden and surrounded the buildings. By the mid 1840s, tree-lined walkways led from the entrance of each building to the foot of the hill to join the roads leading into town. Traces of the "Tan Path," which adjoined the main structure, are still visible today.[32]

The erection of buildings and the beautification of the grounds placed a heavy burden on the financial resources of the Seminary. As a result, the furnishings for the rooms were provided by benevolent individuals and congregations. In 1840, the cost of furnishing a dormitory room amounted to $37.65. Some of the items provided included: a bed, three chairs, a table, washstand, basin, ten yards of up ticking, three pounds of feathers, a shovel, and tongs. The last two items were needed for the maintenance of the most expensive fixture — a heating stove, which cost $13.29 at the time.[33]

The conduct and daily activities of the seminarians were closely monitored.

Schmucker wrote that in order to prepare his charges for their holy duties, "I have endeavored to keep that kind of order in the house and have recommended such habits of personal deportment, as become the dignity of the ministerial character."[34] Evidently, he practiced what he preached. One associate described Schmucker as a "severe moralist" who carried his principles "to an extreme length." He objected to a wide range of amusements and recreational activities, abstained from the use of alcohol and tobacco, and never conformed to modern fashions.[35]

As a rule, there was little interaction between the professor and the students. Dr. Schmucker allotted just one hour a day for personal interviews. If a pupil called at another hour out of necessity, he ran the risk of being censured for his transgression. One scholar recalled that study hours were so strictly enforced "that a man absorbed in his book under the trees would be reprimanded for breaking the rule requiring students to be in their rooms at that time."[36]

Daily exercises commenced at 5 A.M. with an all-inclusive worship service, followed by classes and study hours. Appropriate time periods were set aside during the day for physical fitness and the performance of chores, such as the washing of bed clothes and the cleaning of stove pipes. Private devotions began at 5:30 P.M. The students were required to be in their rooms two hours later for faculty inspections. Attendance at Sunday morning worship services was mandatory, as was a conference in the afternoon during which practical topics of religion were explored and discussed in detail. The first Wednesday of every month was set aside for special prayer and self-examination.[37]

The *Lutheran Observer* fully endorsed this highly structured regime and proclaimed that "No situation in life presents advantages for growth in grace equal to those which may be enjoyed in a Theological Seminary. Here the world may be completely shut out from the mind, and the soul be left to the uninterrupted pursuit of spiritual good."[38]

One early student eagerly embraced this unique learning situation. "The professors are men in every respect calculated to input highly valuable information to the understanding, while at the same time they possess the equally important quality of interesting the feelings and probing the hearts of students," he wrote. "Heartily do I lament that I did not come to this institution a year earlier."[39]

The academic year was comprised of two 20-week sessions. Although the school's constitution specified that the course of study should extend over three years, the majority of the students did not attend classes for more than two years. Most of them had already spent several preliminary years at Pennsylvania College. During the early years of the Seminary there was no

diploma and no formal graduation. In fact, it was not until 1867 that the three years' course went into effect and regular graduation exercises were held.[40]

In the pursuance of their daily studies, young theologians had a ready guide — Samuel Wild's "Directions for the Student of Divinity," published in 1817. Wild stressed the importance of time management and offered a number of rules to follow, among which were the following: never sleep above six hours; keep ceremonies and formal visits to an absolute minimum; avoid indolence, sloth, and idleness; and refrain from reading "useless books," which were defined as those which you either "do not understand, or if you do, afford neither solid improvement nor suitable entertainment."[41]

Not everyone accepted Mr. Wild's theories or quietly acquiesced to the rules and regulations imposed upon them by the Board and the faculty. Student complaints were commonplace. Seeking relief from their rigorous studies, Seminarians often petitioned for longer and more frequent vacation periods. These requests were usually submitted under the clever guise of being "beneficial to the health of both professors and students." The earnest appeals were invariably denied.[42]

The most universal complaint from the student body concerned the quality and cost of the meals provided to them. One theologian bitterly described the unsavory fare to his family and then concluded, "Thus you may judge for yourself with respect to boarding in the seminary and the desirableness for me to remain."[43]

Serious outbreaks of sickness and disease also plagued the institution during the early years. In 1832, during the first year of operations in the new building, diarrhea was so prevalent among the student body that classes had to be postponed. A decade later, an epidemic of typhoid fever resulted in four deaths at the school. As a result of this tragedy, stricter rules for sanitation and personal hygiene were adopted.[44]

Despite these setbacks, the Seminary enjoyed considerable success during its first 20 years of operations. During this period more than 200 students had passed through its halls.[45]

The most serious threat to the continued success of the Seminary involved the deep theological differences which developed between two rival groups. The "American" Lutherans, led by Schmucker, favored a new approach to Lutheranism which de-emphasized its differences from other Protestant denominations. They stressed the importance of unity among Christians and called for a spirit of cooperation. In keeping with this ecumenical outlook, Schmucker became an outspoken advocate for a number of national movements, including temperance, the observance of the Sabbath, Sunday Schools, missionary work, and the abolition of capital punishment.

On the other hand, the more orthodox members of the faith maintained that a strong emphasis should be placed on traditional teachings and the German language. The two sides differed sharply on ideas about worship practices and the proper mode of theological training. At the Seminary, both camps had passionate supporters among the student body, faculty, and the Board of Directors. Even the Schmucker family was divided. Samuel, a spokesman for the liberals, was opposed by his son, Beale, and his brother-in-law, Dr. Charles F. Schaeffer, who were both leaders in the more conservative party.

The growing tensions between the two factions climaxed in 1855 when Schmucker anonymously published a brochure which defined the doctrinal beliefs of leading American Lutherans. The major portion of the *Definite Synodical Platform* was devoted to a recension of the Augsburg Confession, the fundamental

document of the Lutheran faith, to better reflect the views of New World Lutherans. The proposals endorsed in the paper were decisively rejected by the Lutheran Church, considerably weakening Schmucker's once dominant influence.[46]

In the midst of this professional turmoil, Schmucker suffered a severe personal loss when his wife of 22 years died on February 11, 1848, at the age of 40. Mary Catherine Schmucker had given birth to twelve children, eight of whom lived to maturity. A woman of much personal charm, she had proved to be a faithful wife, a loving mother, and the efficient manager of a large household. Samuel's first wife had also died at an early age after giving birth to their first child. The death of his beloved Catherine, coupled with his earlier loss, left him severely shaken.

Nine months later, the grief-stricken professor wrote his son, Beale, "I cannot even now think, as I often do, of the many happy years we spent together, and of the dreary and forlorn condition in which her death has left not only me but also our little children, without tears."[47] In the spring of 1849, Schmucker married for the third time. His union to Esther Wagner of Philadelphia was primarily for convenience, however, as he wanted to provide a mother for his younger children.

In 1850, the Board of Directors hired Dr. Charles Philip Krauth, a conservative, to fill the second professorship. This position had been filled on an interim basis throughout much of the school's early history. For the previous 16 years, Krauth had ably served as president of Pennsylvania College. At the College and Seminary, Charles enjoyed the admiration of both his students and colleagues. One contemporary described him as "one of the purest and best men that ever lived," while a student characterized him as "a cultivated gentleman, whose very presence created an atmosphere of dignity and refinement."[48]

For the next 15 years, Krauth and Schmucker constituted the faculty of the Seminary. Although the two men differed sharply in their theological views, their personal relationship was very cordial. In a period marked by internal discord, Krauth's amiable disposition was as valuable to the institution as his vast experience and teaching skills.[49]

One promising theology student who arrived in Gettysburg during these turbulent times was Franklin Jacob Fogel Schantz, a native of Lehigh County, Pennsylvania, and a graduate of Franklin and Marshall College in Lancaster. Schantz commenced his studies at the Seminary in the fall of 1855. Jokingly, he boasted, "I was certainly the second honor man of my class if not the first, for the simple reason that there were only two members in the class!" After completing his theological studies, Schantz was licensed as an Evangelical Lutheran minister and then embarked on a long and distinguished pastoral career. He fondly remembered his time in Gettysburg as being "two very pleasant years of my life."[50] Six years later, he would return to his alma mater under remarkably different circumstances.

Just as the Lutheran Church and the Seminary suffered from schism after a long period of harmony, the country itself was

Charles Philip Krauth. Courtesy of LTSG.

on a dangerous road toward dissolution. Politically, socially, and economically, the North and South had followed two divergent paths since the founding of the young Republic. Unfortunately, these differences would lead to the most tragic period in the history of the United States. Gettysburg, once the scene of a bitter theological battle, would soon host a far more serious and costly conflict that would shape the future course of the nation.

CHAPTER 2

A House Divided

God is our mighty fortress,
always ready to help in times of trouble.
And so, we won't be afraid!
Let the earth tremble
and the mountains tumble into the deepest sea.
Let the ocean roar and foam,
and its raging waves shake the mountains.
Psalm 46, Verses 1–3

On May 14, 1861, William M. Artz of Mount Pleasant, North Carolina, wrote an impassioned letter to his brother in Hagerstown, Maryland:

This comes to inform you that we are all well and doing tolerably well in our church and mill business. The great political excitement predominates over all other affairs and the duties of religion are much neglected.... The election for Delegates to the State Convention to be held at Raleigh on the 20th of this month came off yesterday ... This State will go out of the general Gov[e]rnm[en]t and go into the Southern Confederacy. We understand that the decree for our subjugation is gone forth; the time is come, and the blow will soon fall. The Old N[orth] State is up and a doing; is preparing to meet it; and to show to the world that she will defend her rights at all hazards. More than 30,000 of her Sons will volunteer their services for her protection. Thousands have already gone....

Our country rings with the sound of war; civil war; the most dreadful calamity that can come upon a nation. We trust that all parties will pause on the brink and hearken to the voice of conscience and to the Gospel of the Son of God which speaks peace and good will to men.... G[od] is our refuge and strength; a very present help in time of trouble. O, that he would bring us deliverance from trouble and restore peace and harmony to our much distracted, unhappy country![1]

William Artz had the distinction of being the very first student matriculated into the Gettysburg Lutheran Theological Seminary's inaugural class.[2] As William predicted, North Carolina seceded from the Union on May 20th, thus becoming the 10th and next-to-last state to merge with the newly formed Confederate States of America. William's son, George, was among the first to enlist.[3]

Three young men who attended the

Seminary just prior to the outbreak of hostilities also took up arms against the Union. George W. Holland enlisted as a private in the 33rd Virginia and Webster Eichelberger joined Company G of the 2nd Virginia. Both of these units would become part of the famous Stonewall Brigade led by the legendary General Thomas J. "Stonewall" Jackson. Meanwhile, Alexander Philippi was elected as a lieutenant in the 29th Virginia. A fourth alumnus, Louis Albert Bikle, served as the chaplain of the 20th North Carolina during the final two years of the war.[4]

Considering the fact that 95 out of the 277 students who enrolled at the Seminary from 1826 to 1860 listed birthplaces south of the Mason-Dixon Line, the number of graduates who enlisted in the Confederate army appears low. However, it must be kept in mind that the majority of these enrollees came from Western Maryland and Northern Virginia, areas that were deeply divided in their sentiments.[5]

On the other hand, 12 students who attended the institution during the antebellum period served in the Union forces at some point during the conflict. Among the first to enlist was Samuel Augustus Holman, an 1855 graduate of Pennsylvania College, who studied at the Seminary with Holland, Philippi, and Eichelberger, who were now his adversaries. Holman, a Pottsville, Pennsylvania pastor, was five days shy of his 30th birthday when he mustered in as chaplain of the 48th Pennsylvania Volunteers on October 1, 1861.[6]

How could members of the same religious faith who shared a common educational background, many of the same values, and a commitment to democratic government take up arms against one another? Politics, geography, and economics all played a role in the sectional strife that led to civil war.

As the young nation emerged as a world power following its struggle for independence, territorial expansion pushed the moral debate of slavery into the forefront of national affairs and threatened to divide the country. This issue, more than any other, became the irrepressible cause of the Civil War.

When President Thomas Jefferson took office on March 4, 1801, the United States contained about 900,000 slaves from a total population of 5,308,000, making it the largest slaveholding country in the world. The President was one of Virginia's wealthiest planters and among its principal slaveholders. His elite social standing was antithetical to his stated principles; he said he regarded slavery as a "hideous evil." He also promoted the abolition of the Southern class structure that empowered an aristocracy based upon wealth and family connections, of which Jefferson himself was a prime example. Thomas inherited both land and slaves from his father, and his mother and in-laws were also members of the genteel class.[7]

This irony is emblematic of the numerous contradictions which characterized Jefferson and the issue of human servitude. While the author of the Declaration of Independence wrote that "all men are created equal," he was convinced that the African race was intellectually inferior to Caucasians. And despite the fact that he had urged the abolition of slavery as early as 1774, Jefferson failed to take an active role in the growing abolition movement.

This inertness can be partly explained by Jefferson's belief in predestination. He was convinced that the dreaded institution would die out on its own, as would other social evils. Reinforcing this faith was his opinion that one generation could absorb only a certain amount of political reform. Thus, he favored the gradual abolition of slavery. The closing of the foreign slave trade in 1808 by his administration would help seal its fate, he thought. Jefferson remained a slaveholder throughout his life, primarily for financial reasons.[8]

Two weeks before his death on July 4, 1826, the former president defended his numerous inconsistencies in regard to the institution that had been such an integral part of his life:

> A good cause is often injured more by ill-timed efforts of its friends than by the arguments of its enemies. Persuasion, perseverance, and patience are the best advocates in questions depending on the will of others. The revolution of public opinion which this case requires is not to be expected in a day, or perhaps in an age; but time, which outlives all things, will outlive this evil [slavery] also.[9]

Two months after Jefferson's death, Samuel Schmucker took time from his busy schedule in Gettysburg to write his wife, Mary Catherine, who had remained behind in Virginia to give birth to the couple's daughter. The letter was filled with expressions of love and affection. "The more I learn of this place the more firm is my conviction that we will be exceedingly happy here—(but the long four weeks!!!! how shall I live without you till then!!!)," wrote the sanguine, but lonely professor.[10]

The letter also contained detailed instructions for the transfer of household goods to the couple's new residence. The property included a number of slaves of which Samuel had become the legal owner through his marriage to Catherine, who came from a prominent and wealthy family in Frederick County, Virginia. Thus, just as Jefferson, Schmucker became a slaveowner by circumstance rather than by choice.

Although Samuel had no intention of retaining his newly acquired status, he strictly adhered to the statutes concerning the transportation of slaves across state lines. The "servants" were indentured before two magistrates in Virginia for vari-

ous lengths of time before their arrival in Gettysburg. One minor named Easter was indentured for six years according to Schmucker's instructions. The professor gradually manumitted all of his slaves after training them for independent life. He also established pensions for those too old to work.[11] British theologian Dr. James W. Massie observed, "Few have made the personal sacrifices which he has conscientiously made to live free from the contamination of slavery."[12] Through his benevolent actions, Schmucker demonstrated the "revolution of public opinion" advocated by Jefferson in an enlightened new age.

Schmucker differed from Jefferson, however, on the intellectual capacity of African-Americans. In fact, one of his most eminent students was Daniel Alexander Payne, a freeman and respected teacher from Charleston, South Carolina. When the education of blacks was outlawed in South Carolina, Schmucker and a number of his students sponsored Payne's relocation to the North as part of a missionary program. Payne arrived in Gettysburg in 1835 and soon became a leader in the Seminary community. He was later elected a bishop in the African Methodist Episcopal Church and served as president of Wilberforce University in Ohio from 1863 to 1876.[13] Payne never forgot Schmucker's liberality; as he wrote years later in his recollections, "Dr. Schmucker was not only a kind instructor, but often exhibited the tenderness of a father by supplying my bodily needs."[14]

Throughout his adult life, Schmucker publicly declared his opposition to slavery. His position on this controversial issue was revealed through his addresses, sermons, and published materials on the subject. He made no effort to hide these views from his students, even though many of them came from the South. Beale Schmucker wrote that his father's "anti-slavery views were

Daniel Payne. Courtesy of LTSG.

by the group encouraged the manumission of slaves and would promote the evangelization of the African continent. He eventually withdrew from the Society when it failed to provide for "the moral and intellectual elevation" of the black population. At the same time, he refused to join the Anti-Slavery Society since he considered the organization's "indiscriminate denunciation and occasionally exaggerated statements" an injustice to Southern Christians.[17]

Indeed, Schmucker never wavered from his moderate position on the issue. The professor clearly endorsed the rights of the individual states in dealing with slavery. In addition, he acknowledged the financial obligation of the Northern states in solving the problem.

Schmucker was convinced that emancipation could not succeed unless the freed slaves were properly prepared for responsible citizenship. This solution entailed granting blacks the right to choose their own means of employment, the right to bargain for their wages, a proper education, and equal protection under the law. Samuel also thought that the former masters should be required to support the old and disabled. In 1839, Schmucker petitioned the state legislature for the passage of a law to provide vocational training for black children. The bill, which he had written himself, was rejected on two different occasions.[18]

The following year Schmucker prepared a formal document entitled "Propositions on the Subject of Slavery" for use in the classroom. In great detail, this unpublished manuscript outlined Schmucker's opinions on the topic. After analyzing the

clearly defined, and not concealed even when they gave offence, and he carried them out to his own pecuniary loss."[15]

The professor believed the institution of slavery was "a reproach to our political system, and a violation of the rights of 'equal' man!" But Samuel did not support the drastic measures proposed by many radicals. He favored measured change and legislative action as opposed to violent revolution. As a native of a slave state, Schmucker was convinced that "those who advocate entire, immediate abolition, do not understand the subject.... The work, in justice to the master, and in mercy to the slave, must be gradual; but its commencement ought to be delayed no longer...."[16]

Schmucker was an early supporter of the American Colonization Society because he believed the measures advocated

Declaration of Independence, the U.S. Constitution, and the Holy Bible, Schmucker concluded that the system of slavery that existed in the United States was composed of "immoral" elements that were "clearly opposed to the character of God."

According to the professor, the institution unavoidably led to a number of evils, such as: the degradation of matrimonial and parental relations, the removal of incentives for industry and honesty, and widespread illiteracy, which effectively shut out the word of God. He concluded with the following admonishment: "It is the duty of every Christian and friend of civil and religious liberty, to exert his influence in every beneficial way to vindicate the right of all God's rational creatures, and by peaceable means and Christian appeals to their consciences, patriotism, and humanity to influence those who are violating those rights."[19]

In 1850, the passage of the Fugitive Slave Law angered many Northerners, even those with moderate views. This act created a Federal police force that was authorized to issue warrants for the arrest of escaped slaves and required citizens of free states to cooperate in these efforts. Samuel Davis Schmucker wrote the following reaction to this controversial legislation:

> In my early life runaway slaves would occasionally come to our house. Father would allow any such to sleep in his barn by day, and I am sure, assisted them, at least to the extent of supplying them with food…. I once asked him what he would do if a fugitive slave were to approach him personally for aid. He replied that he would never assist in returning a fel-

Samuel Schmucker remained a moderate abolitionist throughout his life. Courtesy of LTSG.

low being into bondage, and would succor any such that were in distress, and that if he were prosecuted for it, he would admit the fact and pay the penalty for which the law might make him liable.[20]

The professor justified this civil disobedience with an article of the Augsburg Confession, which stated that "Christians ought necessarily to yield obedience to the civil officers and laws of the land, unless they should command something sinful, in which case it is a duty to obey God rather than man."

Due to the required secrecy of the enterprise and the subsequent lack of documentation, it is difficult to ascertain if the Schmucker property was a designated station on the Underground Railroad or if it was only used infrequently by individual runaways. The above account by Samuel D. Schmucker seems to support the latter; however, the late Dr. Abdel Ross Wentz, who resided in the former Schmucker house for forty years, asserted that the structure served as a regular station and that to this day in the dingy cellar of the house one can see the evidences of the provision that was made for slaves.[21]

The rise of Abraham Lincoln and the Republican Party to national prominence was fueled by the slavery issue. Lincoln took the moderate view, as did Schmucker, that the Federal government should not interfere with slavery where it already existed. He believed that the institution would die off on its own if not permitted to spread into new regions of the country. His classic "House Divided" speech included a prophetic warning: "I believe this government cannot endure, permanently half *slave* and half *free*.... It will become *all* one thing, or *all* the other."[22]

By the time of Lincoln's first inaugural address on March 4, 1861, seven Southern states had seceded from the Union to form the Confederate States of America. Just as William Artz of North Carolina had prayed for the restoration of peace and harmony, Lincoln beseeched his "dissatisfied fellow-country-men" to pause and reflect on their common heritage and values:

> We must not be enemies. Though passion may have strained, it must not break our bonds of affection. The mystic chords of memory, stretching from every battlefield, and patriot grave, to every living heart and hearth-stone, all over this broad land, will yet swell the chorus of the Union, when again touched, as surely they will be, by the better angels of our nature.[23]

Just over a month later, on April 12th, Confederate forces opened fire on a Federal garrison at Fort Sumter in Charleston Harbor. The American Civil War had begun.

Large numbers of Lutherans enlisted in the armed forces of both the Union and the Confederacy during the four years of bloody conflict. By and large, church leaders and parishioners conformed to the prevailing sentiments of the states in which they resided. One notable exception was the Reverend James A. Brown. Born in Lancaster County, Pennsylvania, to Quaker parents and educated at Pennsylvania College, Brown accepted a teaching position at Newberry College in South Carolina in 1859. The Palmetto State was a hotbed for secessionist activity and it was the first Southern state to leave the Union after Lincoln's election.

Following this momentous event, Brown announced to his students that he would resign and return North, and if necessary, enlist in the Union army. A number of prominent citizens feared for his safety and advised him to leave immediately under the cover of darkness. "I came to South Carolina openly, and openly I shall depart," declared the professor. He left the next morning for Pennsylvania on the regular train schedule. True to his word, James served the Union cause as a chaplain in the 87th Pennsylvania Volunteers, and later, at the U.S. Army hospital in York.[24]

Although the Lutheran church in America declined to take an official position on the controversial issues facing the nation, the individual synods (regional governing bodies) were free to express their views on the war and slavery. On October 10, 1861, representatives of the Synod of East Pennsylvania met in Germantown, Pennsylvania, just outside of Philadelphia. The delegates included Drs. Schmucker and Krauth as well as Pennsylvania College president Henry Louis Baugher. Besides addressing church matters, the assembled leaders passed several resolutions on the war, now six months in progress.

The first resolution asserted that in attempting to dissolve the Federal Union, the Confederate States of America were in "plain violation of the Apostle's injunction for all men to be subject to the higher powers which are ordained of God." Moving from this point, it was progressively argued that since "the present war was inaugurated by the party in rebellion in pursuance of their unholy purpose of overturning the benign Government which God ordained," the military policies of the Lincoln administration were justified. In this particular case, the "sword" became the "minister of God" wielded "for the punishment of evildoers." The delegates pledged support for "our brethren in the faith, who have gone to fight the battles of their country" and urged pastors to patriotically appeal to their congregations for donations of blankets, stockings, and other winter comforts.[25]

No mentions of slavery were recorded during the proceedings. In fact, only two district synods, one in New York State and the other in Pittsburgh, declared their opposition to slavery. However, as the most visible leader in the Lutheran church, Dr. Schmucker's views were well known throughout the country.[26]

A letter printed in an 1863 edition of the *Southern Lutheran* vehemently attacked Schmucker: "You doctor, and your abolition friends knew not what you were doing, when your opposition to Southern rights terminated in this unhallowed war. So deadly is this hatred on the part of the South that not only is reconstruction impossible, but Southern men will resist the attempts of the United States to restore the Union to the bitter end."[27]

Amid the patriotic fervor of 1861, a militia company was formed by students of the Seminary and the College. Otherwise, classes went on as usual. In mid-August of 1862, Dr. Schmucker reported to the Board of Directors that the members of his present class "have shown more disposition to take their daily exercise in play-

A bucolic depiction of the Seminary campus circa 1840. Courtesy of LTSG.

ing ball, than their predecessors." While he did not object to the activity, he was concerned by the "unnecessary and unusual amount of noise, which has in some degree changed the usual quietness and solemnity within and around the Seminary itself." Schmucker requested the opinion of the Board as to whether the playing of sports should be allowed on the campus.[28] Throughout the following summer, Schmucker and other Seminary officials would have far greater concerns as the "unthinking multitude" descended upon them.

CHAPTER 3

Wolf at the Door

In times of trouble, you will protect me.
You will hide me in your tent
and keep me safe on top of a mighty rock.
Psalm 27, verse 5

By 1860, the town of Gettysburg had fulfilled the promise detected by the directors of the Seminary over three decades earlier. The population of approximately 2,400 citizens represented a nearly twofold increase during the period.[1] It was a vibrant, prosperous, and thriving community.

The major roads leading into the town intersected at the town square, referred to by the locals as the "Diamond." This downtown area featured brick sidewalks and gas lamps. No fewer than eight nearby hotels catered to weary travelers. The completion of the Hanover, Hanover Junction, and Gettysburg Railroad in 1856 enhanced Gettysburg's role as a transportation center.

A new county courthouse, built in 1859 along Baltimore Street near the square, provided sundry services for the 28,000 residents of Adams County. Three weekly newspapers supplied entertainment and "kept the political agitation active," while ten churches of various denominations ministered to the spiritual needs of the town's population.[2]

A variety of professionals and artisans offered their services and wares to the townspeople. The most important industry in Gettysburg was carriage manufacturing, which employed roughly 15 percent of the wage-earning population. The major market for this booming business was Northern Virginia.[3]

But prior to the Civil War and the great battle for which it is now famous, Gettysburg was best known for its educational institutions. Besides the Seminary and the College, six schools could be found in the community. The higher learning facilities expanded with the town. In 1837, Pennsylvania College moved to larger quarters, just as the Seminary had five years earlier. The old academy building, which had served as the first home of both institutions, became the new site of the Eyster Female Academy, operated by Rebecca Eyster.[4]

The new site of the College was located on an open plain just north of the town. The campus included three structures by 1860: the main edifice, today known as Pennsylvania Hall; Linnaean Hall, erected in 1847; and the newly constructed president's home occupied by Dr. Baugher. In 1835, Christ Lutheran Church was constructed on the south side of Chambersburg Street. This house of worship came to be known as the "college church" since its membership was composed mainly of the professors and students from the Seminary and the College.[5]

One Gettysburg resident recalled that prior to the battle the annual exercises of these two institutions provided a welcome break from the monotony and "quiet tenor of an inland town." She recalled how the influx of strangers during commencement week added "some stir and life to the place, only to have it settle into more irksome quietude after the visitors and their dear boys had left."[6] In hindsight, many residents would have preferred this anonymity to the worldwide fame the town would acquire as a result of the landmark events of 1863.

Despite Gettysburg's economic ties to the South, most of its residents were strong Unionists and supported the Lincoln administration. Nearly 200 free blacks also called Gettysburg home. The proximity of the town to Virginia and Maryland, both slaveholding states, caused a great deal of concern among the black and white population upon the outbreak of hostilities.[7]

Student Michael Colver recalled that the town "was in a state of agitation during almost the whole of my college and seminary life."[8] Henry Jacobs, the son of Professor Michael Jacobs, thought the disturbances were more intermittent in nature. "There were often months when the town was undisturbed as in peace," he wrote, "but there was every now and then an alarm that disquieted people of weak nerves."[9]

From the beginning of the war, loose bands of amateur scouts and home guards kept up a constant vigil, patrolling the

Henry Eyster Jacobs. Courtesy LTSG.

roads leading south into Maryland and watching for enemy incursions through the various gaps in the South Mountain range to the west.

The region's vulnerability was revealed in the fall of 1862 during the Confederate invasion of Maryland. The campaign culminated on September 17th with the bloody battle of Antietam, less than twenty miles from the Pennsylvania line. The booming of the artillery could be distinctly heard in Gettysburg.[10]

An even closer call took place a month later when Confederate General James E. B. "Jeb" Stuart led 1,800 horsemen around the stationary Federal army and raided into Southern Pennsylvania. The troopers destroyed public stores in Chambersburg and scoured the countryside for horses and other supplies before escaping back into Virginia. A squad of home guard cavalry skirmished with the raiders a mere five miles from Gettysburg, taking one captive in the process. This unfortunate soul was a great curiosity to the townspeople and the first Confederate to enter Gettysburg.[11]

The residents of Southern Pennsylvania breathed a collective sigh of relief when the stage of battle shifted southward once again. The results were disheartening to loyal Northerners, however. The battle of Fredericksburg, Virginia, on December 13, 1862, was a disastrous Union defeat. As a result, morale in the Army of the Potomac, the Union's premiere fighting force in the Eastern Theater, sank to its lowest point since the outset of the war.

The following spring's campaign also ended on a dismal note when General Robert E. Lee and the Army of Northern Virginia defeated the newly appointed Union General Joseph Hooker at the tiny crossroads of Chancellorsville, 10 miles west of Fredericksburg, in early May. Although outnumbered by a two-to-one margin, Lee outmaneuvered his adversary in the tangled woodlands and hurled the invading Federals back across the Rappahannock River.

Hooker became the fourth Union commander to taste defeat at the hands of Lee since the Virginian's rise to the top command post in June of 1862. But the victory cost Lee nearly 13,000 men and his most trusted lieutenant, Stonewall Jackson, who died a week after his left arm was amputated near the shoulder. The contending armies returned to their former positions near Fredericksburg to rest and recuperate following the strenuous campaign.[12]

After a month of planning and reorganization, Lee seized the initiative from his stunned opponent. In early June, the Confederate chief began shifting his forces out of their old camps in preparation for a major summer offensive. His objective was Southern Pennsylvania. By shifting the theater of operations away from Northern Virginia, Lee would gain a much needed respite for the war-ravaged countryside, while he replenished his own ragged army in the rich farmlands of the Cumberland Valley.[13]

Marching down the Shenandoah Valley behind the protective screen of the Blue Ridge Mountains, Lee's fast-moving army gained a head start on Hooker. Just prior to this movement, the Army of Northern Virginia had been reorganized into three corps under the leadership of Generals James Longstreet, Richard Ewell, and A.P. Hill. Ewell's Second Corps, previously commanded by the legendary Jackson, spearheaded the invasion. During the middle of June, Ewell's veteran fighters overwhelmed a Federal garrison at Winchester, Virginia, near the northern terminus of the valley. As a result of this decisive victory, the path was cleared for Lee's 75,000 troops.[14]

Reports of Lee's movements caused considerable alarm throughout South-Central Pennsylvania. Reflecting back to his childhood days in Gettysburg, Robert McClean recalled that for some time prior to the battle, "There was an indefinable apprehension, 'something in the air,' arising from rumors or news of the movements of the opposing armies...."[15] Tillie Pierce remembered that this information "caused the greatest alarm; and our hearts often throbbed with fear and trembling."[16] Another Gettysburg youngster, 13-year-old Lydia Ziegler, told a similar story:

> The spring and summer of '63 were days in which the citizens of our quiet village were much disturbed, for scarcely two consecutive weeks would pass without rumors reaching us that the enemy had crossed the Potomac, and were headed in our direction. Anxiety filled every breast. Farmers would flee with their horses to a place of safety and merchants would either ship their valuable goods away or securely hide them. So day followed day, each seeming to bring fresh trouble. The enemy were close at hand.[17]

The Ziegler family resided in the basement story of the Lutheran Seminary during the Civil War. Emanuel and Mary Ziegler served as the steward and matron of the building, respectively. Five children lived with them in 1863, ranging in age from 6 to 16.[18] Lydia and her younger brother, Hugh, left detailed accounts of the family's memorable experiences.

The fears of Gettysburg's citizenry became even more palpable when a telegraph arrived from Governor Andrew G. Curtin on June 15th, directing the residents to move their stores as quickly as possible. Sarah "Sallie" Broadhead, a 31-year-old

housewife, recalled that this official notification "made us begin to realize the fact that we were in some danger from the enemy."[19] Sallie, who came from a prominent and prosperous New Jersey Quaker family, resided with her husband, Joseph, and three-year-old daughter, Mary, in a house on Chambersburg Street near the western limits of town. Joseph was employed as an express messenger on the local railroad.[20] The campus of the Lutheran Theological Seminary stood a short distance from the Broadhead home.

Sallie kept a daily journal "to aid in whiling away time filled up with anxiety, apprehension, and danger." Her entry for June 20th reads in part: "The report of to-day is that the Rebels are at Chambersburg and are advancing on here, and refugees begin to come in by scores.... All day we have been much excited."[21]

Over the next several days, scouting parties, deserters, and groups of civilians encountered detachments of Rebel cavalry in the passes of South Mountain, but it was still uncertain where the main body of the enemy was located.[22] All eyes were trained on the western horizon.

In 1863, the western part of Gettysburg was largely undeveloped and citizens of the town could look directly out the Chambersburg Pike and enjoy an unobstructed view of South Mountain. Henry Jacobs recalled:

Its dark blue wall bounds fully one third of the horizon, forming a background for the lower and greener eminences that intervene, exhaustless in its variety of brilliant effects beneath the

Sarah Broadhead. Courtesy of Clair P. Lyons, Erie Pennsylvania.

glories of the setting sun.... Along these ridges in summer, storms were nursed, which we often watched as they gathered, and then approached with all the fury of a charging army....[23]

In the midst of numerous reports and sightings of enemy activity in Adams County, General Darius Couch, the commander of the Department of the Susquehanna, issued a statement from his Harrisburg headquarters warning the citizens of Gettysburg to seek their own protection. An emergency meeting held in the courthouse placed the county on a full military alert.[24]

Meanwhile, Dr. Schmucker received a personal notification from a friend and former student living in Maryland that the Confederates intended to place him under arrest for his anti-slavery sentiments. The informant exhorted the professor to leave immediately if the enemy moved in his direction. Schmucker decided to heed the warning, and sometime during the third week of June, he fled eastward to York, where he sought refuge with friends.[25]

A nearby resident recalled that, "Prominent men (not liable to service) had fled, such as the venerable Dr. Schmucker, whose books and sermons on slavery had made his name odious as far south as the 'slave block and chain' were known. And not only such men fled, but 500 of our population were colored people who feared the southern rebels more than death. They played hiding and peeping all this time."[26]

Samuel's unceremonious departure drew the censure of some of his colleagues. Dr. Charles Schaeffer, Schmucker's brother-in-law and bitter theological rival, made a particularly denigrating comment about the affair following Schmucker's resignation from the Seminary in 1864: "And so Dr. Schmucker has run away again. That man is my thermometer. His flights show that danger is at hand, and tell me when I must stay to protect my family."[27]

Classes at the Seminary were suspended even though Dr. Krauth and his family remained at home on the campus. Operations at the College continued, but attendance declined measurably due to the patriotism of the student body.[28]

As the Army of Northern Virginia steadily marched towards the border areas of the North with little opposition, President Abraham Lincoln issued a proclamation early on the morning of June 15th calling for 100,000 volunteer militia troops, half of this quota being assigned to Pennsylvania. Later the same day, Governor Andrew Gregg Curtin made a patriotic appeal to the citizenry of the Keystone State "to guard and maintain the free institutions of our country" and "to defend their homes and their firesides ... in this hour of imminent peril."[29]

The notice reached Gettysburg by noon of the following day. The urgent issue was warmly discussed by the young men of the college. E.W. Meissenhelder recalled the transformative effect of the news: "The quiet, peaceful, uneventful current of student-life had met with a rude shock.... Brave words, nobly spoken, were added fuel to the patriotic fire smoldering in each loyal heart. The time for decisive action had come."[30]

A call for volunteers was posted in the local bookstore, and within a few short hours, 57 College students and four Seminarians had signed their names to the list. Dr. Baugher, who had lost a son at Shiloh a year earlier, counseled discretion and advised the youthful patriots to return to their studies. His pleas were in vain, however, for "no human agency could have stayed the ardor of the students."[31]

Among the Collegians were Samuel D. Schmucker and John Morris Krauth, the sons of the two Seminary professors, and two future Seminary professors, Edmund J. Wolf and Thomas C. Billheimer. The Seminary students attached to the unit were Frederick Klinefelter, Henry C. Shindle, Alexander McLaughlin, and Matthias H. Richards. The non-student portion of the company included Henry M.M. Richards of Reading. Young Henry, a mere 14-year-old, became the unit's drummer boy. He enlisted to be with his older brother, Matthias, who celebrated his 22nd birthday by joining the military.[32]

On June 16th, the company assembled in front of Linnaean Hall. Frederick Klinefelter, a Seminary student with prior military experience as a private in the 16th Pennsylvania Volunteers, was elected captain. The 26-year-old York native had always been popular with his classmates. Highly regarded as a gentlemen with an unselfish disposition, he exuded a "peculiar charm and attractiveness."[33]

The following morning Klinefelter and his men gathered in the Diamond to hear a brief farewell address by Professor Frederick Muhlenberg and then boarded the cars for Harrisburg. After traveling about six miles, the cars ran off the track. No one was injured, but the slight mishap shook the patriotism out of a few faint hearts and hastened their return to Gettysburg. The remainder of the recruits reached the capital later the same day and marched to Camp Curtin, located just outside the city limits.[34]

At first, the response of the citizens of Pennsylvania was apathetic, but when the details of the Confederate invasion became more fully known, volunteers flocked to Harrisburg. The minutemen were greatly dismayed to learn that they would only be accepted for a term of six months in the *Federal* service, rather than as state troops. Many were not willing to commit to such a prolonged absence, while others feared

Captain Frederick Klinefelter, Company A, 26th Pa. Emergency Militia. Courtesy of LTSG.

they would be forced to serve outside of the state. As a result, large numbers of the would-be soldiers returned home. The conditions were later modified so that troops could be accepted for the length of the "existing emergency," a rather vague term by any definition.

The Gettysburg company set a patriotic example for others to follow when they stepped forward and freely offered their services. The men were immediately sworn into the service of the United States and thus became the first group of soldiers mustered into the 1863 militia force. The unit was officially designated Company "A" of the 26th Pennsylvania Emergency Militia.[35]

The organization of the regiment was completed by June 22nd. It was composed of 743 men under the command of 25-

year-old William W. Jennings, a veteran of the 127th Pennsylvania Volunteers, who was still recuperating from a wound he received at the Battle of Fredericksburg.

Due to the urgency of the developing situation, Jennings did not have the luxury of instilling much military drill and discipline into his eager charges. On the evening of the 23rd, orders arrived for the unit to be prepared to move out in the morning for Gettysburg.

The next day the men boarded the cars of the Northern Central Railroad and the train sped across the Susquehanna. The journey was interrupted six miles short of Gettysburg when the locomotive plowed into an "unromantic cow" that unwisely stepped onto the tracks. The accident derailed the train and halted any further advance for the remainder of the day. The regiment camped in a nearby patch of woods and a number of the men contented themselves by dining on tough steak.[36]

While the militia troops assembled and organized at Harrisburg, Lee's long columns of infantry slowly, but inexorably, slithered forward. Like a huge viper, the Confederates prepared to strike the exposed underbelly of the state. When Ewell's troops approached the Mason-Dixon line, Lee instructed the Second Corps commander to advance on a broad front towards the Susquehanna River. If Harrisburg came within his grasp, he was to seize it. The remainder of the army would move up to within supporting distance.[37]

On June 25th, Ewell conferred with his three division commanders at his headquarters near Chambersburg to devise plans for the movements of his corps. The chief would accompany the divisions of Edward "Allegheny" Johnson and Robert Rodes as they marched northeast up the valley towards Carlisle and Harrisburg. Meanwhile, his remaining division, under Major General Jubal Early, would travel east over South Mountain to Gettysburg and York.[38]

Early's 5,500 veteran troops, supported by Colonel William French's 17th Virginia Cavalry and Lieutenant Colonel Elijah White's 35th Virginia Cavalry Battalion, also known as "The Comanches," set off on their independent mission on the morning of June 26th. Before crossing the mountain, Early ordered his men to destroy the ironworks owned by Congessmen Thaddeus Stevens at Caledonia Furnace.

Six miles from Caledonia Furnace, a secondary road forked to the left and led to Mummasburg, a small community located five miles northwest of Gettysburg. As his troops neared the intersection, Early learned of the presence of a Federal force of unknown strength at Gettysburg. Accordingly, the Confederate commander sent the brigade of General John B. Gordon and White's battalion of cavalry on the pike towards Gettysburg "to amuse and skirmish with the enemy." "Old Jube" accompanied the rest of his command on the side road to Mummasburg to "get on his flank and rear, so as to capture his whole force."[39]

On the morning of June 26th, in the midst of a pouring rain, the militiamen arrived in Gettysburg from the east as Early's troops marched towards the town from the opposite direction. Despite the dismal weather, the neophyte soldiers "received the admiring attention of professors, pretty girls, etc.," and hot coffee, pies, and sandwiches were freely distributed, making it a memorable homecoming for the boys of Company A.[40]

Although they were warmly greeted, the arrival of the 26th did little to calm the frayed nerves of the populace. Sallie Broadhead spoke for many of her neighbors when she bluntly commented, "We do not feel much safer, for they are only raw militia."[41]

The commander of the Union outpost

at Gettysburg was Major Granville O. Haller, a regular army officer. In addition to the 26th, he had two small mounted forces at his disposal, Captain Robert Bell's Adams County Cavalry and the Philadelphia City Troop, commanded by Captain Samuel Randall.

Unaware of the advancing Confederate force, Haller instructed Jennings to march his green regiment toward South Mountain. "In happy ignorance of our fate and what lay before Gettysburg itself, at 10 A.M., with drums beating, sweethearts, relatives, and friends waving us farewell, we proudly stepped out and passed through the town," recalled drummer boy Henry Richards.[42]

Henry never forgot the serious countenances of Colonel Jennings and Captain Bell of the cavalry troop as the men "marched cheerfully and even gaily" along the Chambersburg Pike past the Seminary campus.[43] The 26th trudged out the pike a distance of about three miles through a drizzling rain, then halted along the road in a swampy field bordering Marsh Creek. The militiamen, unused to such physical exertion, cheerfully stacked arms and commenced pitching their tents. Jennings, sensing danger, rode to the top of a low ridge on the opposite side of the road and anxiously scanned the countryside through his field glasses.

Shortly after noon, a distant column of horsemen exploded into view from the west. The enemy was coming! Jennings galloped over to his regiment with the alarming news.[44] Suddenly, loud and excited commands broke the stillness: "Fall in, fall in!" followed quickly by "Forward!" One reluctant warrior wrote: "[W]e did not feel disposed to join battle — a thousand green militia against ten thousand bronzed and scarred veterans. We were brave, *but not to rashness*."[45]

The experienced Union officer had no intention of fighting the seasoned troops about to descend upon him. His primary concern was saving his regiment from annihilation or capture. Jennings led his soldiers cross country through muddy fields and over fences in an effort to bypass Gettysburg and reach the railroad on the eastern side of town.[46]

As the majority of the infantrymen took flight to the northeast, White's Comanches overtook Bell's cavalry and the rearguard of the 26th. It was a short and bloodless contest. The historian of the Comanches described the action:

> Our battalion came with barbarian yells and smoking pistols, in such a desperate dash that the bluecoated troops wheeled their horses and departed ... without firing a shot, while the infantry ... followed their example, and those who could not, threw down their bright new muskets and begged for quarter. Of course, nobody was hurt, except one fat militia captain who was stepped on by a horse and bruised somewhat.[47]

The Confederate horsemen, flushed by their easy victory, thundered ahead towards Gettysburg in pursuit of the Union fugitives. The noisy diversion allowed Jennings and the main body of his unit the opportunity to escape undetected. In the late afternoon, the weary soldiers stumbled onto the Mummasburg-Hunterstown Road near the Henry Witmer farm, located about four and a half miles due north of Gettysburg.

Jennings called for a halt near the farm to give his exhausted troops a much-needed rest. While most of the men collapsed on the wet ground, others visited the house in search of food and water. A few energetic souls climbed into a nearby row of cherry trees to pluck the ripening fruit.[48]

Suddenly, French's 17th Virginia Cavalry appeared on a small rise known as "Bailey's Hill" just to the southwest. Hastily, Jennings attempted to form his men

The Henry Witmer Farm. Author's collection.

behind a rail fence along a sunken lane opposite the farmhouse.[49] In the ensuing confusion, "everyone gave orders and no one obeyed."[50] A number of the Pennsylvanians became separated from the group and were quickly scooped up by the advancing cavalry. Those who reached the fence fired a ragged volley at their pursuers. Most of the rounds passed harmlessly over the heads of the enemy as they formed in line of battle near the farm.[51]

In the midst of their first combat action the militiamen "were full of excitement, most of them yelling at the top of their voices, some loading and firing without any pretense as to aim ... while others were so thoroughly worked up as to place the powder on top of the ball, rendering their piece useless, or possibly neglecting to take out their ramrod, fire it away."[52] One soldier in the 26th later admitted that he fired a shot "more to try whether my gun would go off than anything else."[53]

The Confederates sat firmly on their horses in straight and compact lines, calmly returning the fire. The youthful curiosity of Henry Richards was aroused by the balls whistling by his head. During the peak of the skirmish, he turned to his older brother, who was lying on the ground exhausted, and inquired if he thought one particular missile sounded like a hummingbird. With a look of utter scorn on his face, Matthias retorted, "You idiot! you will find out soon enough whether it is a humming bird if it hits you."[54] No doubt at that moment, the Seminarian longed to be back in school listening to one of Schmucker's tedious sermons or staring into Dr. Krauth's piercing black eyes as he drove home an important theological argument.

Fortunately for the 26th, the contest was of short duration. By most estimates, the fighting lasted between 20 and 30 minutes. About 120 militiamen, including the cherry-pickers and those inside the Witmer home, were taken prisoner, while a private in Company C sustained a wound to his face. The Pennsylvanians claimed to have killed or wounded several of the Confederates during the brief engagement.[55]

Once again, Jennings decided that discretion was the better part of valor, as he knew the Confederate infantry could not be far behind. At an opportune time the regiment retreated rapidly and took a straight path through the wooded hills and open valleys. For the next two days, the 26th marched almost nonstop in an effort to reach the safety of the Harrisburg defenses. The men avoided the public highways whenever possible. The retreat route led through Petersburg (York Springs), Dillsburg, Lisburn, New Cumberland, and finally, to Fort Washington on the west shore of the Susquehanna, opposite the capital.

For most of the arduous journey, the men were deprived of food and rest. The majority had discarded their tents and blankets at the beginning of the retreat, and were at the mercy of the elements.[56] Although it rained for much of the time, fresh water was scarce. Henry Wirt Shriver recalled "drinking water from every mud puddle we found in the road." On one occasion, he had to spit out the mud after swallowing a gulp of water, but felt no disgust whatsoever.[57]

In many ways, the 50-mile forced march to Harrisburg was more of an ordeal than the brief, but frightening, engagement with the Rebels. In hindsight, one member of Company A deeply regretted that he was not taken captive by the enemy and thereby spared of the hardships of the march.[58] It was indeed a severe test for troops unaccustomed to the rigors of campaigning. "We were so stiff and exhausted that every step was painful," recalled Shriver. "I never thought I could bear what I have gone through."[59]

There were numerous close calls and false alarms during the retrograde movement. Captain Klinefelter recorded one particularly humorous incident:

> We came to Conewago Creek, over which was a foot-log with a dilapidated handrail as guide. About half of Company A had crossed when the tramp of horses was heard in the rear, and a rush was made for the bridge, knocking many into the water, while others endeavored to ford the stream. We who had crossed came near firing on our comrades as they rushed through the water, mistaking them for cavalry. Later the rear of the regiment gave us another scare. Having separated from us in the darkness, and forded at another point, they suddenly brought the wrong end to the front. After a good deal of challenge and counter-challenge we opened order and passed them to their place, each laughing at the other's fears....[60]

Henry and Matthias Richards became separated from the regiment when they took temporary refuge with a farm family in Petersburg on June 27th. They experienced a variety of adventures in their efforts to overtake the command. By this time, Ewell's main body had penetrated up the Cumberland Valley to Carlisle. At one point the brothers donned homespun clothing provided by a friendly farmer to disguise themselves as Rebel soldiers. The subterfuge did not produce the desired results; the boys were twice arrested as enemy spies on June 30th near Mechanicsburg, shortly after a rearguard of Confederate horsemen had vacated the town. Much to the amusement of their comrades, the pair eventually reached the regiment near Harrisburg while still wearing their Rebel outfits.[61]

The remainder of the regiment's service was comparatively uneventful. After performing guard duty at various points along the Susquehanna, the 26th marched down the Cumberland Valley to Greencastle

Monument of the 26th Pa. Emergency Militia near Chambersburg Street. Author's collection.

Taking considerable poetic license, he then asked, "Who can deny that these occurrences were not instrumental in the salvation of the entire nation?"[63]

In truth, the regiment's actions had a limited impact on the outcome of the campaign. Jubal Early hit closer to the mark. "It was well that the regiment took to its heels so quickly," he wrote, "or some of its members might have been hurt, and all would have been captured."[64]

In spite of the unit's limited military accomplishments, the patriotism and bravery of its soldiery cannot be denied. The directors of the Lutheran Theological Seminary praised the "heroic conduct" of the four Seminary students who served with the regiment.[65] Tillie Pierce defended the men of the 26th, particularly the local company, when she wrote, "Though inexperienced, the stand they made, and the valor they displayed before an overwhelming force, cannot fail in placing the loyalty and bravery of her citizens in the foremost rank."[66]

The feeble resistance of the 26th Militia led to the first occupation of Gettysburg by enemy forces. It was an event the townspeople would never forget. The first hint of trouble came at around 3 P.M. when Bell's troopers and the supply wagons of the militia came thundering back along the Chambersburg Pike in full retreat. White's Comanches, numbering about 200 men, arrived in Gettysburg about a half an hour later.

Residing on the western outskirts of town, Sallie Broadhead was among the first to observe the invaders. "[T]hey came with

to cooperate in the pursuit of Lee's army following the Battle of Gettysburg. The Army of Northern Virginia escaped across the Potomac, following which the emergency troops were mustered out of service on July 30, 1863.[62]

In later years, former members of the militia took great pride in their role as the first defenders of the state. Henry Richards proclaimed that he and his comrades were "the first troops to oppose the entrance of the Rebels into Pennsylvania; the first to meet the enemy at Gettysburg and the first to draw blood in that historic combat."

such horrid yells that it was enough to frighten us all to death," she recorded.[67]

An instant later, the Rebels entered the town and "rode rapidly through the principal streets flourishing their guns in a threatening fashion."[68] Professor Michael Jacobs bitterly recalled the horsemen "shouting and yelling like so many savages … firing their pistols, not caring whether they killed or maimed man, woman, or child...."[69]

One of the Comanches admitted that most of his fellow riders were heavily intoxicated by this point and in this "half-horse, half-wildcat condition … each man imagined himself to be the greatest hero of the war." Some were overheard recounting to the horrified citizens of Gettysburg "the immense execution they had done with the saber in a hundred battles."[70]

Brigadier General John Gordon's Brigade of six Georgia regiments followed the cavalry into town. They were far superior in numbers, but considerably more disciplined than their mounted companions. "I shall never forget the June afternoon when I stood on the Seminary steps with my parents and other persons to see a Confederate host marching in the Chambersburg Pike," recalled Lydia Ziegler. "It seemed as if pandemonium had broken loose." One can only imagine the horrible thoughts that raced through the mind of the slender teenager as she stared aghast at the "ragged and unkempt set of men" marching towards her home. When an advance squad of the invaders learned that the large four-story brick edifice on the low ridge ahead was a theological school, a guard was placed around the structure as the troops filed past. For the time, Lydia and her family "felt perfectly safe."[71]

The loyal Unionist residents of Gettysburg were mortified when the jubilant Rebels raised the Stars and Bars on the tall flagpole in the center of the Diamond as a nearby band struck up a medley of Southern tunes. The humiliation was complete when a squad of the militiamen marched past surrounded by an armed guard.[72]

General Early requisitioned large quantities of food and supplies from the community, including 1,000 pairs of shoes and 500 hats. In lieu of these items, a ransom of $10,000 was levied. The town council informed the general that both the requested provisions and the sum of cash were beyond their means to supply, but they offered to make their limited inventory of wares available to the invaders. The solution appeased Early.[73]

In addition to what they gathered from area merchants, the Confederates discovered the rations intended for the militia in a group of railroad cars near the depot. After the unloading and distribution of the provisions, the cars, engine house, and the railroad bridge over Rock Creek were set ablaze. The resulting conflagration lit the night sky with an eerie red reflection.[74]

Sallie Broadhead characterized the evening of June 26th as "the most uncomfortable night of my life." She was alone with her young daughter while "surrounded by thousands of ugly, rude, hostile soldiers." Her anxiety was heightened by the fact that her husband was en route to Hanover Junction, a small railroad station located about 25 miles east of Gettysburg. Sallie feared that he might be taken prisoner before he could return.[75]

On the morning of June 27th, much to the relief of Gettysburg's remaining citizens, the enemy forces disappeared as suddenly as they had came. Before he swung east towards York and perhaps even larger prizes, Early assembled an estimated 175 militiamen in the town square and scolded them: "You boys ought to be home with your mothers, and not out in the fields where it is dangerous and you might get hurt."[76] After being paroled, the hapless soldiers trudged north to Carlisle and then to Harrisburg. Along the way they suffered the further indignity of having their shoes stripped from them.[77]

Although the invaders had generally behaved well during the brief occupation and no violent acts or "wanton destruction of property" occurred, the town was now completely isolated from the outside world as a result of the severed rail and telegraph lines and the disruption of mail service. Henry Jacobs described the feeling of help-lessness which pervaded the community at the time:

> The town was as quiet as it could well be. All business was paralyzed. Everything was in a state of expectancy. It was the calm that preceded the storm.[78]

Another resident wrote, "Now we knew beyond peradventure that the 'wolf was at the door.'"[79]

CHAPTER 4

The Armies Converge

Armies may surround me, but I won't be afraid;
war may break out, but I will trust you.
Psalm 27, verse 3

On June 26, 1863, as Gettysburg experienced an enemy invasion for the first time, Robert E. Lee established his headquarters in a patch of woods on the eastern outskirts of Chambersburg. For the next four days, this area would serve as the nerve center of the Army of Northern Virginia. It was here that Lee fine-tuned his strategy for the invasion of Pennsylvania. Longstreet would continue up the valley and support Ewell in an assault on Harrisburg, while Hill's men traveled east in Early's wake, crossed the Susquehanna below Harrisburg, and destroyed the railroad and communications linking the state capital with Philadelphia.[1]

Lee was riding an impressive string of victories, and a sense of invincibility pervaded his thinking. Before the campaign, he had written to one of his division commanders: "There were never such men in an army before. They will go anywhere and do anything if properly led."[2] He had every reason to expect continued success in the final days of June.

In reciprocation, the officers and men of the Army of Northern Virginia displayed an almost universal affection for their chief. Colonel Edward Porter Alexander summed it up best: "We looked forward to victory under him as confidently as to successive sunrises."[3]

This unwavering faith reached a zenith during the final stages of the Gettysburg Campaign. One South Carolina officer asserted, "I have little doubt that we had now the finest army ever marshaled on this side of the Atlantic, and one scarcely inferior to any Europe has known."[4] Another officer doubted whether "any army ever marched into an enemies country with greater confidence in its ability ... than the army of Gen. Lee."[5] Observing the fighting men around him, a Confederate surgeon from North Carolina boasted, "How can they be whipped?"[6]

The fighting spirit and tenacity of the Confederate invaders was perhaps best exemplified by Major General Isaac Ridgeway Trimble. At age 61, he was among the oldest generals in either army, but Trimble displayed the ambition and restlessness of many men half his age. He was straightforward and accustomed to getting his way. Isaac's perpetual scowl, broad mustache, bull voice, and fancy manner of dress punctuated an eccentric personality.[7] Nevertheless, a junior officer declared that he was "as gallant a man as ever drew a sword" and that "there was fight enough in old man Trimble to satisfy a herd of tigers."[8]

A man of firm convictions, Trimble developed a bitter hatred for the North and the Republican party. He vehemently asserted that the seceded Southern states could "*never* join the North in political hands much less in brotherly kindness." The differences between the two regions were impossible to reconcile because "the Union was at variance with our feelings, tastes, pursuits, honorable aims & religion and time instead of removing these, has strengthened them."[9]

Born in Culpeper County, Virginia, Trimble

Major General Isaac Trimble, CSA. Courtesy of Library of Congress.

graduated from the United States Military Academy at West Point in 1822, at the age of 20. He then served for 10 years in the Old Army before tendering his resignation. For the next three decades, Isaac tapped into the unlimited growth opportunities of the burgeoning railroad industry. As chief engineer he supervised the construction and operation of a number of lines in the Mid-Atlantic region.

Trimble was residing in his adopted state of Maryland at the outbreak of the Civil War. He immediately allied himself with the Confederacy by burning the railroad bridges north of Baltimore, so as to disrupt the transportation of Federal troops to Washington. In May 1861, Trimble returned to his native Virginia and accepted a commission as colonel of engineers. In this capacity, he assisted in the design of defensive works at Norfolk and at other strategic locations. These behind-the-scenes operations did not suit his fiery temperament, however, and by the end of the summer, he had wrangled a promotion to brigadier general. In November, he was placed in command of a brigade in a division that was led by General Richard S. Ewell. In March of 1862, Ewell was ordered to assist Stonewall Jackson in the Shenandoah Valley.[10]

During the spring and summer campaigns, Trimble earned a reputation as an aggressive and relentless fighter. These traits made him a favorite of the usually dour Jackson. Early in the war, the energetic Trimble informed his younger mentor that before the close of the conflict he intended "to be a Major General or a corpse."[11] At the battle of Second Bull Run or Manassas on August 29, 1862, he nearly achieved both objectives when an exploding bullet struck his left leg just above the ankle, causing severe damage. After the battle, Stonewall recommended Trimble for the promotion he so dearly coveted.

Much to his dismay, Isaac's recovery was protracted. The damaged limb was often inflamed or infected, and pieces of bone surfaced from the wound months later. Examining surgeons even hinted at amputation, but doses of laudanum and "lead water as a wash" were prescribed instead.[12] The general's advanced age and restlessness further complicated his condition.

In spite of his feeble health, Isaac returned to the field on February 1, 1863, to take command of Jackson's old division. On April 13th, he contracted a severe cold from exposure and was stricken with a near fatal case of erysipelas. Ironically, 10 days later, his promotion to major general was approved by the Senate. As a result of his serious condition, Trimble was sidelined during the Chancellorsville campaign.[13]

Afterwards, General Lee placed the recuperating officer in charge of the Valley District, where Jackson had once reigned supreme. But when Trimble entered the region during the third week of June to assume formal command, he discovered that it had been stripped of troops during the northward movement. Although still not fully recovered from his ailments, Isaac could not accept the prospect of missing another battle.[14]

He rode north and caught up with his commander near Berryville, Virginia, and Lee invited him to join the invasion. Upon reaching Chambersburg, the two officers pored over area maps. Trimble shared his extensive knowledge of the topography from his railroading days. According to Isaac, Lee laid his hand on the map over Gettysburg and predicted that a great battle would be fought in this vicinity. Lee then suggested that the Marylander ride ahead to Carlisle and join his old chief, Lieutenant General Richard Ewell, as a volunteer aide and military advisor.[15]

Ewell's troops arrived in Carlisle on Saturday, June 27th, and the Second Corps commander planned to capture Harrisburg within the next two days. Trimble, full of fight as ever, offered the opinion that the city could be successfully stormed with one brigade of infantry.[16]

Not every soldier in the Confederate army was as eager for the fray as old man Trimble. Major Henry Kyd Douglas, the 24-year-old assistant adjutant general of General Johnson's staff, entered Pennsylvania with a degree of apprehension. "I could not get over the feeling that an invasion of the enemy's territory, however tempting, was the wrong policy for us," Douglas wrote in his memoirs. The origin of his foreboding was readily traceable. "I was conscious of the fact that I was doubting everything since [Stonewall] Jackson was gone and rather ashamed of it," he admitted.[17] Except for their mutual reverence for the fallen Jackson, the youthful Douglas and the pugnacious Trimble were polar opposites in almost every respect.

Tall, dashing, and handsome, Kyd Douglas was the beau ideal of a soldier. His charisma and geniality, combined with his boyish good looks, made him popular with nearly everyone he met. Women found him alluring, men sought his friendship, even the enemy enjoyed the company of this effervescent young man. Following the war, one Union soldier paid Douglas the

Major Henry Kyd Douglas, class of 1858, Franklin & Marshall College. Courtesy of FM.

highest tribute when he pronounced that he "never knew a man who more deserved the too-often used words, 'a soldier and a gentleman.'"[18]

Henry had enjoyed an idyllic childhood roaming the fields and woods near Ferry Hill Place, the family plantation, situated in Southwestern Maryland directly across the Potomac River from Shepherdstown, Virginia, his place of birth. Harpers Ferry, Antietam Creek, and the upper reaches of the Shenandoah Valley were familiar haunts.

He received his early education at the Shepherdstown Classical School, where he received instruction in Latin, Greek, advanced Mathematics, Philosophy, Chemistry, and Theology. His principal de-

scribed him as "a young man of irreproachable moral character, of studious habits, and agreeable manners."[19] Douglas entered the junior class of Franklin and Marshall College in Lancaster, Pennsylvania, in 1856. During his college years he cultivated the friendship of many Northerners.

Upon his graduation in 1858, Douglas concentrated on Law, studying at Lexington, Virginia, and at Hagerstown, Maryland. After his admittance to the bar in 1860, he moved to St. Louis, Missouri, and began a practice.[20]

Young Douglas discounted the dire predictions of national fractionalization which followed Lincoln's election, since he did not believe "our people would ever take up arms against each other." While he firmly believed that any state had the Constitutional right to secede, he could not come to grips with a dissolution of the Union, "perhaps because I was so much opposed to it," he reflected later.[21]

But when his native state of Virginia adopted the Ordinance of Secession on April 17, 1861, the budding attorney returned home and enlisted as a private in Company B of the 2nd Virginia Infantry, which was recruited from the Shepherdstown area. Together with four other regiments, the 2nd became part of the famous "Stonewall Brigade."[22]

Henry was one of those rare individuals who could succeed at any undertaking. His leadership qualities quickly earned him promotions. Within four months he had ascended to the rank of second lieutenant.

The bright young officer attracted the attention of Stonewall Jackson after he completed an epic 105-mile ride through rain, mud, and impenetrable darkness to deliver an important dispatch to General Ewell at the outset of the legendary Valley Campaign. Douglas completed the vital mission in less than 24 hours, and soon afterwards, fainted from exhaustion. He used five horses during the journey, one of them falling dead under him. Afterwards, an appreciative Jackson appointed him the assistant inspector general of his staff.

The lively Douglas and the reticent Jackson constituted an odd pairing, but the former lawyer quickly developed into one of Stonewall's most trusted subordinates. Douglas was by Jackson's side in the Valley, at Cedar Mountain, Second Manassas, Harpers Ferry, and Antietam, and in one instance, he may have saved the general's life during a surprise encounter with Union cavalry.[23]

Henry missed the battle of Fredericksburg due to illness, but he was in the thick of the fighting at Chancellorsville. Here, he experienced two close calls. During the early stages of the campaign a shell fragment just missed him, cutting his bridle and halter reins in two. After the bloody fighting of Sunday, May 3rd, Douglas discovered that a ball had entered his brand new cap just above the visor, but fortunately the projectile exited harmlessly, only clipping off a lock of his hair. This followed on the heels of a similar experience eight months earlier; Henry became increasingly superstitious and swore never again to wear new headgear into combat.[24]

His conduct during the battle elicited praise from two of his superiors. Both officers mentioned his gallant behavior, good conduct, and valuable assistance in their official reports of the battle. Colonel John H. S. Funk added that Douglas' "daring example caused the greatest enthusiasm among the men."[25]

Following Jackson's death on May 10, 1863, Douglas and other former members of the general's staff accompanied Mrs.

Jackson to Richmond with the remains of the fallen hero. When Henry returned to the army in mid–May, he received a promotion to major and joined the staff of General Johnson.

Throughout his military service, Douglas had little difficulty filling his insatiable appetite for two things: literature and female companionship. In less than three years Henry read over three hundred books, including works by Nathaniel Hawthorne, Walter Scott, James Fenimore Cooper, Edgar Allan Poe, Victor Hugo, and numerous others. In nearly every town through which the army passed the handsome bachelor met beautiful young ladies, a number of whom became his "military advisors."[26]

To the casual observer, Douglas's military exploits read like a novel, chock-full of adventure and romantic intrigue. But as the Gettysburg campaign commenced, Henry's gaiety had been subdued by a stern dose of reality. An untold number of his friends and comrades had given their lives for the Southern cause and the blighting hand of war had wreaked havoc upon his own family. In the aftermath of the battle of Antietam, Union forces occupied Ferry Hill Place. The estate sustained considerable damage, and worse, Henry's elderly father was accused of spying for the Confederacy. The elder Douglas endured a six-week imprisonment at Fort McHenry before being released. Henry always maintained that the brutal incarceration contributed to his father's death near the end of the war. And now, as the army neared another showdown with the Yankees, even the indefatigable Jackson was no more.

These losses and his own brushes with death placed young Henry in close touch with his own mortality. Nevertheless, when the soldiers of Ewell's corps liberated Winchester, Virginia, an elated Douglas accepted a homemade cap from a grateful female admirer despite his streak of bad luck with new headgear.[27]

On the evening of June 28th, Robert E. Lee received a shocking piece of intelligence. A spy hired by Longstreet at the outset of the campaign revealed that the Army of the Potomac was no longer in Virginia, but instead, situated near Frederick, Maryland, only a one or two day's march from the Pennsylvania border.[28] With his forces spread out in a huge arc across 60 miles of Pennsylvania countryside, Lee realized he was in a vulnerable position. He immediately issued a set of orders to reunite his forces along South Mountain near Cashtown.

Lee seemed prepared for this contingency. He could easily pull his troops together within 24 hours, while he expected the enemy to arrive in Pennsylvania "broken down with hunger and hard marching, strung out on a long line and much demoralized."[29]

The residents of Gettysburg needed no official notification to inform them of the proximity of the opposing army. In the large clearings dotting the eastern slope of South Mountain, the camp fires of Southern troops were clearly visible. There were also constant rumors of Rebel foraging parties roaming the surrounding countryside.[30]

Therefore, it was with much trepidation that Martin Luther Culler and Washington Van Buren Gotwald accepted a request by the pastor of the Emmitsburg charge for two Gettysburg Seminary students to fill the pulpit at Fairfield, Pennsylvania, for the morning and evening services scheduled for Sunday, June 28th. The village of Fairfield was located near a gap in South Mountain only ten miles south of Cashtown. During the journey it was decided that Gotwald would preach in the morning since he was senior to Culler in both age and in years of study at the Seminary.[31]

Near the close of the morning service, a contingent of Confederates dashed into the village, greatly frightening the citizens, who did not hang around for the benediction. The curiosity of the students was greatly aroused, however, and in the early afternoon they walked towards the Rebel camp near the outskirts of the town for a closer look. From a respectful distance, they cautiously observed the Southerners. Suddenly, two Union scouts rode up and halted nearby. The Yankees took cover behind a hedgerow, discharged their carbines at the enemy troops, and dashed away unobserved. The Confederates immediately returned the fire in the direction of the rising white smoke. The bullets passed dangerously close to the students, and the pair immediately scampered into a nearby house. A moment later, an angry group of Southern soldiers burst through the door, thrusting their weapons into the faces of the suspected gunmen. The prisoners were marched out of the house, where they were met by a Rebel captain.

Gotwald, visibly shaken by the experience, was speechless. Conversely, his companion maintained his composure. After respectfully saluting the officer, Culler earnestly narrated the true sequence of events and the mistaken identity which had occurred in the midst of the confusion. The captain admitted that the story seemed plausible, but he did not appear entirely convinced of the innocence of the two young men. A painful silence followed.

Acting decisively, Culler cleverly turned the tables on his interrogator. "Captain, you do not arrest ministers of the gospel, do you?" he asked forcefully.

The surprised captain immediately queried, "Are you men ministers?"

In replying in the affirmative, the Seminarian did not believe he had told an egregious lie. They were, after all, ministerial students, and they had indeed come to the town for the express purpose of preaching.

Feeling more at ease with the polite officer, Martin pointed to the Lutheran church and stated: "Do you see that brick church yonder? There we were holding religious services this morning. This man whom you see with me was preaching. Your men rushed into town and disturbed our worship. Now you occupy the town and this hinders me from preaching the splendid sermon which I intended to preach this evening."

The captain smiled and replied that he did not arrest ministers of the gospel unless they were bearing arms. He then inquired as to the quality of the horse they had ridden into town on. "It is old, blind, and poor in flesh," Culler answered, "We are Yankees enough to know better than venture anywhere near your army with a good horse." The officer laughed heartily and assured the "ministers" that they could return home undisturbed on such a specimen. Later, Culler conceded that the Fairfield congregation did not "lose much" in missing his sermon.[32]

When they reached home following their adventure, the two theologians found their community in the clutches of nervous anxiety once again, as the eventful month of June 1863 neared a close. Daniel Skelly related that he and his neighbors expected enemy troops to march into their town at any moment. As of yet they had no word on the whereabouts of the Army of the Potomac.[33] Everyone seemed to be asking the same question: "Where is our army, that they let the enemy scour the country and do as they please?"[34]

Although greatly relieved by the safe return of her husband, late in the evening of June 29th, Sallie Broadhead's apprehensions returned the following day. She confided her gloomy outlook to her diary: "It begins to look as though we will have a battle soon, and we are in great fear. I see

by the papers that General Hooker has been relieved, and the change of commanders I fear may give great advantage to the enemy, and our army may be repulsed."[35]

No one was more surprised at this latest development than Major General George Gordon Meade. Stirred from his tent at 3 A.M. on the morning of June 28th, the 47-year-old Philadelphian suspected that he was being removed of command or placed under arrest for his open criticism of Hooker following the Chancellorsville campaign. The groggy corps commander was stunned when the order was read that placed him in command of the army.[36]

Four hours later, from his headquarters near Frederick, Maryland, Meade wired General-in-Chief Henry W. Halleck in Washington that he would "move toward the Susquehanna, keeping Washington and Baltimore well covered, and if the enemy is checked in his attempt to cross the Susquehanna, or if he turns toward Baltimore, to give him battle."[37] On the 29th, his 90,000-man force streamed northward on a broad front in an effort to locate Lee and bring him to battle.

The army was grouped into three wings to facilitate rapid movement and flexibility. The left wing, consisting of the First, Third, and Eleventh Corps, was led by Major General John F. Reynolds, a native of Lancaster, Pennsylvania, highly regarded as one of the army's most intelligent and capable corps commanders. His own First Corps formed the vanguard of the infantry advance, and on the morning of June 30th, its three divisions moved off from their overnight bivouacs near Emmitsburg, Maryland, crossed the Mason-Dixon line, and halted about five miles south of Gettysburg.[38]

In the lead was Brigadier General James Wadsworth's stalwart First Division. One of Wadsworth's two brigades was the famous "Iron Brigade," which consisted of three regiments from Wisconsin, one from

Indiana, and one from Michigan. The tough Midwesterners received their sobriquet in recognition of their stubborn fighting at Brawner's Farm, Second Bull Run, South Mountain, and Antietam.[39]

The other brigade of the First Division was commanded by Brigadier General Lysander Cutler. Although Cutler's New Yorkers and Pennsylvanians were not nearly as well known as their Western counterparts, they were proven fighters, with one exception. The 380 men of the 147th New York were untried in battle. The unit was present at Chancellorsville, but like most regiments in the First Corps, it saw only limited action.[40]

Brigadier General John C. Robinson's Second Division was also a first-class combat unit. By contrast, the Third Division was for the most part an unknown commodity. This all–Pennsylvania organization was led by Major General Abner Doubleday. Only two of the six regiments supervised by Doubleday had played a major role in a battle prior to Gettysburg. The remainder had spent much of their service time performing guard duty near Washington.[41] But as a South Carolina officer pointed out later, they were "Pennsylvanians fighting for everything they held dear." The same officer noted that these were not ordinary soldiers, but were generally "more intelligent" than those his men had encountered in the past.[42]

This intelligence and promise was exemplified by two young officers in the 142nd Pennsylvania. On July 31, 1862, at the tender age of 17, Andrew Gregg Tucker graduated from the University at Lewisburg (present-day Bucknell University). His family tree was filled with notable examples of civic and military service. Andrew had been named in honor of his distinguished grandfather, U.S. Senator Andrew Gregg. His father, Charles, had been the pastor of the Tabernacle Baptist Church in Philadelphia prior to his death

in 1850. Pennsylvania Governor Andrew Gregg Curtin was his first cousin, and two other cousins, John Irvin Gregg and David McMurtrie Gregg, served as generals in the Cavalry Corps of the Army of the Potomac. Andrew continued the family tradition when he received a commission as a second lieutenant during the formation of the 142nd Pennsylvania in August.[43]

The day before Tucker received his diploma in Lewisburg, Jeremiah Hoffman attended commencement exercises at Franklin and Marshall College in Lancaster, Pennsylvania. Hoffman planned to enter the law profession, but for the present, national issues took precedence. Jeremiah and 25 of his neighbors from the Schaefferstown area reported to Harrisburg, where they became part of Company K of the 142nd. Hoffman was elected as first lieutenant of this unit.[44]

The commander of the 142nd, Colonel Robert Parson Cummins, was held in high esteem by his officers and men because he led by example without seeking personal recognition. At the outbreak of the war, the 34-year-old husband and father of seven resided in Somerset, Pennsylvania, where he operated an apothecary. A respected pillar of the community, Robert also served as a school director and as justice of the peace. Cummins gained valuable military experience during a stint as a captain in the 10th Pennsylvania Reserves.

Cummins was a burly, athletic man, and a skilled horseman. Despite his imposing stature, he was kind and unpretentious. Just as importantly, he strove to perform his duty at any sacrifice of comfort and at whatever risk the situation demanded.[45]

During the Battle of Fredericksburg, he rose from his sick bed and joined his troops in their first combat action. His sudden and unexpected appearance elicited a burst of applause from the rank and

Colonel Robert P. Cummins, 142nd Pa. Vols. Courtesy of PSA.

file. During the fierce encounter, Cummins had his horse shot from under him. The following spring, at Chancellorsville, he narrowly escaped once again when his mount was struck in the head by an artillery shell.[46]

As the colonel continued to gain the respect and affection of the men, his junior officers continued to develop leadership skills and to master the details of military life. In February 1863, Andrew Tucker was appointed acting adjutant of the regiment, and a month later, he was promoted to first lieutenant. Captain Charles Evans, a friend and fellow alumnus of the University at Lewisburg, remarked on Andrew's rapid progress. "He was the most brilliant one I ever saw and was fast developing into a man. The office of adjutant gave him something to do, and well did he do it."[47]

The bitter defeats at Fredericksburg and Chancellorsville did not diminish the resolve of the Pennsylvanians. In response to growing opposition to the war in the North, Tucker authored an open letter to his hometown newspaper in which he proclaimed that he and his comrades in Company E would not "shirk from dangers and death in defense of our principles."[48]

The other regiment in Doubleday's division that could boast of combat experience was the 121st Pennsylvania. Led by Colonel Chapman Biddle, a prominent Philadelphia lawyer, this unit was assigned to the Third Division at the same time as the 142nd and was also heavily engaged at Fredericksburg.[49]

Although not as seasoned as the 121st and 142nd, the remaining four regiments in the division were well-drilled and would certainly fight well on their home soil. The 143rd, 149th, 150th, and 151st Pennsylvania joined the division in February 1863 as replacements for the battle-weary Pennsylvania Reserves, which took their place in the defense of Washington.[50]

The 149th and 150th Pennsylvania were known as the Bucktail Brigade. These regiments hoped to build on the reputation of the original "Bucktails," the 1st Pennsylvania Rifles, a unit made up of skilled marksmen from the Northern Tier counties of the Keystone State. In imitation of their highly admired predecessors, the new recruits affixed deer tails to their headgear.[51] The 143rd Pennsylvania under Colonel Edmund L. Dana joined the Bucktails to form the Second Brigade of the Third Division.

Captain Brice Blair, Company I, 149th Pennsylvania, was a typical Bucktail officer. The owner of a thriving mercantile business and tannery, he left behind his family and business interests to offer his services for the Union. The company under his command had principally been raised in the vicinity of his home at Shade Gap, a valley hamlet nestled among the mountains of southern Huntingdon County. Captain Blair was 42 years old "while his boys, as he called them, were an average of 21 years. He felt deeply for their welfare."[52]

Not all of the new Bucktails were rugged outdoorsmen. Henry Chancellor, Jr., was born in Philadelphia on June 23, 1842, the youngest son of Henry Chancellor, Esq., "a wealthy and estimable citizen." Henry Junior grew up in the Germantown district in the luxury and ease of a fine city home and was educated at a classical academy in Lawrenceville, New Jersey. On August 19, 1862, he entered the army as sec-

ond lieutenant of Company B, 150th Pennsylvania. Less than three months later, he received a promotion to first lieutenant.

Although of slender build and "unused to the rougher sides of life ... he endured the longest marches, lived upon the hardest fare, and underwent all the hardships of a campaign equal to the most robust and embrowned among them."[53] When orders came for his regiment to join the Army of the Potomac in Virginia, Henry had just received a 10-day furlough to visit home. The young officer turned down the opportunity to rest and endured the toils of the Chancellorsville campaign with his comrades. A second furlough was received the day before his command was ordered to march north in pursuit of Lee. Again, Chancellor refused the leave, and he somehow persevered during the severe and exhausting marches from Virginia to Pennsylvania. The delicate, but determined, youngster would not shirk his duty.[54]

Unlike the other regiments in the Third Division which had enlisted for three years, the 151st Pennsylvania was a nine-months regiment and its term was due to expire at the end of July. Its commander, Lieutenant Colonel George Fisher McFarland, described his mixed emotions in a letter to his wife, dated June 19th: "My anxiety to see home and the dear ones there is growing with the flying moments. I resist the feeling all I can, for I know it can do no good, while it makes me more uncomfortable and more likely not to encourage the men as I should. Reason and feeling are in direct conflict.... But I will try to do my duty until regularly dismissed by the proper order."[55]

Lieutenant Colonel George F. McFarland, 151st Pa. Vols. Courtesy of PSA.

Throughout his military service, McFarland struggled with

the conflicting ideals of duty to his country and devotion to his family. It was only after serious thought and anxious prayer that he had decided to join the Union army in early September of 1862. It was an agonizing choice for the 28-year-old school teacher as it meant leaving behind his beloved wife, two young children, and his academy in McAlisterville, Pennsylvania, of which he was the principal and proprietor. But, George concluded, "The continuance of the blessings now enjoyed seemed to depend upon the integrity and perpetuity of the union of our fathers, and this was now in jeopardy and only to be rescued by force of arms."[56]

The 151st suffered its first battle casualties during several minor skirmishes at Chancellorsville. Although the regiment's performance was shaky, George predicted that his men would "stand the next fire much better."[57]

On the eve of battle the Third Division was augmented by the addition of the 20th New York State Militia (80th New York Volunteers). This veteran unit had spent the past five months on assignment with the Provost Guard after being decimated through hard service at Second Bull Run, South Mountain, Antietam, and Fredericksburg. In the emergency of Lee's invasion, the regiment, also known as the Ulster Guard, was reassigned to the First Corps. Colonel Theodore Gates and his 300 New Yorkers joined the 121st, 142nd, and 151st Pennsylvania in General Thomas Rowley's First Brigade. The Pennsylvanians were performing picket duty about two and a half miles west of the Emmitsburg Road.[58]

The ranks of the 20th were composed of many farmers from the agricultural regions of Ulster and Green Counties in Southeastern New York. The cultivated landscape of orchards, meadows, and grain fields probably reminded many of their own homes.[59]

Among those who may have experienced such nostalgic feelings was Corporal Abram Swart, a 19-year-old farm laborer from Platte Mountain who served in Company I. As he settled into his new surroundings, Abram's thoughts might have reverted to his mother and three young sisters. Sarah Swart Bemis had suffered great hardships in her 50 plus years. Twice a widow, she had buried her second husband, the father of all of her children, in 1849. She remarried shortly thereafter, but her third husband abandoned the family in 1858, leaving her destitute. In feeble health, Sarah depended upon the charity of neighbors and the limited income of her eldest son for support. It was an act of faith and patriotism on her part when she watched her son go off to war in 1861. Throughout his military service, Abram directed a local bank cashier to pay out part of his wages to his mother. By June 1863, these allotments totaled $172.66.[60]

Swart and his comrades were led by veteran officers such as Captain Daniel McMahon of Company D. A native of London, England, the 24-year-old officer had served in the English Army during the Crimean War. McMahon enlisted to defend his adopted country immediately after the firing on Fort Sumter in April of 1861. He served as a private during the original three-month term of the 20th Militia. When the unit was reorganized as a three-year regiment in the fall, he was elected as captain of his company.

McMahon received a slight wound in his right hip on September 1, 1862, at the Battle of Chantilly, Virginia. After recuperating in a Washington hospital, he was granted a leave for twenty days, during which time he returned home and was married.[61] The new husband looked forward to the expiration of his military service and the start of a new life with his bride, but he realized there was grim work ahead.

General Lee was only partly correct in assessing the condition of the Federal army on the final day of June. The strenuous marches of the past three weeks had certainly exacted a large toll. This was particularly true of the beginning of the campaign, which took place in the midst of a severe heat wave in Virginia. The subsequent marches through Western Maryland were characterized by rainy weather and muddy roads.

For the numerous Pennsylvanians in the First Corps, the fact that they were now back on their home soil buoyed their spirits. But this feeling was not unique to the troops from the Keystone State. The historian of the 76th New York recorded that he and his comrades "felt that they were now called upon to fight, not merely for an abstract principle, but for their own hearth-stones, — not only to sustain the government, but for their own families, and to preserve their homes from the desolation of war."[62]

Although they were not as outwardly confident as their Southern rivals, Colonel Lucius Fairchild of the 2nd Wisconsin proclaimed that there was no "better disciplined, better equipped, better behaved army in the world" than the Army of the Potomac.[63] The long string of bitter defeats and the poor leadership it had long suffered under had imbued its members with a grim determination to succeed. The adversity and personal hardships they had endured together had created a deep reservoir of resilience. One officer compared the army to an English bulldog: "You can whip them time and again, but the next fight they go into, they are in good spirits, and as full of pluck as ever. They are used to being whipped, and no longer mind it. Some day or other we shall have our turn."[64]

The camp fires observed by Gettysburg residents on the eastern slope of South Mountain belonged to the division

of Major General Henry Heth of A. P. Hill's Corps, which had arrived in the Cashtown area on the 29th. The next morning Heth sent Brigadier General James J. Pettigrew's brigade to Gettysburg in search of supplies with strict orders not to precipitate a fight if any organized resistance was encountered.[65]

Meanwhile, the Cavalry Corps of the Army of the Potomac was attempting to pinpoint the specific location of the enemy. Screening the advance of the left wing was Brigadier General John Buford's First Division. A Kentucky native, West Point graduate, and former Indian fighter, Buford was among the Union's most reliable cavalry officers. After bivouacking near Fairfield on the evening of the 29th, Buford's 2,950 troopers pushed forward towards Gettysburg.[66]

Pettigrew's troops arrived on the western outskirts of town during the mid-morning of the 30th. The head of the column halted near the Seminary as skirmishers were thrown forward to check for enemy troops.[67] Sallie Broadhead had a good view of the Confederates from her home and at any moment expected to hear the booming of cannon, as she feared the Confederates would commence shelling the town.[68] At the same time, Henry Jacobs was observing the enemy force with the aid of a telescope from the garret of his home on the corner of Washington and Middle Streets. As he scanned the terrain to the west, Henry detected movement along the Chambersburg Pike. He described his exciting discovery and the subsequent events in his memoirs:

> A glance showed that something interesting was happening. On the further hill, horsemen were seen moving.... But a brief pause, and they have descended the ravine, and mounted the hill nearest me. They are on the crest of Seminary Ridge. I distinguish two officers examining the country, and then lingering,

with their field glasses turned towards the south-east. Back of them, I can indistinctly see a considerable force with a piece of artillery in front. Suddenly they all turn, and have retraced their way into the ravine. A minute or two more, and I hear a great cheering in the street. Running downstairs, I am too late to see the head of the procession. Buford's division of Federal troops has come in the Emmitsburg Road....[69]

Having spotted Federal cavalry approaching Gettysburg from the south, Pettigrew ordered a countermarch back to Cashtown in compliance with his orders. After entering the town, the blue-clad horsemen turned off the Emmitsburg Road onto Washington Street and then galloped west along Chambersburg Street in the direction of the enemy infantry. One squadron cautiously followed the Confederates to make sure they were retiring.[70]

Buford noted that he "found everybody in a terrible state of excitement on account of the enemy's advance upon this place."[71] After being visited by the enemy twice in the past four days, the citizens of Gettysburg were overjoyed by the arrival of the cavalrymen. They were comforted by the fact that at least a portion of the Army of the Potomac had finally arrived. Tillie Pierce and her classmates stood outside of their school on West High Street as the long column trotted past. "It was to me a novel and grand sight, " she wrote, "I had never seen so many soldiers at one time. They were Union soldiers and that was enough for me, for I then knew we had protection, and I felt they were our dearest friends."[72]

The dust-covered liberators were serenaded with patriotic songs, while other residents expressed their pleasure by waving flags, cheering heartily, or by tossing bouquets of flowers at the mounted column. The liberal distribution of water, bread and butter, fresh meat, pies, cakes,

and other treats was also greatly appreciated by the hungry and thirsty riders.[73] A New York trooper wrote that the warm reception "made the blood flow quicker in our veins, as we thought of those at home, and that we were there to defend Northern soil...."[74]

Although his horses and men were "fagged out," Buford immediately sent out patrols to ascertain the strength of the enemy in the area.[75] He thoroughly examined the surrounding terrain and established outposts to cover all of the principal roads leading into the area. Of primary concern was the Chambersburg Pike, the exit route for Pettigrew's troops. This road also led to the important pass in South Mountain at Cashtown, which was wide enough to allow easy passage of troops, artillery, and supplies. Colonel William Gamble's larger First Brigade was assigned the defense of this critical area, while Colonel Thomas Devin's Second Brigade fanned out to cover the northern approaches.

The main body of the cavalry force gathered near McPherson's Ridge, about one mile west of the town square. The six 3-inch guns of Lieutenant John Calef's Battery A, 2nd U.S. Artillery, unlimbered on the low ridge on either side of the pike. Located just a quarter-mile to the east, the prominent cupola of the Lutheran Seminary functioned as an observation post and as a signal station.[76]

The Union horsemen not employed on patrol or outpost duty set up camp in the swale south of the pike between McPherson's and Seminary Ridge. Their presence drew a considerable amount of attention from the local residents. The closest neighbors to the new military community were the members of the Ziegler household residing at the Seminary. "We gave them a royal welcome," recalled Lydia. "How well do I remember the happiness it gave me to hand out the cakes and pies that our kind mother made until late at night for those boys in blue who seemed almost famished for a taste of 'home victuals,' as they called them."[77]

The ever opportunistic cavalrymen took full advantage of the natural curiosity of ten-year-old Hugh Ziegler and his friends. Years later, Hugh fondly recalled that the "boys of Gettysburg, including myself, would often ride the soldiers' horses down to the watering trough in town, and sometimes the soldiers would give us money with which we would buy them knickknacks or something to eat."[78]

From his headquarters at the Eagle Hotel on Chambersburg Street, Buford analyzed the wide array of intelligence information gathered from his patrols and through spies and scouts operating in the region. As he weighed his available options, there is no doubt that the veteran officer considered the strong potential of the high ground south of the town: Culp's Hill, Cemetery Hill, Cemetery Ridge, and the Round Tops. In addition to giving an advantage in battle, these heights controlled the roads over which Meade's infantry would be arriving. Buford realized he did not have the manpower to fight a passive defensive battle on this choice ground. Instead, he decided that the best way to preserve this highly desirable position was to deploy his troopers at a considerable distance west and north of the town. By utilizing a series of low ridges and other natural obstacles, his small force could fight an effective delaying action until Reynolds and the infantry of the left wing, about 30,000 strong, arrived on the scene.[79]

By evening, Buford had a fairly accurate picture of the enemy forces confronting him. Near 11 P.M., he sent the following dispatch: "A. P. Hill's corps, composed of Anderson, Heth, and Pender is massed back of Cashtown, 9 miles from this place. His pickets ... are in sight of mine....

Major General John Buford, U.S.A. Courtesy of MOLLUS, USAMHI.

Rumor says Ewell is coming over the mountains from Carlisle.... Longstreet, from all I can learn, is still behind Hill."[80]

Pinpointing the location of the three infantry corps comprising the Army of Northern Virginia did little to ease Buford's anxiety over the developing crisis; rather, it deepened his sense of foreboding. One staff officer recalled that his chief "seemed anxious, more so than I ever saw him." In a conversation with Colonel Devin, the cavalry commander predicted gloomily, "They'll come early in the morning, with skirmishers three deep, and you'll have to fight like the devil to hold your own till support arrives ... the enemy knows the importance of this position and will strain every nerve to secure it."[81]

As Buford gathered valuable intelligence information for the Federal army, Pettigrew reported the results of his expedition through the chain of command. Neither his division commander, General Heth, nor his corps commander, A. P. Hill, believed that any portion of the Army of the Potomac was in Gettysburg. Much to Pettigrew's disconcertment, they insisted that he had probably observed a small detachment of cavalry and perhaps some militia troops. Near the conclusion of the meeting, Heth turned to Hill and stated, "If there is no objection, I will take my division tomorrow and go to Gettysburg...." With considerable nonchalance, Hill replied, "None in the world."[82]

Lydia Ziegler climbed up into the cupola of the Seminary and took in the grand spectacle spread out below her. Over the course of the next several days, famous generals and their staff officers would occupy this same perch to survey the surrounding hills and fields in all directions. The Gettysburg teenager left behind a moving account of what she saw and heard on that memorable evening:

And, vividly, too, do I remember that

night of the 30th of June when I stood in the Seminary cupola and saw, as in panoramic view, the camp fires of the enemy all along the Blue Mountainside, only eight miles distant, while below us we beheld our little town entirely surrounded by thousands of camp fires of the Union Army. As we stood on that height and watched the soldiers on the eve of battle, our hearts were made heavy. Many of the soldiers were engaged in letter writing, perhaps writing the last loving missives their hands would ever pen to dear ones at home. In the near distance we could see a large circle of men engaged in prayer, and as the breezes came our way, we could hear the petitions which ascended to the Father in heaven for His protecting care on the morrow. However, many of the boys seemed to be utterly oblivious to the dangers threatening them, and were singing with hearty good will "The Star Spangled Banner" and many of the other patriotic songs which we loved to hear.[83]

The arrival of the Union cavalry did much to ease the nervousness of the townspeople. Henry Jacobs recalled how "our optimistic temper persuaded us that Gen. Buford could readily repulse, if not capture" any enemy force that descended upon the town.[84] These sentiments were echoed by Daniel Skelly, who wrote: "We thought surely now we were safe and the Confederate army would never reach Gettysburg ... the people ... settled in their homes with a sense of security they had not enjoyed for days and with little thought of what the morrow had in store for them.... We little dreamed of the momentous events which were soon to happen right in our midst." [85]

The backgrounds, values, and dreams of the 2,400 residents of Gettysburg, those of the Union soldiers who sought to protect them, and those of the Confederate invaders were as diverse as the young nation itself. As in the climax of a dramatic play, fate and circumstance combined to bring

Lydia Ziegler. Courtesy of the Rev. R. Donald Clare.

this rich cast of characters together for a brief, but white-hot instant in time. Not all of them would survive the coming cataclysm; those who did would find their lives forever altered.

The stage on which they were destined to meet — the campus of the Lutheran Theological Seminary — was certainly an improbable setting for the horrible scenes about to unfold. Here, ignited by intense emotional and physical stress, the most heroic and the most horrific aspects of humanity bubbled to the surface.

CHAPTER 5

July 1, 1863:
The Battle Opens

You teach my hands to fight
  and my arms to use a bow of bronze.
You alone are my shield. Your right hand supports me,
  and by coming to help me, you have made me famous.
You clear the way for me, and now I won't stumble.
                                    Psalm 18, verses 34–36

During the early morning hours of April 12, 1861, Henry Jacobs, then a junior at Pennsylvania College, awoke after experiencing a strange dream. He dreamt that war had broken out between the North and the South, and that a great battle was being fought around Gettysburg. The Northern troops were led by one of Henry's professors, Dr. Frederick Muhlenberg. After making a desperate stand on the western outskirts of town, the Northerners retreated through the college campus, leaving the grounds strewn with the dead and the wounded.

The next day, Gettysburg residents learned of the Confederate bombardment against Fort Sumter near Charleston, South Carolina. Henry was startled by this revelation, as he was not superstitious by nature. He chalked it up to a strange coincidence and went back to his studies. Little did he realize that when he awoke on the morning of July 1, 1863, his premonition of two years earlier would soon be eerily fulfilled in nearly every detail.[1]

Actually, the likelihood of a clash of arms near Gettysburg increased significantly as the two armies drew near one another. As Robert E. Lee concentrated his forces east of South Mountain and George Meade advanced his army on a broad front to engage the Southerners, it was inevitable that the two commanders would utilize the vast road network which converged at Gettysburg. Thus, the same physical characteristic that had played a role in the town's selection as the site of the Lutheran Seminary now drew two great armies towards the community like a magnet attracts steel.

The events which led to this historic showdown were set in motion during the early morning hours of July 1st. At 4 A.M., General John Reynolds was awakened by an aide after enjoying a few hours of

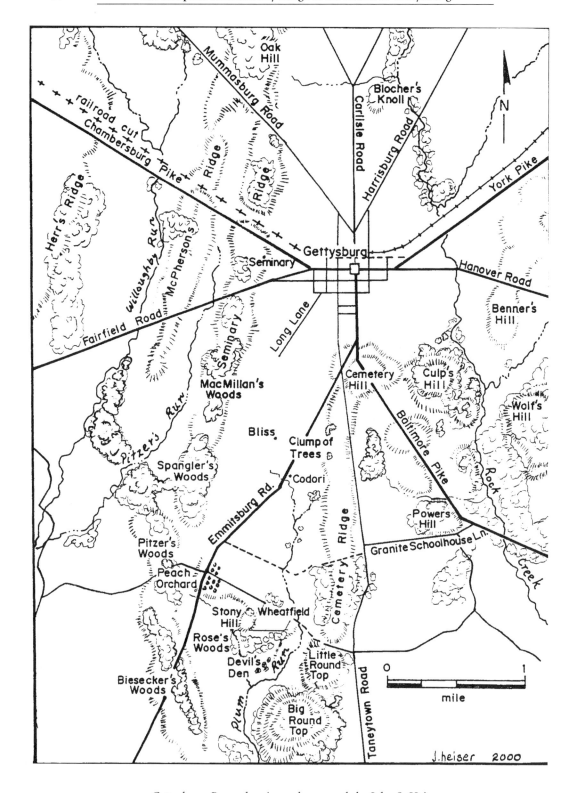

Gettysburg, Pennsylvania, and surrounds by John S. Heiser.

much-needed sleep. He was read a dis-patch from army headquarters which out-lined the prescribed marches for the seven army corps. Reynolds was particularly in-terested in the instructions pertaining to the left wing. The orders specified that the First Corps, followed closely by Oliver O. Howard's Eleventh Corps, should march to Gettysburg in support of Buford's cav-alry division. The Third Corps under Major General Daniel Sickles was ordered to replace the Eleventh Corps at Emmits-burg. The remaining four infantry corps were positioned to react to developing cir-cumstances. They would be approaching Gettysburg from the south and southeast.[2]

A short time later, the First Corps camps began to stir with activity amid a slow drizzle. As the soldiers prepared breakfast, a blood red sun broke through the clouds and illuminated the eastern horizon. The air was "charged with mois-ture" making it feel "intensely sultry" even at this early hour.[3]

The first troops to hit the road were the veterans of Wadsworth's division. With Cutler's brigade in the van, they pushed north on the Emmitsburg Road at around 7:30 A.M. Reynolds galloped forward to ac-company his lead division, entrusting Abner Doubleday to supervise the move-ments of the remainder of the corps. This act was characteristic of the Pennsylvan-ian; it was his nature to direct affairs from the front.

About an hour later, the rest of the corps was underway. Robinson's Second Division, followed by most of the corps ar-tillery brigade under Colonel Charles Wainwright, continued in Wadsworth's wake up the Emmitsburg Road. Mean-while, General Rowley, acting in Double-day's stead, led the Third Division on a parallel course just west of the main thor-oughfare.[4]

The Confederates were also on the move during the early morning of July 1st.

General Heth seemed quite eager to reach Gettysburg, as his troops were up before dawn and on the road by 5 A.M. Heth's ad-vance along the Chambersburg Pike was led by his artillery battalion. The brigades of Generals James Archer and Joseph Davis led the infantry advance, followed by Pet-tigrew's North Carolinians, with Colonel John Brockenbrough's Virginians bringing up the rear. Major General Dorsey Pender's hard-hitting division followed within sup-porting distance of Heth.

Heth later admitted that it was care-less of him to march with his batteries in the lead, but he did not expect to en-counter any serious opposition, perhaps only a few regiments of local militia.[5] This light-hearted air seemed to filter down through the ranks. An artillery captain noted that, "The morning was lovely. A soft, fresh breeze rippled over wheat fields stretching on either side of us. We moved forward leisurely smoking and chatting as we rode along, not dreaming of the prox-imity of the enemy."[6]

Other elements of the Army of Northern Virginia also began to converge on the town. Later in the morning, Richard Ewell received word of A. P. Hill's advance on Gettysburg. In response, he turned his two divisions off to the south instead of continuing on to Cashtown. Meanwhile, Longstreet's entire corps and Johnson's di-vision of Ewell's corps were stacked up along the pike from Cashtown west to Chambersburg in what would become a major traffic jam.[7]

At the Seminary, the Ziegler house-hold was also up bright and early provid-ing whatever items they could for the com-fort of the soldiers. Lydia recalled that "the sun shone in all its splendor over the wheat fields which were of a golden hue and ready for the harvest. All nature seemed to be offering praise to God for his manifold blessings."[8]

Young Hugh Ziegler and other boys

from the town were much too busy to partake of nature's splendor. They were having a grand time running errands for the cavalrymen. One trooper assisted Hugh onto his horse and then handed him some money to purchase a loaf of bread. The youngster was in no great hurry to complete his mission. He recalled that he purposely selected the most distant watering trough in town before going to the bakery.[9]

As Union and Confederate forces converged on Gettysburg from nearly every direction, Lieutenant Aaron B. Jerome, a young signal officer on Buford's staff, climbed up two flights of stairs and a ladder to reach the cupola of the Seminary. From his lofty perch, he could see for miles in every direction. Jerome was not there to enjoy the view, however. Buford had instructed him to seek out a prominent point and watch for movements of the enemy. Through his previous service in the signal corps, Jerome had earned a reputation for aggressiveness, dependability, and resourcefulness.[10] His efforts during the Gettysburg Campaign elicited more praise from his commander, who noted in his official report that he "was ever on the alert, and through his intrepidity and fine glasses on more than one occasion kept me advised of the enemy's movements when no other means were available."[11]

The surrounding country was made up of gently rolling farmland, broken occasionally by wood lots and small streams. Viewed from above it resembled a giant patchwork quilt. The golden yellow of the ripening wheat intermingled with various shades of lush greens and the sparkling blue of the meandering waterways. Radiating from the town in every direction, the major thoroughfares added thick brown strokes to the vibrant landscape in the near distance, then thinned, before gradually disappearing from view. The Virginia worm fences bordering the fields and the

more stout post and rail fences lining the roads stitched the living tapestry together.

The entire length of Seminary Ridge was crowned with hardwoods. Looking north over the apex of the building's roof line, Lieutenant Jerome spotted Oak Hill, a prominent knoll at the terminus of the ridge about one mile away. Shifting his gaze slightly to the northeast, he viewed an open plain of cultivated fields and meadows through which the Carlisle and Harrisburg Roads entered the town. It was expected that Rodes' and Early's divisions would be advancing upon Gettysburg from this direction. Turning around 180 degrees, the officer often peered south down the spine of the narrow ridge towards the Emmitsburg Road for any signs of dust or movement that would indicate the welcome arrival of the First Corps.

The ground dropped off sharply from the east side of Seminary Ridge, providing the lieutenant with a bird's-eye view of Gettysburg and its gridiron pattern of streets and alleys. His attention was drawn toward two commanding heights located a short distance south of the town. In the foreground was Cemetery Hill, so named for the local cemetery situated on its southern slope. This open height was bisected by the Taneytown Road from the south and the Baltimore Pike from the southeast. From Jerome's vantage point, a rugged, wooded elevation appeared to rise up directly behind the first hill, though in reality, a half-mile valley separated Culp's Hill from Cemetery Hill.

Looking southward from Cemetery Hill, the signalmen followed the two-mile course of Cemetery Ridge. This low, mostly treeless swell ran parallel to Seminary Ridge at a distance of about one mile. The intervening space was dotted with large barns, grain fields, meadows, and orchards.

At the southern end of Cemetery Ridge, a pair of distinctive heights could be

Lieutenant Aaron Jerome (seated on top of log in full uniform) with the Signal Corps at Elk Mountain near Sharpsburg, Md. Courtesy of MOLLUS, USAMHI.

seen towering above the countryside. The open, boulder-strewn western slope of Little Round Top rose 150 feet above the valley floor. As its name implies, Big Round Top, essentially a small mountain, protruded an additional 120 feet above Little Round Top. Unlike its smaller cousin, this massive height was entirely covered with trees.

Although he was certainly aware of

the strategic potential of the heights situated south of the town, Jerome had no way of knowing the important role this ground would play in the coming struggle. For now, these topographical features, however distinctive, were just part of the terrain.

During the early morning hours of July 1st, Jerome spent the majority of his time scanning the western horizon with his field glasses, since the first appearance of the enemy was likely to come from this direction. Directly below him, the ground sloped away gently into a marshy swale, where the camps of the cavalrymen began to stir with activity. The aromatic odors of boiling coffee, frying meat, and burning hardwood wafted into the atmosphere.

The most distinctive terrain feature of the country west of the town was the series of north-south ridges which rippled like waves from the towering heights of South Mountain. Roughly 500 yards from the Seminary, McPherson's Ridge would function as the primary Union defensive position. The ridge was composed of two distinct crests, a higher western crest upon which were situated the house, barn, and outbuildings of the Edward McPherson farm, and a slightly lower eastern crest.

Edward McPherson, a former newspaper editor and two-term U.S. Congressman, served as deputy commissioner of internal revenue in 1863, and did not live on the ridge which bore his name. Tenant farmer John Slentz managed his nearly 100 acres of pasture, orchards, and woodlands, and tended to the livestock and poultry. Assisting with the farm chores were his wife, Eliza, and five children under the age of 12. On the morning before the battle, John left his family in an attempt to hide his horses from the invading armies. His efforts were in vain, as his prized equines were seized by a group of disreputable soldiers.[12]

Although the triangular grove of mature oak and chestnut trees located just south of the farm is commonly referred to as "McPherson's Woods," it was actually owned by a neighboring farmer, John Herbst.[13] Herbst's Woods covered the ridge about halfway between the Chambersburg Pike and the Hagerstown Road. These two roadways cut through the ridge from the northwest and southwest, respectively. Jerome could stare straight ahead into Herbst's Woods from the Seminary cupola.

Most of the officer's attention, however, was directed along the Chambersburg Pike towards the more distant ridges. Running roughly parallel to the pike, several hundred yards to the north, was the bed of an unfinished railroad. The project, commonly called the "Tapeworm Railroad" by Gettysburg residents, had been suspended in 1839. By this time most of the grading work to level a bed for the tracks had been completed.[14] There were several deep cuts along the ridge lines. The deepest cut was located just north of the Seminary, with two shallower ones near the two crests of McPherson's Ridge.

As ghostlike tendrils of mist rose towards the heavens, Jerome could see the high, open crest of Herr Ridge, located about one mile from McPherson's Ridge. A quarter mile beyond was the Belmont Schoolhouse Ridge. Whistler's Ridge, which overlooked Marsh Creek, rose about a half mile still farther west. It was in this vicinity that Buford formed his advance line of pickets.

At around 7 A.M., with his glasses trained on the pike near Marsh Creek, Lieutenant Jerome espied the advance pickets of Heth's Division. Even though this sight was expected, it quickened the pulse of the young officer. He immediately dispatched a courier to notify Buford of this important development.[15]

A short time later, the general climbed up into the cupola and borrowed Jerome's powerful field glasses. As he watched the Rebel column marching steadily towards

A turn-of-the-century view looking west from the Seminary. Union regimental monuments are visible on McPherson's Ridge. Herbst's Woods is located near the center of the image. Courtesy of Ken and Sue Boardman.

him, the Kentuckian realized that the time of crisis had arrived. With positive information on the enemy's position, the gritty commander scrambled down to make final arrangements "for entertaining him until General Reynolds could reach the scene."[16] Soon the first scattering shots of the great battle rang out in the distance as the Confederate skirmishers exchanged long-distance shots with the Yankee sentries.

Gamble's camp in front of the Seminary was suddenly a scene of heightened activity as the company buglers belted out the command "Saddle and Mount." It was "a sound that struck terror to the hearts of all who heard it," recalled Lydia Ziegler. "All was excitement; company after com-pany, regiment after regiment, fell into line, and accompanied by the strains of music, the march began towards the front."[17]

As he rode west on the pike following his errand in town, Hugh Ziegler became caught up in the confusion as scattered troopers dashed off from all directions to rejoin their units. One cavalrymen pulled up alongside of him, struck his horse with a saber and shouted, "Hurry up with that horse!" When Hugh reached Seminary Ridge at a full gallop, the anxious horse owner was waiting for him. The trooper hastily assisted the boy off the horse, snatched the loaf of bread from his hands, then mounted up and rode away to join the forming battle line.

The inquisitive 10-year-old, still ignorant as to the cause of all the commotion, hiked the several hundred yards to McPherson's Ridge for a better view. He was instantly drawn to a section of Calef's battery on the north side of the pike. As he watched, the artillerymen coolly and methodically moved about the pieces. Suddenly, the shiny black guns came alive, exploding with a belch of fire and smoke as they leaped backwards from the violent recoil. Greatly frightened, the youngster ran back towards the Seminary as fast as his short legs could carry him. Hugh had inadvertently witnessed the first Union artillery shot of the battle.[18]

The volume and tempo of the firing west of the town gradually increased as Gamble reinforced his advanced skirmish line with additional squadrons and Heth deployed his infantrymen from column formation into a line of battle on both sides of the pike. The Confederate artillery began to hurl exploding shells at the fleeting blue forms dashing to and fro on the hills to the east. As Buford wrote later, his men had "the advantage of position" while the enemy enjoyed the superiority of numbers.[19]

General Gamble formed his main battle line on Herr Ridge, where he dismounted his men behind stone walls and fence lines. Every fourth trooper was designated as a horse holder and took position just behind the firing line. When the enemy approached at too close a distance, the cavalrymen could mount up quickly and ride to another location. By forcing Heth to deploy his men, Buford was already buying valuable time, but the outcome of the fighting was inevitable. Eventually, the longer Confederate line would overlap the outnumbered blue horsemen. One question remained—could they delay the enemy long enough for John Reynolds and the First Corps to arrive on the scene?

Buford's men fought tenaciously. The cavalry chief wrote in his official report that at one point in the battle, his troops "had to be literally dragged back a few hundred yards to a position more secure and better sheltered."[20] Inevitably, this stubborn resistance produced some casualties. Thomas Day of the 3rd Indiana remembered that one of his wounded comrades was placed upon a milk white horse to be transported back to a hospital, possibly the Seminary. The blood gushed from his wounds to such an extent that it nearly turned the horse red.[21] Another casualty was Private Lyman Shaw, 12th Illinois Cavalry, who was shot in the leg and both arms.[22]

As Hugh Ziegler dashed back towards his home a soldier passed him with blood streaming down his face. When he reached the Seminary his mother was positioned at the water pump assisting several wounded soldiers as they washed blood from their hands and faces. It is quite possible that Mary served as the first nurse at the battle of Gettysburg.[23]

Most Gettysburg residents were going about their daily activities as the fighting escalated. Sallie Broadhead was up early baking bread when she heard the rumbling of artillery fire. Panicked townspeople scurried about in all directions and rumors began to circulate that the town would be shelled. A number of neighbors advised that it would be safer to retire to a less exposed section of town, but Joseph Broadhead believed it was best to stay put.[24]

Another segment of the population was more concerned about missing the greatest event that had ever taken place in their town. Martin Luther Culler and the small contingent of Seminary students still residing on campus decided to climb up into the cupola for a panoramic view of the action. "We saw the battle open with a puff of smoke from the mouths of booming cannon, several miles west of the Seminary," wrote Culler. "We watched the advance of the Confederates, until shells from their guns, aimed at a Union army signal tower, made it unsafe to remain longer."[25] For Martin, it was the second close call within the past three days.

At nearby Pennsylvania College, the few remaining students attended morning prayer and classes as usual. Their suspicions were soon aroused, however, by the presence of a signal corps officer in the tower of the building. Eventually, the distraction proved to be too much for President Baugher. In the middle of a recitation, the professor abruptly announced, "We will close and see what is going on, for you know nothing about the lesson anyhow."[26]

As student Michael Colver was walking towards Linnaean Hall, Horatio J. Watkins called to him from an upper window and asked whether he heard the shooting. Michael instantly heard the ominous sounds and proposed that they go to the cupola of the Seminary for a closer observation. Watkins' suggestion that they should first obtain permission from the faculty brought forth a crude reply from his classmate. "Let the faculty go to grass and you come on," insisted Colver.[27]

Joined by a third student, the collegians cut through the open fields surrounding the campus, crossed the unfinished railroad, and followed the pike out to the Seminary. Apparently, Lieutenant Jerome had plenty of company throughout the morning. Invariably though, his unofficial visitors did not remain long. Colver claimed that he and five others enjoyed a number of thrilling sights during their brief visit: the exchange of shots between the advance pickets of the two forces, Calef's battery swinging into action, and the initial charge of Heth's line upon Buford's dismounted troopers. Their amusement was cut short by a Confederate shell whizzing by the cupola. The assembled students descended from the ex-posed perch "rather unceremoniously" and passed rapidly out of the building.[28] The hasty departures of the Seminary and College students no doubt provided some comic relief for the anxious signal officer as he watched the enemy's inexorable advance upon Gettysburg.

The Seminary cupola was not the only vantage point utilized by concerned civilian spectators. Daniel Skelly positioned himself on Oak Ridge near the railroad cut just north of the Seminary. By this point, the ridge was crowded with men and boys "all eager to witness a brush with the Confederates." Daniel scaled a large oak tree to gain a better view of the action. The firing grew progressively louder as Buford's men fell back slowly, contesting every inch of ground. At around 9:30 A.M., the final defensive line on McPherson's Ridge engaged the advancing Confederates. A round of shells fired from the enemy guns on Herr Ridge triggered a general stampede towards the town. One projectile passed dangerously near the tree Skelly had climbed.

As he retreated eastward through a field adjacent to the railroad cut, a cannon ball struck the earth fifteen or twenty feet from Daniel. The projectile showered dirt all around the teenager and quickened his pace. As he sprinted along the Chambersburg Pike, a general and his staff galloped past in the opposite direction.[29]

Just moments before, Jerome had spotted the same entourage of horsemen galloping up the Emmitsburg Road. A quick glance with his field glasses revealed a large red flag emblazoned with a white circle, the symbol of the First Corps. It was General Reynolds riding at the head of his infantry column! His arrival was very fortuitous, for as Jerome recalled, "The enemy pressed us in overwhelming numbers, and we would have been obliged to retreat...."[30] The elated officer quickly informed Buford of the glad tidings, and once again, his superior joined him in the cupola.

Reynolds was highly regarded as one of the army's best horsemen, and he must have presented an inspiring sight as he rode towards the point of danger. The handsome 42-year-old Pennsylvanian looked every inch an officer. He stood over six feet tall, with a narrow waist, and his dark complexion, hair, and eyes were accented by a neatly trimmed beard. In the saddle, he appeared tall, arrow-straight, and graceful.[31]

More important than his physical appearance was that the Lancaster native was deeply beloved by his officers and men. Major Thomas Chamberlin pointed out that underneath his "cold and somewhat haughty exterior was hidden a personality of wonderful attraction.... His ruling passion seemed to be devotion to his country and his calling."[32] Another soldier considered the First Corps chief "one of the soldier generals of the army, a man whose soul was in his country's work."[33]

This devotion to duty burned at a fever pitch as Reynolds rode through the town in the midst of panicked civilians, the sound of booming artillery and the sharp crackle of musketry filling his ears. When he reached the Seminary, Reynolds halted under the cupola and inquired of his old friend Buford, "how things were going on" and received the characteristic answer, "let's go and see."[34]

Another version of the conversation is as follows:

Reynolds: "What's the matter, John?"
Buford: "The devil's to pay!"[35]

Regardless of the exact words that passed between them, the two officers rode forward to examine the state of affairs

Major General John F. Reynolds, U.S.A. Courtesy of FM.

from the eastern crest of McPherson's Ridge. Along the way Buford informed Reynolds that he had been engaged with Heth's Division of Hill's Corps since dawn and that his scouts had reported the advance of Ewell's Corps from the north. After examining the surrounding terrain and absorbing the tactical and strategic situation, Reynolds made a momentous decision. Against heavy odds, he would commit the First Corps to the growing battle in a desperate bid to save the town and the high ground to the south.[36]

Reynolds fired off a dispatch to Meade: "The enemy is advancing in strong force, and I fear he might get to the heights beyond the town before I can. I will fight him inch by inch, and if driven into the town I will barricade the streets, and hold him back as long as possible."[37]

Aides and orderlies also dashed off with instructions for Howard and Sickles to hasten their movements towards Gettysburg. One aide was sent into the west end of the town to warn the residents of the impending danger. The citizens were implored to leave their homes and seek shelter in the less exposed sections of the borough.[38]

Shortly afterwards, Reynolds galloped south to direct his leading division to the front. Robert McClean enjoyed a close-up view of the general at the foot of Chambersburg Street. Nearly half a century later, he wrote that "His restless dark eyes are pictured still in my mind's retina."[39]

Upon reaching the farm of Nicholas Codori, on the Emmitsburg Road about a half mile from town, Reynolds directed his escort to tear down the fences lining the road. From this point his arriving infantrymen could save precious time by marching across the fields directly towards the Seminary. Soon Cutler's brigade, followed by Captain James Hall's 2nd Maine Battery and the Iron Brigade, came pounding up the road at the double-quick.

After a brief consultation, Reynolds ordered General Wadsworth to turn his division off the road and march toward the sound of battle. Pioneers armed with axes rushed forward to fell the fences along the route. The sweating infantrymen moved cross-country toward the swelling chorus of bursting shells and peals of musketry. There was a rattle of jingling ramrods as the men attempted to load their weapons on the run.[40]

Apparently, Reynolds' warning to seek shelter went unheeded by the majority of Gettysburg's populace. From the garret of his home, Henry Jacobs watched the thrilling display unfold at around 10 A.M. White spheres of exploding shells could be seen high in the air beyond the Seminary as the First Corps arrived at the south edge of the town. Henry watched intently as the 3,800 men of the First Division marched diagonally towards the crest of Seminary Ridge.[41]

As the men of the 147th New York passed by the Schmucker house, a number of soldiers stopped to receive cool drinks of water being handed out by two ladies at a fence gate. Several officers quickly rode forward and kicked over the water pails to eliminate the unwanted distraction.[42]

From the doorway of the Seminary, the Ziegler family watched the long column of blue infantry heading directly towards them. Lydia asked her father how the soldiers would traverse the high fence surrounding their garden. "I did not have long to wait until my curiosity was satisfied," she wrote, "for the General [Reynolds] came at rapid pace, urging his men to follow, and the fence fell as if it were made of paper as the men pressed against it with crowbars and picks."[43]

The few intrepid souls remaining in the cupola and in other elevated positions enjoyed a magnificent spectacle as the infantrymen swept forward across the crest of the ridge with their bayonets "scintillating and flashing back the rays of that bright July morning sun."[44]

Not everyone was enjoying the pageantry of the scene. Eliza Slentz had just placed a loaf of bread in the oven when news of the approaching battle reached the McPherson farm. She quickly gathered up her five children, and driving the family cow herd before them, they fled towards Gettysburg. In typical motherly fashion, Eliza worried that the children were bareheaded and without shoes or stockings in their haste to depart for safer environs. Before the family reached the town, the cattle were lost, and mother and children were forced to take refuge in the cellar of the Seminary.[45]

The First Corps arrived just in time to relieve Buford's beleaguered troopers on McPherson's Ridge. Hall's battery unlimbered on the westernmost crest of the ridge to engage the enemy's guns on Herr Ridge. Reynolds then personally directed the deployment of Cutler's brigade. Three regiments—the 56th Pennsylvania together with the 76th and 147th New York— crossed the Chambersburg Pike and the railroad cut to form a line of battle facing west. Shortly after getting into position, the 56th Pennsylvania unleashed the first Union volley of the battle as Davis' Mississipians and North Carolinians ascended a low swell in the open ground in their front. Cutler's remaining units, the 14th Brooklyn and the 95th New York, took position near the McPherson farm.

Suddenly, Reynolds spotted Archer's Brigade advancing into Herbst's Woods towards the exposed left flank of Cutler's brigade. Fortunately, at that very moment, Meredith's Iron Brigade was pushing towards the front from the Seminary. The general sent two aides to hurry them along. He met the lead unit, the 2nd Wisconsin, near the crest of the ridge. As they charged into the woods, the men were momentarily staggered by an enemy volley, but continued to advance.[46]

The regiment suffered 233 casualties at Gettysburg.[47] Corporal Luke English, a 21-year-old member of Company E, was shot in the left hip joint. The musket ball emerged near the anus and then penetrated his right thigh.[48]

Reynolds turned in his saddle to look for the remaining Iron Brigade units. As he did so, a bullet struck him in the head near the right ear. His horse bolted forward and the general tumbled to the ground. Sergeant Charles Veil and two orderlies carried their beloved commander back towards the Seminary in hopes of getting medical assistance. It is likely that Reynolds gasped his last breath before the party reached Seminary Ridge.[49]

Meanwhile, the 7th Wisconsin, the 19th Indiana, and the 24th Michigan slammed into Archer's line in successive waves. They drove the stunned Confederates out of the woods and back across Willoughby Run. In the process, the Midwesterners captured a large number of enemy troops, including a much chagrined General Archer.[50]

As this attack was taking place, Lydia Ziegler quietly slipped to the edge of the wooded grove in back of the Seminary. It was a unique opportunity since the youngster "always had a desire to see something of a battle." She was thoroughly enjoying the awe-inspiring scene when a bullet flew so near her head that she could hear a whizzing sound as it passed by. The close call and the admonishment of Lieutenant Jerome from the cupola sent Lydia speeding for home. She discovered that her entire family and the Slentz household had taken refuge in the cellar. A short time later, two shells struck the building.[51]

The fighting north of the pike was not as one-sided as the fighting in Herbst's Woods. Davis' longer line overlapped the right flank of Cutler's brigade. As a result, the three Union regiments positioned north of the railroad cut were in danger of being surrounded. Consequently, General Wadsworth ordered Cutler to reform his troops farther to the rear on Oak Ridge.

The 147th New York did not receive the order and found themselves facing three Confederate regiments alone. The New Yorkers were exposed to enemy fire from the front and both flanks. Casualties mounted at an alarming rate. Lieutenant J. Volney Pierce proclaimed, "Not a man flinched; none left the field except the wounded; the untouched living and the dead remained.... Never was a grander fight made against triple odds; never greater readiness to do and die on duty's line...."[52]

After a half of an hour of this unequal contest, orders finally arrived for the 147th to retire. Part of the unit retreated directly east through the railroad cut while others dashed through the adjoining fields on either side.[53] As he started towards the rear, Lieutenant Pierce discovered the badly wounded Edwin Aylesworth lying prostrate with a fractured right thigh. The 21-year-old sergeant begged the officer to assist him off the field. Pierce and another soldier attempted to carry Aylesworth, but had to abandon him a short time later to avoid being captured. "His piteous appeal, 'Don't leave me, boys,' has rung in my ears and lived in my memory these five and twenty years," recalled Pierce.[54]

The heroic stand cost the 147th dearly. Two officers and 42 men were killed; 10 officers and 153 men were wounded.[55] Without infantry support, Hall's gunners pulled back from their exposed position. Although greatly disorganized, the jubilant Southerners raced pell mell towards Seminary Ridge in pursuit.

Colonel Rufus Dawes and the 300 plus men of the 6th Wisconsin viewed the action from their position just west of the main Seminary building. Shortly after his arrival, General Abner Doubleday had held the regiment back as a reserve while the remainder of the Iron Brigade swept forward into Herbst's Woods. This force was soon augmented by the 100 men of the brigade guard. As the emergency unfolded, Doubleday ordered Dawes to change front and engage Davis' men.[56]

Advancing at the double-quick, the 6th halted at the fence bordering the Chambersburg Pike. Resting their guns on the rails, they poured a devastating volley into the ranks of the unsuspecting Rebels. The enemy line swayed and bent. The Confederates abruptly broke off their pur-

suit of Cutler's troops and dove into the nearby railcut for protection. From behind the grading, Davis' men laid down a withering fire on the exposed Union troops along the pike.

In desperation, Dawes ordered a charge. Simultaneously, the 95th New York and the 14th Brooklyn attacked to the left of the 6th Wisconsin. The distance between the turnpike and the cut was about 200 yards.[57] Dawes stated that his charging line was a "v-shaped crowd of men, with the colors at the point, moving hurriedly and firmly forward, while the whole field behind is streaming with men plunging in agony to the rear or sinking in death upon the ground."[58]

Out of the 420 men under Dawes' command, only about 240 reached their objective. Levi Stedman of Brookville, the tallest man in the 6th Wisconsin, presented a conspicuous target to the enemy riflemen. An enemy bullet pierced his right lung. Another casualty was stout Abe Fletcher of Company K. The kind-hearted corporal, who had frequently carried extra knapsacks to help the "little fellows" during long marches, fell to the ground when a projectile fractured his muscular left thigh.[59] Nearby, Corporal John A. Crawford of the same company received a serious wound in his right knee.[60]

Upon reaching the embankment, the survivors of the unit leveled their muskets at their foes and shouted for them to surrender. When a squad of Dawes' men sealed off the eastern end of the cut, over 200 Mississipians reluctantly complied.[61] The remainder of Davis' command retreated towards Herr Ridge. The initial fighting of July 1st was done and a lull settled over the field.

With the death of Reynolds, command of the field devolved upon Abner Doubleday. After he positioned the Iron Brigade in Herbst's Woods and reformed Cutler's scattered command, the general eagerly awaited the arrival of the Second and Third Divisions. Even then, he could expect to face roughly two-to-one odds when the remainder of Hill's and Ewell's Corps reached the battlefield.[62]

Doubleday reasoned that since Reynolds "had formed his lines to resist the entrance of the enemy into Gettysburg, I naturally supposed that it was the intention to defend the place."[63] The New Yorker fervently hoped that his men could hold on long enough to buy the time necessary for the rest of the army to arrive.

The initial Union success had been costly. The First Corps had suffered numerous casualties, including the beloved Reynolds. The price tag would continue to escalate as the day progressed.

The sturdy and commodious Seminary building immediately attracted the attention of Union medical personnel. Dr. George New, the Surgeon in Chief of the First Division, noted that he opened the first field hospital at Gettysburg inside the Seminary. "The first wounded of the battle were then admitted and properly cared for," he wrote. Shortly afterwards, New rode into town and "took possession of several more rooms, halls, hotels, etc."[64]

The proximity of the Seminary to the front lines made it readily accessible to the wounded, but this advantage was offset by its susceptibility to artillery fire. Ideally, a field hospital was located one or two miles behind the lines to safeguard against this hazard. During the opening day's battle, the Seminary served as a collection point and primary aid station. Soldiers with minor wounds could easily walk back to this facility, while the more seriously wounded were carried by stretcher.

During the Gettysburg Campaign, the medical staff of most Union infantry regiments consisted of a surgeon, one or two assistant surgeons, a hospital steward, and several orderlies. Each regiment supplied a hospital detail of 10 men. Together with the regimental musicians, these soldiers served both as nurses at the field hospitals and as stretchermen.

A chief surgeon was assigned to each infantry division. These staff officers had a number of important duties. Besides selecting sites for field hospitals and supervising surgical personnel at the time of an engagement, they were responsible for sanitary inspections, the maintenance of medical supplies, and the compilation of morbidity and casualty reports. Each army corps had its own medical director and medical inspector. At the top of the chain of command was Dr. Jonathan Letterman, the medical director of the Army of the Potomac.

After a hospital site had been established, the medical staff busily prepared for the influx of wounded. The soldiers detailed as cooks would heat water, prepare hot beverages, and soak sponges. The hospital steward readied the instruments and supplies, which included such items as chloroform, brandy, aromatic spirits of ammonia, bandages, adhesive plaster, needles, silk thread, knives, forceps, scalpels, scissors, probes, and tourniquets.

Once the fighting started, the stretchermen canvassed the field to locate the wounded and transport them back to the primary aid stations. Generally, only basic first aid procedures were performed at these stations—dressing open wounds and stopping the flow of blood from severed arteries through the use of tourniquets. Liquor was often administered to help alleviate pain and shock. It was also common practice to give the wounded an opium pill or small doses of morphine. Elaborate surgical procedures were generally not undertaken at this time. After the patient was stabilized, he was transported by ambulance to a hospital farther to the rear, where thorough examinations and operations were performed.[65]

Among the first patients received into

the Seminary Hospital were Lyman Shaw of the 12th Illinois Cavalry and Private Stedman, Corporal Fletcher, and Corporal Crawford of the 6th Wisconsin. Lieutenant Pierce would have been relieved had he known that Sergeant Aylesworth also reached the hospital. A number of the seriously wounded, such as the 2nd Wisconsin's Luke English, were scattered in remote locations or left in buildings such as the McPherson barn. These men would not be located until many hours after the fighting. English remained on the field overnight before being conveyed to the Seminary the next day.[66]

In addition to the main Seminary building, both professors' homes were occupied. The first floor of the Krauth house was soon filled with wounded enlisted men, while the upper story was occupied by the surgeons and wounded officers, forcing Dr. Krauth, his wife, Harriet, and Sallie, the couple's 13-year-old daughter, to take refuge in the cellar. Richard Meade Bache of Philadelphia, a member of Reynolds' staff, was among those who cared for the wounded in the house.[67]

As the wounded from the morning's battle received treatment, the first Union reinforcements arrived on the scene. At around 11 A.M., Colonel Roy Stone's Bucktails panted up Seminary Ridge at the double-quick by the same route utilized by Wadsworth's men. While the troops were halted near the Seminary, Generals Doubleday and Rowley delivered patriotic addresses. The two commanders reminded the Pennsylvanians that they were fighting on their home soil and that the eyes of the commonwealth were upon them. The men cried out in response, "We have come to stay!"[68] The three regiments moved forward and took position on the right of the Iron Brigade. McPherson's Ridge was alive with bursting shells as Stone deployed his brigade.

Colonel Langhorne Wister of the 150th Pennsylvania instructed the drum-

mer boys of his regiment to assist the medical staff by serving as stretcher bearers. He reminded the musicians that by doing so they were "just as much helping the battle on as if you were fighting with guns in your hands." Drummer boy Harry Kieffer recalled that he and his comrades reported to the Seminary, which was "rapidly filling with the wounded," to obtain stretchers from the ambulances. He surmised that the enemy could not know that a hospital was in operation there or else "they wouldn't shell the building so hard!"[69]

Meanwhile, the First Brigade, now under the command of Colonel Chapman Biddle, reached the field via the Hagerstown Road. Doubleday instructed Biddle to occupy the open eastern crest of McPherson's Ridge to the left rear of the Iron Brigade. Lieutenant Colonel McFarland noted that the "enemy whom we had hunted for several days, were found, and we all felt that a decisive struggle was about to take place."[70]

The last elements of the First Corps, Robinson's division and the remainder of the corps artillery brigade, reached the field shortly before noon. Doubleday directed Robinson to station his division in reserve at the Seminary. The men of Gabriel Paul's brigade hastily constructed a barricade of fence rails, stumps, and earth near the front of the wood lot that extended west of the main building. The semicircular line of works stretched a distance of roughly 300 feet. Although "weak and imperfect," the position was strengthened by an existing stone fence located farther to the east, which originated near Professor Schmucker's house and ran southward along the crest of the ridge.[71] If his front line troops were driven back from McPherson's Ridge, Doubleday could rally his forces on Seminary Ridge before falling back through the town to Cemetery Hill.

The lead brigades of the 9,200-man strong Eleventh Corps arrived in Gettys-

burg at about 12:30. By virtue of his se-
niority, General Howard assumed command of the field, and established his
headquarters on Cemetery Hill. He agreed
with Doubleday's decision to hold his front
line beyond Gettysburg for as long as possible. In order to protect the First Corps
from an attack by Ewell from the north,
Howard instructed his acting corps commander, Major General Carl Schurz, to
march two divisions through Gettysburg
and occupy Oak Ridge and Oak Hill. The
remaining Eleventh Corps division was
held in reserve on Cemetery Hill.

Before this plan could be carried out,
a sudden explosion of artillery fire echoed
from Oak Hill. Robert Rodes' 8,000-man
division had fortuitously arrived on the
vulnerable right flank of the First Corps.
As Ewell and Trimble looked on, Rodes
prepared to pitch into the Union troops
spread out below. After losing the race for
Oak Hill, Schurz's men deployed on the
open plain north of town. They would
soon have their hands full with Early's division and could offer little assistance to
Doubleday's hard-pressed soldiers.[72]

From the cupola, Jerome watched
anxiously as Rodes' troops approached
Oak Hill from the north. He immediately
sent the following message to Howard by
flag signals: "Over a division of the rebels
is making a flank movement on our right;
the line extends over a mile, and is advancing, skirmishing. There is nothing but
cavalry to oppose them."[73]

Doubleday was forced to send Robinson's entire division to Oak Ridge to deal
with this threat. To replace these troops,
Doubleday detached the 151st Pennsylvania
from Biddle's brigade and placed it behind
the breastworks erected by Paul's men near
the Seminary. Lieutenant Colonel McFarland's 467 officers and men represented the
last reserve force available to the First
Corps.

Shortly after 2 P.M., Rodes' infantry

emerged from the cover of Oak Hill. The
initial attacks were poorly coordinated and
repulsed with heavy losses to the Southerners. Brigadier General Alfred Iverson's
Brigade of North Carolinians was nearly
annihilated by Robinson's men, who fired
deadly volleys into the Tarheels from behind a low stone wall. Farther to the west,
General Junius Daniel's Confederates attacked the railroad cut near the McPherson
farm. Colonel Stone pulled the 143rd and
149th Pennsylvania out of line and placed
them along the Chambersburg Pike to
meet the assault. Heavy casualties were incurred by both sides, but ultimately, the
Pennsylvanians prevailed. Once again, the
First Corps line held. The tide was about
to shift.

At around 2:30 P.M., the Confederates
finally launched a coordinated assault
upon the thin Union defensive line. Heth's
Division, with the endorsement of General Lee himself, stepped off from Herr
Ridge. Heth's new attack on McPherson's
Ridge was spearheaded by General James J.
Pettigrew's 2,500 North Carolinians, the
largest brigade in the Army of Northern
Virginia at Gettysburg. Pettigrew was supported on his left by Colonel John Brockenbrough's small Virginia brigade. General Dorsey Pender's division followed
within supporting distance. Meanwhile,
Rodes prepared his units for another strike
from the north.

Throughout the afternoon of July 1,
the odds were deeply stacked against the
First Corps. The three Confederate divisions aligned against them numbered
nearly 20,000 men, supported by 75 artillery pieces. To oppose this force, Doubleday had fewer than 8,700 men with 28
guns and one brigade of Buford's cavalry.[74]

Major Chamberlin of the 150th Pennsylvania recalled that the "the enemy was
formed in continuous double lines of battle, extending southward as far as the ac-
cidents of the ground permitted the eye to

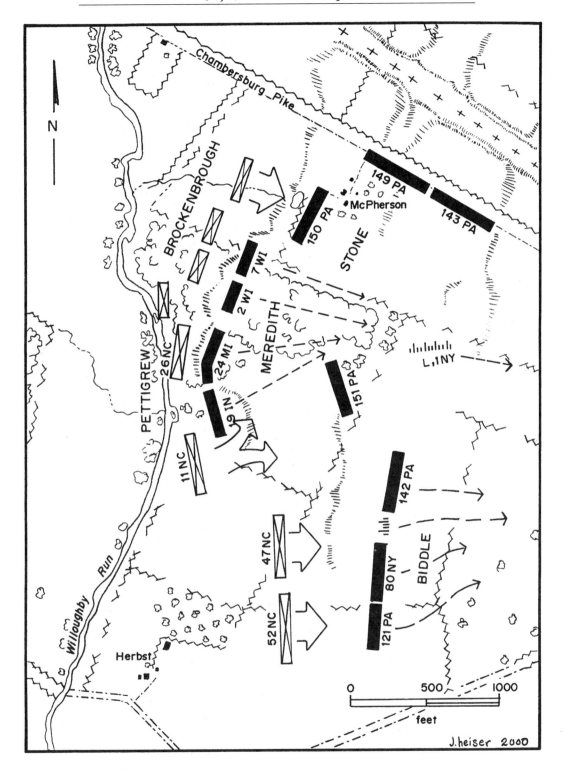

The fight for McPherson's Ridge by John S. Heiser.

reach, with heavy supporting columns in the rear."[75] From his position near the Seminary, Colonel Charles Wainwright, the First Corps artillery chief, despaired that Pettigrew's line "outflanked us at least a half mile on our left." The veteran artillerist predicted "there was not the shadow of a chance" of holding McPherson's Ridge.[76]

A number of the surgeons gathered at the Seminary, who were far less astute in military matters, thought the position could be held indefinitely. One pointed to the west during Stone's successful defense against Daniel's men and remarked enthusiastically, "See how we are driving them." Surgeon Bache was considerably less optimistic. "When I looked at the impending masses beyond, I did not feel so certain of the event," he wrote. Bache supervised the evacuation of the transportable wounded to more secure locations inside the town previously selected by Dr. New. This work was completed by shortly after 3 P.M.[77] Christ Lutheran Church on Chambersburg Street was among the first of these structures.[78]

The renewed Confederate attack was preceded by a heavy artillery barrage of the Union position. Exploding shells whistled through the air near the Seminary and solid shot ricocheted through the grove of hardwoods where the 151st Pennsylvania crouched behind the low breastwork. Lieutenant Colonel McFarland quietly sat on the ground taking notes "while the shells were flying in all directions."[79]

Colonel Wainwright's dire prediction proved very accurate as Pettigrew's long line of infantry lapped around Biddle's exposed flank on McPherson's Ridge. The 52nd North Carolina delivered a crushing fire into the line of the 121st Pennsylvania, which was positioned on the extreme left of the First Corps position. As the officers attempted to change front and meet the attack, "the ranks were broken and became massed together" in the face of the leaden storm. Its organization shattered, the regiment's survivors bolted for the cover of the Seminary woods.[80]

The retreat of the 121st subjected the 20th New York Militia to a destructive enfilading fire as the 47th North Carolina blazed away at the unit from the front. Corporal Abram Swart, the young farmer who had been sending part of his army pay home to his mother, received a bullet in the right thigh. As the killed and wounded fell to the ground, the survivors closed up on the colors until more than half of the regiment became casualties. Realizing the position was untenable, Colonel Theodore Gates ordered a fighting withdrawal towards the Seminary.[81]

During the retrograde movement, Lieutenant Alfred Tanner toppled to the ground as a bullet struck his left leg below the knee. Lieutenant Edward Ross wrote, "I stopped to help him from the field not expecting our forces would fall back farther than the hospital." Upon reaching the Seminary, Ross hastily tied a dampened rag around his comrade's wounded leg. The lieutenant then dashed to a nearby window in an effort to locate his regiment.[82]

The 142nd Pennsylvania, the last of Biddle's regiments in line, was also engaged in a close-quarters battle with the enemy. Mounted on horseback, Lieutenant Andrew Tucker presented an easy mark for the enemy riflemen. During one of the initial volleys, he was shot in the right forearm and his horse was severely disabled.

Opposite: *Officers of the 20th New York State Militia. Lieutenant Edward Ross is standing second from the left, Lieutenant Alfred Tanner is lying on the ground on the far right. Also pictured are Surgeon Robert Loughran (the officer with the full beard in the center of the group) and Captain John D. S. Cook (seated second from the left). Courtesy of MOLLUS, USAMHI.*

Captain Charles Evans, Andrew's friend and former classmate, ordered him to the rear. Instead, the young officer remained with the regiment "cheering and urging the men by going into the thickest of the fight himself." A short time later, Lieutenant Jeremiah Hoffman was incapacitated when a projectile struck his right hip, cut through his pelvis, and lodged near his spine. Tucker pushed Hoffman up onto his wounded mount and sent him off to the Seminary for medical assistance.[83]

The stalwart soldiers of the 142nd were "mowed down by the terrible fire" as the North Carolinians converged upon them. When Colonel Biddle noticed the line of Pennsylvanians wavering under the increasing pressure, he darted into the ranks, seized the regimental flag, and led the men forward in an ill-fated countercharge. The Confederate rifles "turned on the mass and seemingly shot the whole to pieces."[84]

In a last-ditch effort to rally the survivors, Colonel Cummins pointed to the colors with his sword and shouted "rally round the flag!" A knot of men halted long enough to fire a round at the oncoming Confederates. The seemingly invincible Cummins fell with a chest wound an instant later. Several of his loyal soldiers attempted to carry his lifeless body off the field. They were shot down in succession until only one remained.[85] Realizing that he could not perform the task alone, the survivor unbuckled his commander's sword and sprinted for Seminary Ridge. An enemy minie ball struck him during his flight. An officer who witnessed the scene wrote that as the intrepid soldier ran past him "the blood was streaming out of his mouth, and tears down his cheeks. But with the courage of an infuriated lion, he was swearing eternal vengeance on our enemies."[86] The lifeless form of the beloved colonel was abandoned between the hostile lines.

While Biddle's three regiments were being swept from the eastern crest of McPherson's Ridge, the Iron Brigade was locked in a deadly struggle with the remainder of Pettigrew's brigade and Brockenbrough's Virginians for the possession of Herbst's Woods. From their naturally strong position, the Midwesterners poured repeated volleys into the ranks of the advancing Confederates. As Biddle's line collapsed, however, the 11th North Carolina worked its way around the flank of the 19th Indiana on the left of the brigade line. One by one, the Union regiments were forced back through the woods. The veteran officers reformed their troops in the depression between the two ridges.

As Doubleday watched his McPherson Ridge line begin to fall apart, he decided to take a drastic measure. He ordered McFarland's 151st Pennsylvania to move forward from the Seminary in a last-ditch effort to stem the Confederate tide. Observing the approach of the Pennsylvanians, the Iron Brigade fell back slowly towards Seminary Ridge.

The 151st engaged the 26th North Carolina and elements of the 11th North Carolina in the southeastern corner of Herbst's Woods. The two forces exchanged volleys at a distance of about twenty paces. The untried Keystoners inflicted severe casualties upon their adversaries, but as McFarland later wrote, "the fire of the enemy … was severe and destructive, and my gallant officers and men fell thick and fast."[87] The former schoolteacher held his men in line until the regiment was nearly surrounded. He then ordered a withdrawal to their original position near the Seminary.

Among the unit's numerous casualties was Musician Michael Link of Company E. Link was fighting in the ranks when a bullet smashed into his left eye, passed under the bridge of his nose, and emerged near his right eye. The blow knocked him to the ground, and he lost

Musician Michael Link, 151st Pa. Vols. Courtesy of Dale E. Biever, USAMHI.

major combat action, but casualties steadily mounted as overwhelming numbers of enemy troops converged upon their exposed position.

The ferocity of the fighting made it difficult for the stretchermen to perform their duty. Drummer boy Harry Kieffer recalled that while he moved off to examine a wounded soldier, a shell struck his stretcher and tore it to pieces. When the 16-year-old musician crept up to the McPherson's log house, he felt a hand upon his shoulder. Colonel Wister gently admonished him, "Keep back, my boy; no use exposing yourself in that way."[89]

During one bold counterattack, Major Thomas Chamberlin sustained a dangerous wound to his right shoulder. Five volunteers retrieved the badly wounded officer and carried him into the McPherson house. Sergeant William Ramsey never forgot the gallantry of the major as he addressed the rescue party with the following words: "Now boys, raise my head up, give me a drink of water and go out to your work."[90]

consciousness. Recovering a short time later, Michael made a horrifying discovery. One of his eyes had "run out" and the other was hanging down over his cheek. Three of his comrades carried him back a short distance and placed a knapsack under his head. As they departed, Link, now totally blind and helpless, overheard a remark that he was "done for."[88]

At about the same time, Stone's brigade was finally forced to relinquish its position near the McPherson farm. Throughout the afternoon, the Pennsylvanians had faced attacks from two different directions. The brigade fought heroically in their first

Later, as the 150th pulled back from its advanced position, Lieutenant Henry Chancellor, the frail youngster who had refused to take a sick furlough, was shot through the left thigh and sustained a painful fracture of the limb.[91] A large number of the brigade's wounded were left behind in the McPherson house, barn, and outbuildings as the Pennsylvanians retreated along the Chambersburg Pike.

Others were assisted off the field by their unwounded comrades. Captain Brice Blair of the 149th Pennsylvania was struck in the left arm near the shoulder as his unit held the ground just east of the McPherson barn. The blow shattered the bone to pieces, nearly severing the arm. Blair remained with his beloved "boys" until he nearly collapsed from loss of blood. He then called upon Sergeant Levi Graham to assist him off the field. The wounded captain could not walk fast and it would be a long time before the pair reached the sanctuary of the Seminary.[92]

As the 151st Pennsylvania and Stone's brigade withdrew from McPherson's Ridge, the 7th Wisconsin formed the rear guard of the Iron Brigade. Lieutenant Colonel John Callis looked back and saw the large brick Seminary on the ridge behind him. Making this landmark his objective point, he issued the order, "by the right of companies to the rear, march."[93]

During the fighting withdrawal, the 7th received a direct fire from the front and an enfilading fire from both flanks. A ball struck Private John Shultz of Company H in the right upper jaw and lodged near his skull behind the right ear. Sergeant Francis Jefferson Coates, a 19-year-old sergeant in the same company, received a ghastly wound similar to the one sustained by Michael Link of the 151st Pennsylvania. A ball hit him near the right temple and emerged on the opposite side of the head. The inch-and-a-half diameter wound tore away nearly the entire orbital plate and severed the optic nerves.

Coates was left behind during the retreat "sightless and defenseless with blood streaming" from his eye sockets. A short time later, an enemy soldier jabbed him with a bayonet. Another began to remove his shoes, but was prevented from completing the act by Francis' frantic kicks and screams of protest. Finally, a compassionate Rebel carried the wounded sergeant under a shade tree and gave him some water. In grateful appreciation, Coates supplied his merciful foe with a portion of his coffee.[94]

Through its stubborn defense of McPherson's Ridge, the First Corps inflicted severe losses upon their attackers and delayed the Confederate advance by about an hour and a half. The cost of this success was staggering, however. Most of the Union regiments had lost more than 60 percent of their men, while four had lost over seventy percent.[95]

Shortly before 4 P.M., the weary infantrymen regrouped on Seminary Ridge for a final defensive stand. The units maintained roughly the same alignment they had fought in earlier. Colonel Wainwright lined up 21 artillery pieces from the Seminary north to the railroad cut to bolster the new position.

As Doubleday's men dug in for another battle, the surgeons and medical personnel inside the Seminary worked frantically to treat the mangled and bleeding bodies collected inside the building. Most of the patients were soldiers from the First and Third divisions who had participated in the desperate contest for McPherson's Ridge. The overtaxed surgeons would have precious little time to ply their trade.

The difficult task of storming the last Union stronghold west of the town was assigned to General Dorsey Pender's division, which had closely followed Heth's division throughout the day. Also known as the "Light Division," this unit had earned a reputation as a crack combat unit. Pender organized a three-brigade attack to assault Seminary Ridge. Colonel Abner Perrin's 1,600 South Carolinians formed the center of the battle line and his four regiments would advance directly towards the main Seminary building. General Alfred Scales' North Carolinians lined up on Perrin's left, while another Tarheel brigade under General James Lane held the right flank.[96]

At about 4 P.M., Perrin's men passed through Pettigrew's depleted ranks and ascended McPherson's Ridge. Lieutenant

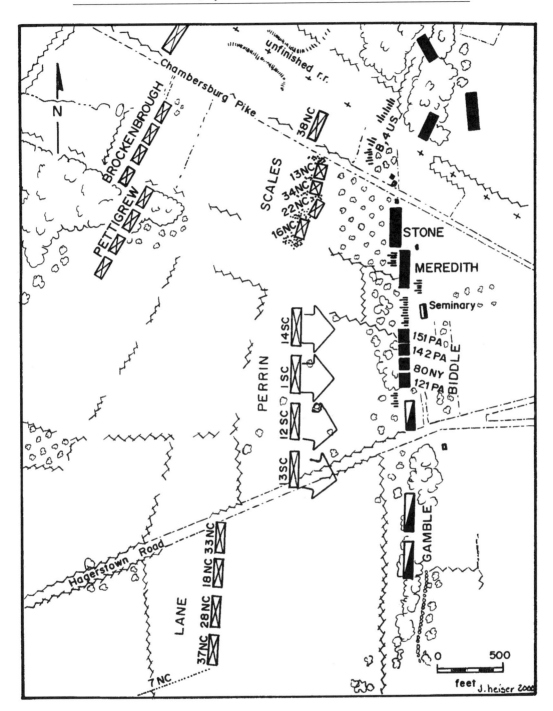

Seminary Ridge: Last Stand of the First Corps by John S. Heiser.

Colonel Joseph Brown, 14th Carolina, described the spectacle:

In front and in view amid the grove of trees was the Seminary now changed from the halls of learning to a scene of bloodshed and carnage. Beyond was a beautiful town partly concealed from view by the shade trees surrounding the Seminary.... Beyond and to the south of the town rising still higher was Cemetery Heights, so soon to become historic ground. It was but the glance of the eye for a moment and then grandeur was lost in the tumult of battle.[97]

In the few brief moments before the fighting erupted, the Union soldiers admired the view from the opposite direction. Colonel Rufus Dawes penned, "For a mile up and down the open fields in front, the splendid lines of the Army of Northern Virginia swept down upon us. Their bearing was magnificent. They maintained their alignment with great precision."[98]

The parade ground pageantry was short-lived. The moment the Southerners popped into view, the vast array of Union artillery on Seminary Ridge exploded with sheets of flame and smoke. Scales' Brigade had the misfortune of advancing directly into the teeth of the deadly cannon. The Yankee artillerists enjoyed a splendid field of fire and the crew members served their pieces with considerable enthusiasm.

After a number of salvos, the blinding smoke shut out the sun and completely enveloped the view to the west. When the smoke lifted, a ghastly scene appeared. According to a Union infantrymen, "Only the dead and dying remained on the bloody slopes of Seminary Ridge."[99] Scales' command was virtually destroyed. The general and every field officer in the brigade, except one, was wounded. The survivors were pinned down several hundred yards from the Union line.

The attack on the right also ground to a halt as Gamble's dismounted troopers held Lane in check below the Hagerstown Road. Thus, the entire success of the assault depended upon Perrin's men. When the brigade reached the shallow depression between the ridges, they were entirely unsupported. The full force of the Union artillery fire was concentrated upon them. Still, the well-disciplined troops surged forward.[100]

When the South Carolinians approached a fence 200 yards from the grove, they received what Perrin rated as "the most destructive fire of musketry I have ever been exposed to,"[101] as the line of breastworks in their front erupted into "a sheet of fire and smoke."[102] The noise was deafening, as violent popping rips of musketry volleys mingled with the thunderous booms of the artillery.

After several desperate charges, Colonel Perrin realized that the position could not be carried by a frontal assault. While the 14th stood its ground opposite the Seminary, he directed the 1st South Carolina to shift to the right around the breastworks and flank the position. The movement was executed successfully, and the Confederates raked the Union line with a destructive fire.[103]

Following a brief consultation with Colonel Gates, Colonel Biddle determined that it would be impossible to remain any longer without sacrificing the brigade. The line slowly collapsed from left to right. The fugitives rushed down the eastern slope of Seminary Ridge towards the town in a frantic attempt to reach Cemetery Hill.[104]

Private Henry Mull, Company A, 121st Pennsylvania, was firing at the South Carolinians from behind the Schmucker house when an enemy soldier crept up on him and demanded his surrender. Instead, he darted around the side of the structure only to encounter two more Southerners. Quickly reaching the conclusion that he "would rather be a live prisoner than a dead hero," Mull capitulated.[105]

As Captain John D. S. Cook of the 20th New York Militia passed the Seminary building, he spotted Captain Daniel McMahon, "one of our best and bravest officers," lying on the ground with a shattered left thigh. Kneeling beside McMa-

Artist Alfred Waud's sketch of the 151st Pennsylvania locked in combat with the 14th South Carolina just west of the main Seminary building. Courtesy of Timothy Smith.

hon was a faithful enlisted man who was unwilling to leave him behind. Cook described the desperate effort to rescue his fellow officer:

> The captain entreated me to help him away and I could not resist his appeal. His soldier took off a belt and with it bound his legs together, then taking him by the legs I took one shoulder and a man of my company ... took the other and we carried the captain around the building and started down the walk that sloped from its front across the lawn. The weight was too much for us but I stopped a Pennsylvanian who came running after us and he took my place while I held up the captain's head. It was soon evident that we could not get very far with him, much less keep up with our retreating troops and I directed our course toward a small house on the left of the lawn where I meant to leave him. Just as we turned the corner of its door yard fence we all fell in a bunch, two of the men

wounded. I looked back and saw the line of the enemy in front of the Seminary.... The attention of the enemy was however diverted ... and hastily arranging McMahon in the ditch in which he was lying, I bade him good bye....[106]

The 142nd Pennsylvania retreated moments after the 121st Pennsylvania and the 20th New York. In their haste to depart they were "compelled to leave the lifeless bodies of ... our brave, loyal, and much-beloved Colonel R. P. Cummins and Acting Adjutant Tucker."[107] Later, a Confederate officer ordered four captured soldiers to carry their wounded colonel into the Seminary. Cummins, perhaps in a state of delirium, exhorted his listeners, "For God's sake men rally, we can whip them yet!"[108]

Tucker had been struck in the middle of the back during the withdrawal. He was then assisted towards the Seminary; within

Private Henry Mull, 121st Pa. Vols., pictured on the right with an unidentified companion. Courtesy of Beutonne McKean.

Captain Brice Blair, 149th Pa. Vols. Courtesy of USAMHI.

Sergeant Levi Graham, 149th Pa. Vols. Courtesy of Charles Faust, USAMHI.

40 paces of this structure, another ball passed through his lower back and bowels. Somehow, the young officer gained entrance to the building.[109]

Indeed, reaching the sanctuary of this field hospital soon became an extremely hazardous undertaking. By the time Sergeant Graham and the badly wounded Captain Blair reached the west side of the Seminary, "the bullets were knocking holes in the wooden steps so rapidly that they went around the big brick building and went up the stairs." Graham assisted Blair

into one of the student dorms. Then, acting quickly, he smeared blood on one of his arms and placed it in a makeshift sling to deceive the enemy.[110]

At about this time, the 20th New York's Lieutenant Ross peered out a window from inside the Seminary. Having been preoccupied with caring for Lieutenant Tanner, he was shocked to discover enemy troops swarming around the building. Since he was cut off from his comrades, the New Yorker decided to remain inside and assist the wounded.[111]

The last of Biddle's regiments to fall back was the 151st Pennsylvania. Following in the wake of his men, Lieutenant Colonel McFarland halted about twenty paces from the northwest corner of the Seminary. At this point, he stooped down and peered southward under the thick curtain of smoke to observe the movements of the enemy. Suddenly, a group of pursuing

Confederates unleashed a volley at the fleeing Union troops. McFarland was struck in both legs, and he fell heavily to the ground.

An instant later, Private Lyman Wilson scooped up his commander and hastily made for the north end of the Seminary building. The devoted private nearly paid the ultimate price for his brave act — a minie ball clipped off a button from McFarland's coat sleeve while the colonel's arm was draped around his neck. Miraculously, the pair reached their destination.[112]

One of McFarland's men, 40-year-old Private Anson Miller, had been hit four times by enemy bullets and left behind as his comrades retreated towards Gettysburg. A party of opportunistic Confederates robbed him of some of his clothing, blankets, food, and other personal items. The severely wounded Pennsylvanian happened to be a member of the Freemasons. In desperation, he called out the distress signal known only to other members of the ancient fraternal organization. Immediately, a Confederate Mason from Tennessee stepped forward and came to Miller's assistance. He secured his Union brother's property and returned later with food and water. After he was removed to the Seminary, other Confederate Masons continued to look after his safety and personal needs as best as they could.[113]

As the line to their left gave way, the veteran troops of the Iron Brigade joined in the retreat. Colonel Henry Morrow of the 24th Michigan reported that Lieutenant Newell Grace, "one of the bravest men I ever saw," was shot through the abdomen near the rail barricade just prior to the regiment's withdrawal. Inside the Seminary, Newell was informed that his wounds were mortal.[114]

By 4:20 P.M., the entire Union line was collapsing. As Perrin's South Carolinians rolled up the First Corps line near the Seminary, Rodes' troops finally wrested

Oak Ridge from Robinson's division. Meanwhile, the Eleventh Corps was routed from its position north of the town. Some of Schurz's troops fled through the campus of Pennsylvania College, thus fulfilling the premonition of Henry Jacobs.

From the commanding height of Oak Ridge, Isaac Trimble was thrilled by the spectacle of fleeing Union troops pouring through Gettysburg from the north and west towards Cemetery Hill. As he and General Ewell followed their victorious troops into town, they passed a large body of Federal prisoners. Tauntingly, Isaac remarked to one of the captured officers, "Fortune is against you to-day." His adversary replied grimly, "We have been worse whipped than ever."[115]

Trimble could envision the end of the war and Southern independence if the attack was pressed vigorously. Ewell was not as sanguine as his volunteer aide. His troops were bloodied from the severe fighting and many units had become disorganized during the pursuit through Gettysburg. A substantial portion of his manpower was also needed to guard thousands of prisoners.

With only a few hours of daylight remaining, the time for decisive action had arrived. Rising eighty feet above the town, Cemetery Hill was now the key position on the battlefield. If the Union forces were given time to regroup and fortify this naturally strong position, they could hold out until reinforcements arrived. Thus, the earlier an attack could be mounted, the better the chances of success for the Southerners.[116]

As Ewell, surrounded by his staff, pondered the difficult situation, Major Henry Kyd Douglas spurred up to the party of officers, which now included General John B. Gordon. Henry delivered a message from General Johnson that his division was less than three miles from Gettysburg "in prime condition and was ready to put it in as soon as he got there." Excitedly, Gordon pointed to Cemetery Hill and exclaimed that he could support an attack with his brigade. Laconically, Ewell instructed Douglas to inform General Johnson that upon his arrival he was to await further orders. The group of assembled officers fell into a stunned silence. As Douglas departed, a staff officer remarked to him, "Oh, for the presence and inspiration of Old Jack for just one hour!"[117]

Characteristically, Trimble refused to remain silent. He urged his long-time associate to take immediate action. When his vigorous efforts failed, Isaac rode off to reconnoiter the surrounding terrain.[118]

At about 4:30 P.M., General Robert E. Lee arrived on Seminary Ridge where he witnessed the disorganized Union retreat. Unaware of the enemy's strength and the fighting condition of Ewell's troops, he instructed his commander "to carry the hill occupied by the enemy, if he found it practicable, but to avoid a general engagement until the arrival of the other divisions of the army...."[119] Accustomed to the late Jackson's rigid command style, Ewell was perplexed by Lee's confusing directive. He had also received a report that a fresh body of Union troops was advancing towards him via the Hanover Road. Understandably, the general was in no mood for any unsolicited opinions. Trimble offered his anyway. After inspecting the area, he counseled Ewell to seize Culp's Hill — the rugged, wooded eminence located just east of Cemetery Hill. This elevation did not appear to be occupied and it dominated the surrounding terrain.

The excited Trimble offered to take the hill with one brigade. When Ewell demurred, Isaac retorted, "Give me a good regiment and I will take that hill!"[120] The testy commander shot back, "When I need advice from a junior officer, I generally ask it."[121] His pride injured, the enraged Marylander threw down his sword and stormed away.

By the time Johnson's 6,400 fresh troops arrived, the sun was sinking below South Mountain. Ewell ordered his division commander to march his men around Gettysburg and take possession of Culp's Hill. In the gathering twilight, Johnson exercised caution and deployed his four brigades a mile away from this elevation.[122]

In truth, the window of opportunity for the Confederates was extremely limited. By 5 P.M., the survivors of the First and Eleventh Corps had begun to receive substantial reinforcements, and by nightfall, nearly 30,000 Union troops were on the scene with considerable artillery support. Even if Ewell had been able to mount an attack, it would have been very difficult to dislodge the Federal forces.[123]

As night settled over Gettysburg, the ever adventurous Douglas rode into town. He was soon hailed by one of his former college mates, who invited him into his home. Douglas' Northern acquaintance offered his opinion that the Army of the Potomac was ruined and could not understand Henry's expectations of "rough work ahead."[124] The young officer's trepidation was well-founded. Although the Confederates had emerged triumphant on the opening day of the battle, the fruits of victory would prove elusive in the critical days ahead.

At various times throughout the day, the residents of the Seminary vacated the campus in search of safe havens away from the bloody fighting. From her home on the corner of Washington and High Streets, Catherine Mary White Foster observed a group of civilians "running down the hill faster than 'Double quick'" as the First Corps arrived on the scene near 10 A.M.[125] These fugitives were undoubtedly the students who had been scared out of the cupola by the stray Confederate artillery rounds.

Martin Culler and his Seminary classmate Mahlon Horine observed the final

stages of the July 1st fighting from Cemetery Ridge. "The play of battle all along the
eastern slope of Seminary Ridge was a
thrilling scene," wrote Culler. For the remainder of the battle the pair resided at a
home on Baltimore Street at the foot of
Cemetery Hill.[126]

It is difficult to ascertain precisely
when the Ziegler family vacated their place
of refuge in the cellar of the Seminary.
Hugh Ziegler asserted in both of his post-
war accounts that the family left the building near noon during a lull in the fighting.
His sister Lydia placed the departure later
in the day as the First Corps was being driven back towards the town.[127]

Mary Ziegler and the older children
wisely snatched up some loaves of bread
as they exited the Seminary. Lydia recalled
the march through town as "heart-sicken-
ing" and she would never forget the
"groans and cries of the suffering men as
they lay at our feet."[128] The most memorable scene for Hugh took place at the town
square, where a band on horseback played
military tunes amid the sound of booming
cannon, screaming shells, and the rattle of
musketry.[129] The family first sought refuge
in the woods on Culp's Hill, until shells
and bullets drove them off. After a brief
stop at Spangler's Spring, the family hiked
to Wolf's Hill. There, Mary divided the
bread among the tired and hungry children. During the late afternoon, the party
arrived in Two Taverns via the Baltimore
Pike as General Henry Slocum's Twelfth
Corps marched north. Lydia wrote that
"the shades of night had fallen ere we
reached the home of a friend who kindly
gave us shelter."[130]

Eliza Slentz and her small children
remained in the Seminary throughout the
battle and "subsisted on one small piece of
bread daily."[131] Perhaps they had nowhere
else to go or were too frightened to venture
outside.

Probably out of concern for their

property, the Krauth family remained at
home until the last possible moment. As
the wounded filled up both stories of the
residence, Charles, Harriet, and Sallie retired to the basement. Shortly after 4 o'-
clock, as the Union line began to crumble,
a Yankee officer urged the family to vacate
the premises. When the trio emerged from
their sanctuary, a Confederate soldier was
shot dead almost at their feet; he was later
buried in the yard a few feet from the back
door.[132]

Cut off from the town, the Krauths
struck off for the countryside by traveling
northwest on the Mummasburg Road.
"After almost incredible escapes from destruction and death," the family found
shelter at several farms, including the Han-
key farm, a little over a mile from their
home. Upon their arrival there on the
morning of July 2nd, they partook of their
first meal since breakfast of the previous
day.[133]

Major Eugene Blackford, of the 5th
Alabama, related a remarkable story concerning the Schmucker house during the
Confederate occupation of Seminary
Ridge. On the morning of July 3rd, after
getting a drink of water from a well near
the house, Blackford stopped to pluck
some flowers from an adjacent greenhouse.
According to the major, "the ladies within
observing this mark of humanity in a
smoke begrimed soldier, and being ready
to grasp at straws eagerly besought my
protection against some of the Yankee soldiers wounded within ... one had drawn
his pistol and threatened to shoot them,
they poor creatures were too much scared
to see that they had but to keep out of the
same room where he lay and they would be
safe enough as he had lost a leg."[134]

The officer succeeded in having the
wounded transferred to another location.
"They were very grateful," recalled Blackford. "Upon inquiring my name they were
very much struck by it, and asked at once

A modern view of the Krauth house. Author's collection.

if I was related to Caroline B. of Lynchburg. They then told me that their name was S[ch]mucker, and that they were related to the Steenbergens."[135]

Concerned about the danger of artillery fire, the major asked the ladies if they had any yellow flannel from which a hospital flag could be fashioned. After a long search, they could only produce a red flannel petticoat. Blackford climbed onto the roof and attached the garment to the lightning rod. "The presence of one of the yankees within too dangerously wounded to be moved justified me in this," he wrote, "I would not otherwise have done it [but] for the protection of the women." When he returned later in the day following the cannonade, Blackford found the house deserted.[136]

Sallie Broadhead returned to her house on Chambersburg Street during the early evening of July 1st. While her husband had remained at home, Sallie had taken her young daughter and retired to the home of a friend in a safer section of town when the infantry fighting heated up. As she passed back through the town, the young housewife found the streets littered with clothing, blankets, knapsacks, cartridge boxes, dead horses, and the bodies of several slain soldiers. "As I write all is quiet, but O! how I dread tomorrow," Sallie confided to her diary that evening.[137]

Nowhere was this dread and uncertainty more pronounced than within the walls of the Lutheran Seminary. Inside this field hospital, several hundred wounded Union soldiers fought for their very survival. Trapped behind enemy lines, they now faced perhaps a greater test of their courage and endurance than they had ever faced on the battlefield or on the march.

CHAPTER 6

The Hospital During the Battle: July 1–July 4, 1863

My God, my God, why have you deserted me?
Why are you so far away?
Won't you listen to my groans and come to my rescue?
I cry out day and night, but you don't answer,
and I can never rest.

Psalm 22, verses 1–2.

Nearly 4,000 Union soldiers were wounded during the fierce fighting of July 1st. Most of the patients in the field hospitals were left behind during the retreat. Worse, a number of the more severe cases were scattered across the battlefield with no shelter from the elements.[1]

Seminary Ridge, the last stronghold of the First Corps, now formed the main battle line of the Army of Northern Virginia. The ridge would be the staging area for Confederate attacks throughout the remainder of the battle. General Lee established his headquarters at Mary Thompson's small stone house, situated along the Chambersburg Pike a short distance north of the Seminary. Although the Confederates had enjoyed a smashing success on the opening day of the battle, the outcome of the contest was still undecided.

The wounded Union POWs inside the Seminary Hospital also faced a very uncertain future. Lieutenant Colonel McFarland described the grim situation:

As soon as the rebels took possession of the hospital, they seized and carried off all the instruments, chloroform, and appliances and thus deprived Surgeon Blakeslee and his assistants, who had generously remained behind to share the captivity and alleviate the sufferings of the wounded, the means of amputating shattered limbs or dressing painful wounds.... For three days we were left without food, drink, or attendance to listen with painful anxiety to the booming of cannon and the din of battle.... For a time there seemed to be no hope, and we all awaited our fate with resignation.[2]

Both General Abner Doubleday and his successor, Major General John Newton, praised Surgeon J. Theodore Heard, the medical director of the First Corps, and Medical Inspector Thomas H. Bache for remaining behind with the wounded. In his official report, Newton wrote that both deserved "the highest praise for their zealous and unremitting attention to the wounded."[3]

It was a rare occasion when the medical staff received such accolades. They were far more accustomed to receiving the stinging criticism of the very men they were laboring to save. "My first recollection of the hospital at Gettysburg Seminary is that our doctors had no instruments," recalled Lieutenant Jeremiah

Lieutenant Jeremiah Hoffman, 142nd Pa. Vols., pictured in 1862 upon his graduation from Franklin & Marshall College. Courtesy of FM.

Hoffman. "They were taken prisoner, and in the hurry and excitement of battle, neither of the parties recollected that it was necessary to attend to the wounded. The Rebels had to attend to their own, and the Union doctors found it much more safe to hide in the cellars and behind large trees than to stand and argue the point of international law as to the exemption of doctors, while acting in their professional capacity, from the fate of ordinary prisoners...."[4]

While the lieutenant's comments may have been partly accurate, at least a few of the Union doctors at the Seminary refused to remain passive. The Reverend Isaac W. Monfort, an agent of the Indiana Military Agency, described the resourcefulness of Assistant Surgeon Abraham Haines of the 19th Indiana in a contemporary newspaper article:

> He was left without supplies of any kind. Calling upon the [Confederate] Medical Purveyor for supplies, he was told that there was none. Finding in the cellar of a deserted house a crock of lard, he filled an empty fruit can with lard — took a sheet from a bed, and tearing off a strip, a wick was prepared and soon a lamp was burning. By this light he dressed wounds for the first evening. Having no bandages he went into the town, and entering a house, took from the beds fine sheets, which were soon converted into bandages and lint for his patients.[5]

Although front line surgeons often endured the same privations and dangers as the fighting men of the army, they were rarely the recipients of promotions, rewards, or even recognition for their efforts. Like those of common soldiers, the lives of regimental medical officers fluctuated between long periods of relative inactivity, when their duties took them less than an hour a day to complete, to frantic periods, when they labored incessantly until nearly overcome by physical and mental exhaustion.

When judged by today's standards, doctors of the mid–19th century failed miserably in a number of areas, most notably in sanitation and hygienics and in surgical techniques. One reason for this deficiency was the fact that Civil War–era doctors were poorly trained. The standard medical course lasted less than three years and most of the subjects relied heavily on lectures, lacking any substantial laboratory or clinical instruction.[6]

The background of 37-year-old Amos Blakeslee, the regimental surgeon of the 151st Pennsylvania, was above average. Educated at the Yale Medical Institute, Blakeslee had served as the resident physician of the Connecticut General State Hospital and then operated successful private practices in New Haven, and later in Wyoming County, Pennsylvania, prior to his military service. His two younger assistants, Warren Underwood and Jonas Kauffman, had studied at Jefferson Medical College in Philadelphia, a leading educational facility of the day.[7] At Gettysburg,

Surgeon Amos Blakeslee, 151st Pa. Vols. Courtesy of PSA.

Blakeslee and his staff faced a daunting task. The 151st Pennsylvania's tally of 211 wounded was unsurpassed by that of any other Union army regiment present at the battle.[8]

It is doubtful that additional schooling would have proved beneficial to the army medical personnel of the 1860s. A substantial time lag in medical knowledge existed between Europe and America, and the pioneering research of Louis Pasteur, Robert Koch, and Joseph Lister was still off in the future or not yet fully understood. Although anesthesia had been introduced to the United States nearly two decades earlier, precious little was known about the spread of bacteria and the importance of antiseptics in surgery.

Modern surgeons and operating assistants routinely scrub their hands, wear sterile gowns, and use sterile instruments, dressings, and sutures. By contrast, Civil War surgeons cleaned their instruments by periodically rinsing them with water, usually at the end of the day. Remarkably, they rarely paused to wash the blood from their hands before moving on to the next patient. Typically, the operator wiped the blood and other material from his knife with a quick swipe across the front of his large apron, which was usually stained with blood and pus from prior sessions.[9]

There were many other blunders. Medical journals of the period recommended using a finger to examine a wound as well as for removing the projectile, dirt, and other debris from the area. Nurses normally used the same sponge and basin of water to clean the wounds of every patient in their ward. Dressings and lint applied to protect a wound against contamination were rarely aseptic, as was the case with the makeshift items procured by Surgeon Haines.

Not surprisingly, germs and infections were quickly spread from one patient to another. The appearance of "laudable pus," a creamy and odoriferous pus excreted from a wound following treatment, was considered a positive sign. In fact, this suppuration indicated a bacterial infection caused by the doctor's dirty hands or instruments or perhaps a non-sterile dressing or a washing with contaminated water.[10]

Besides their deficiencies in medical knowledge and general lack of surgical experience, the effectiveness of Civil War surgeons was compromised by the prevalent combat tactics, weaponry, and the physical properties of the projectiles. In battle, Northern and Southern armies advanced to within close range in compact formations to mass their fire power. These outdated tactics were a holdover from an era when notoriously inaccurate smoothbore rifles were the standard arm. However, the new rifle muskets carried by most Civil War infantrymen could kill a man at a distance of one thousand yards. On numerous occasions at Gettysburg, opposing regiments exchanged volleys at distances less than 50 yards![11]

The projectile commonly used in these new weapons was a conical-shaped, soft lead bullet known as a Minie ball. In contrast to high velocity, steel-jacketed modern bullets which drill a small sterile hole before passing out of the body, Civil War projectiles traveled at slow speeds, readily lost their shape on impact, carried dirt and debris into the wound, and often lodged deep inside the body. When these balls mushroomed, they created gaping wounds, destroying muscle, tissue, and arteries, and shattering bones.[12]

Bullet wounds accounted for a whopping 94 percent of all reported Civil War combat injuries. In 7 out of 10 cases, the soldier was struck in the arm or leg. This statistic partly explains the tremendous number of amputations performed during the four years of conflict. Although this extreme measure generated a great deal of controversy, it was often the only recourse if a limb was badly lacerated or if a bone was irreparably splintered.[13]

It was generally thought that major operations should be performed within 24 hours of the time the wound was incurred, since waiting for longer periods dramatically decreased the survival rate. One surgeon recorded that in 19 cases when amputation was delayed for two days or more, only one patient survived. On the other hand, in 19 instances when the operation was performed immediately, all of the men survived.[14] With several hundred wounded patients in their midst, the deprived Union surgeons must have been extremely frustrated by their predicament.

The initial concern of many of the patients, however, was the more immediate danger of friendly fire. Shortly after his arrival, Lieutenant Jeremiah Hoffman was approached by a number of men who informed him that their own artillery was firing upon the building. Thinking quickly, the officer noticed Mary Ziegler's red flannel petticoat lying nearby. He ordered an unwounded soldier to climb up into the cupola and attach the largest piece he was able to tear from the garment to indicate that the structure was a hospital. "Thus, it happened during the fight and for some days after, the undergarment of our hostess floated over the building," recalled an amused Hoffman.[15]

Apparently, the Southerners also made an effort to identify the building's function. On July 2, a Union officer on Cemetery Ridge could clearly see the Seminary with the Confederate's yellow hospital flag floating above the building. That same day, *Boston Journal* correspondent Charles Carleton Coffin climbed up to the roof of the Evergreen Cemetery Gatehouse to familiarize himself with the area. From this commanding height, he spied the Seminary cupola from which he recalled a yellow flag was flying.[16] Despite the visibility of the signal from different vantage points,

The Seminary building shortly after the battle. Note the hospital flag visible in the cupola and the shattered window pane directly below. Courtesy of ACHS.

the menacing threat of artillery fire was not altogether mitigated.

On the second day of the battle, a shell burst near the entrance door. Lieutenant Hoffman was then lying on the floor in the southeastern corner of the first story. He remembered that the entry and adjoining rooms filled with smoke and panicked men cried out in false alarm, "The building is burning!" In desperation, some of the seriously wounded attempted to drag themselves outside to escape the dreaded flames. One cantankerous individual, who had pretended to be in excruciating pain, suddenly made a dramatic recovery. He jumped up from his position on a lounge, rudely pushed aside the crippled patients in his path, and scrambled down the flight of stairs leading to the cellar.

Hoffman was the beneficiary of his comrade's cowardice when order was restored. The partly paralyzed officer was placed upon the comfortable lounge vacated by the "skulking dog." From his new position, Jeremiah could gaze out the window towards Cemetery Hill and Cemetery Ridge, where he observed the smoky discharges of the cannon by day and the flashes of flame by night. He frequently watched shot and shells bound through the yard, knocking down sections of fence and clipping off tree limbs.

At least three shells entered the building, the most remarkable of which was a 24-pound solid shot discovered inside a closet in the "Historical Room" following the battle. The projectile had penetrated several layers of brick before finally losing its momentum. The location of this room is not known, but the evidence seems to indicate it was on one of the upper floors. Lieutenant Colonel McFarland recalled that one shell passed through the second story room in the southeast corner of the building. After the battle, Dr. Schmucker wrote that the main edifice "was perforated by several balls, and large portions knocked out of the North East gable corner."[17]

Along with food, water, and surgical care, much-needed sleep was difficult to obtain inside the Seminary. Anxiety and fear were omnipresent, and heart-rending scenes were commonplace. One pathetic incident narrated by Hoffman took place during one of the first nights at the hospital. A patient on an upper floor was heard crying out desperately for water. When no one responded to his urgent pleas, the anguished soldier could be heard shuffling across the floor and then coming downstairs with a pronounced thump as he painfully rolled from step to step. The remainder of the story is related by Hoffman:

> His motions were slow, and his voice became each time more hollow and unearthly than before. By the time he came to the bottom, he could utter only a whisper. We heard his voice grow less and less and finally we had our former stillness. In the morning the man was found dead at the foot of the stairs. We had all lent him our voices, but not one in our room was able to go to his assistance, and the nurses, if there were any, were out of hearing, resting after severe labor in carrying wounded.[18]

The young officer was also touched in a more personal manner. Colonel Cummins was placed upon a bed directly across the hall from Hoffman. The colonel was in great anguish from his internal injuries.

Writhing and groaning, he would cast his arms about wildly and sometimes sit upright. When he did so, Private Chester Cammer, an unwounded soldier who was serving as his attendant, implored him to lie down. "No, No," responded Cummins, "only let me hang my legs over the bed."[19]

Early the next morning, Cammer reported to Hoffman that the colonel's hands and feet were becoming cold to the touch. Jeremiah ordered the private to search the upper floors of the building for a doctor. Two surgeons from the First Brigade examined Cummins near daybreak. The prognosis was grim; the colonel was dying and it was advised that he should not be disturbed. Hoffman could see his commander, but was not able to converse with him. Any final words uttered by the officer were never recorded by Private Cammer. The same morning the inspirational leader was buried in the Seminary garden. His vacant bed was then occupied by Colonel McFarland, who had been lying on the bare floor in his own blood since the previous afternoon.[20]

McFarland believed the Confederates deserved much of the blame for the deplorable conditions at the Seminary. In addition to seizing precious medical supplies and instruments, he later wrote his wife that "the rebs were very ugly, taking away our hospital help and leaving some poor fellows there [for] days on the field of battle."[21] According to George, "the rebel commanding officer ordered every sound or slightly wounded Union soldier out to be paroled, and though promising to return them as hospital nurses, he marched them off, leaving over three hundred helpless wounded men without a single attendant!" He decried this action as "unchristian and barbarous" and felt it was the direct cause of death in some cases and of unnecessary suffering in many others.[22]

Among those rounded up was Lieutenant Edward Ross of the 20th New York

Militia. Early on the morning of July 2nd, a Confederate lieutenant entered his room and asked if he was wounded. When the New Yorker replied that he was not injured, the enemy officer informed him that he would need to leave with the remainder of the prisoners to be paroled.[23]

Ross had plenty of company. Sergeant Levi Graham's wounded arm ruse was soon detected, and he was forced to leave the side of Captain Blair. Other parolees included Private Cammer and Private Lyman Wilson, McFarland's angel of mercy. These soldiers joined about 1,500 others who agreed "not to bear arms against the Confederate government until they were released from the obligation they were about to assume."[24] The group was supplied with provisions and marched under escort to Carlisle and then to Harrisburg. Since there was uncertainty as to whether the U.S. Government would recognize these arrangements, as many as 3,500 Union captives refused to accept the parole conditions. These men were marched south into captivity.[25]

Along with a number of other prisoners, Lieutenant J. Quincy Carpenter, 150th Pennsylvania, was marched a mile or two out the Chambersburg Pike and then spent the night in a barn, possibly on the Samuel Lohr farm. The next day he was permitted to roam the battlefield and assist the wounded. It was through his efforts that Lieutenant Chancellor was carried into the McPherson barn, where he joined Major Chamberlin and others of his brigade.[26]

Contrary to McFarland's testimony, there is strong evidence that the Confederates retained a number of captured Union soldiers to serve as hospital nurses at the Seminary. In an affidavit, Surgeon Robert Loughran, 20th New York Militia, listed 17 enlisted men from his command who were on duty at the hospital from July 1st through the middle of August.[27]

These attendants enjoyed considerable freedom during the battle. On the afternoon of the 2nd, Private George Bisbee and two companions walked to McPherson's Ridge, where they discovered the Southerners had buried the dead of their regiment in shallow graves the previous evening. The trio was able to identify the remains of a friend by his black silk handkerchief.[28]

The Confederates employed some of the Union captives in scouring the field for guns and ammunition. One prisoner on this detail discovered a loaded weapon. He waited patiently for the right moment and then shot one of his guards through the heart without being detected. A similar misdeed took place when a Rebel private shot and killed a Union soldier who was bringing in a badly wounded comrade from the field. The gunman pulled his hat over his eyes and slipped away. A number of patients in the Seminary reported the incident to Confederate officers, but the transgressor never returned to the scene.[29]

Along with these cold-blooded acts, there were deeds of compassion. Lieutenant Alexander Douglas of the 13th South Carolina was in charge of the infirmary corps of Perrin's Brigade. Like their Northern counterparts, these men were assigned the often hazardous duty of conveying the wounded to the field hospitals. On the morning of July 2nd, Perrin's troops were positioned on Seminary Ridge near the McMillan farm. Following a sharp skirmish, a wounded Union soldier was left abandoned between the hostile lines. Lying in the hot sun, he cried out loudly to be removed. Responding to his urgent pleas, Lieutenant Douglas and four volunteers sallied forth to rescue the Yankee. The party became the target of Federal sharpshooters until the purpose of their mission was recognized. The unidentified Union infantryman was carried into the Lutheran Seminary a short time later.[30]

In another instance, a Confederate soldier came to the assistance of an Irish sergeant of the 121st Pennsylvania who had been lying in the open for over a day without water. The sympathetic Rebel dragged the Irishman under a tree and filled his canteen with water. The sergeant's right thigh bone had been fractured by a minie ball. This rugged soul was carried into Lieutenant Hoffman's room on the fourth. His wound was badly infested with worms.

Jeremiah recalled with disgust that by this time maggots were especially plentiful on his floor. He wrote of another soldier of the 121st "from whose wound the worms jumped as fast as you could snap your fingers." He had been struck in the side and the ball had lodged in his back. His wound was in a position that didn't allow him to attend to it himself, and nurses were scarce.[31]

As revolting as it may sound, these loathsome creatures were actually performing a beneficial service for their unadmiring hosts. Maggots feed only on the diseased tissue of a wound, leaving it clean and healthy. The benefits of larval treatment had actually been discovered during the Napoleonic Wars, only to be forgotten. A group of Confederate surgeons near Chattanooga, Tennessee, rediscovered the phenomenon by accident towards the end of 1863, and thenceforward encouraged the process, while their Northern counterparts continued to eradicate the insects.[32] Thus, by unintended neglect the lives of a number of infested soldiers in the Seminary might have been saved.

The handicapped Union surgeons did what they could to succor the wounded. The Confederates could not take away one instrument that was deemed valuable and effective — the human finger. With this handy device, and perhaps with appliances hidden from the enemy, the medical officers went to work. Two bone fragments were extracted from the right thigh of Corporal Luke English, though the search for the invading missile proved unsuccessful, and a musket ball was removed from the skull of Private John Shultz.[33]

Due to the lack of instruments and supplies, amputations appeared to be infrequent among the Union patients at the Seminary during the battle. One of the first documented cases involved Corporal John Crawford of the 6th Wisconsin, who had been shot in the right knee during his regiment's assault on the railroad cut. The following day it was determined that his limb was fractured beyond repair and would require amputation about eight inches below the hip joint.

Assuming it was available, the operation commenced with the administration of chloroform, the chief anesthetic used during the Civil War. A small quantity of the substance was dropped on a folded cloth or into a paper cone with a small sponge inserted inside. The cloth or cone was slowly lowered towards the patient's nose and mouth until the sleep-inducing fumes brought on full anesthesia.

A tourniquet was applied to Crawford's upper right thigh and the surgeon sliced through the skin and muscle, front and back, with a surgical knife, leaving two flaps of skin. Next, he reached for a bone saw, and after a few quick strokes, the mangled leg was severed. The large arteries were then tied off with undisinfected silk thread to prevent bleeding. At this point, a skilled operator would carefully scrape the rough edges of the bone until smooth before he pulled the flaps of skin over the stump and sewed them together. The operation was complete with the application of a bandage and plaster.

Moments later, the Wisconsin corporal regained consciousness and realized he would spend the remainder of his life as an amputee. Unfortunately, his operation had been performed by an inexperienced or careless surgeon who left a

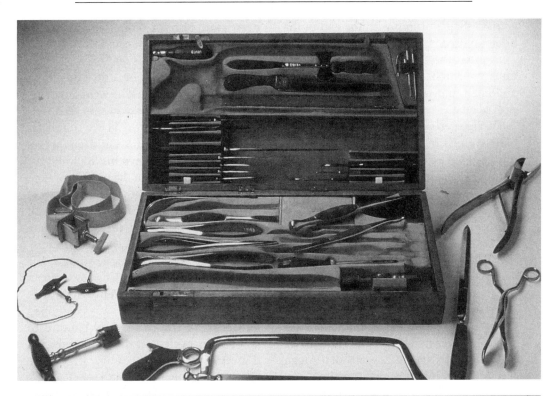

Top: *A Civil War surgeon's kit. Courtesy of NMHM.* Bottom: *A medical kit with anesthesia items. Courtesy of NMHM.*

conical-shaped stump with the end of the bone exposed.[34]

Often there was little that could be done, good or bad. Gunshot wounds in the abdomen and the bowels nearly always proved fatal. The general consensus among medical experts of the day was that "when balls are lost in the capacity of the belly one need not amuse himself by hunting for them."[35] The Iron Brigade's Lieutenant Newell Grace succumbed to his abdominal wound on July 3rd inside the hospital. An examining surgeon informed Andrew Tucker that he too did not have long to live. The officer replied resolutely, "I am a very young man, but I am willing to die for my country."[36]

For those who managed to survive a penetrating abdominal wound, the pain could be interminable. Corporal Charles H. Smith, 76th New York, was shot through the left side, injuring his intestines and colon. Smith was initially treated in a private home, then admitted to the Seminary. Three years later, he complained that fecal matter, food, and wind escaped from the wounds caused by the ball. An examining physician reported that "a largely offensive and ill-conditioned discharge now constantly escapes, and at present disables him more than the loss of a hand or foot."[37]

Chest wounds were also extremely dangerous. Injuries to this region proved fatal in about six out of every ten cases.[38] As evidenced by Colonel Cummins' agonizing death, the victims would often experience a great deal of pain. Captain James Weida of the 151st Pennsylvania was shot in the right side. The bullet broke a rib, injured his liver, and passed through the base of his right lung before lodging inside the body. Surgeon Blakeslee probed into Weida's chest and removed what foreign material he could reach. Lying nearby, Private Aaron Smith testified that his captain "was very low and often complained to me of great pain in the region of his heart [and] also [of] pain in his arms and legs. He was short in his breath and could not speak above a whisper."[39]

Somehow Weida beat the odds. Near the beginning of August he was convalescing at his home in Long Swamp, Pennsylvania. He lived another 44 years and fathered four additional children before intestinal cancer claimed his life in 1907.[40]

Intermingled with the numerous First Corps soldiers inside the Seminary were several representatives of the Eleventh Corps. Among these patients was a private from the 134th New York who had the misfortune of suffering a unique wound. His unit was part of Colonel Charles Coster's brigade of Adolph Von Steinwehr's division. The Second Division was positioned on Cemetery Hill by General Howard to serve as the nucleus of the Union position if a retreat became necessary. In the late afternoon of July 1st, Howard sent Coster's small brigade forward to cover the withdrawal of his remaining two divisions. During a brief stand near John Kuhn's brickyard on the northern outskirts of town, the 134th New York lost 42 killed and 151 wounded.[41]

At some point in the heat of battle, Private John H. Miller of Company I drew the ire of his captain. The enraged officer struck Miller on the top left side of the skull with his sword. The blow caused a deep indentation an inch in diameter. When Miller reached the hospital simple dressings were applied to the wound. Miller continually suffered from convulsions and partial paralysis of his right side. In late November, he underwent a procedure known as "trephination," which involved perforating a circular section of the skull. His disability was declared to be permanent, and he was discharged from the service the following spring.[42]

These types of wounds were extremely rare; fewer than one percent of reported wounds were caused by the saber or bayonet.[43] Adding to the oddity of this particular case was the fact that the damage had been inflicted by a "friendly" blade. Interestingly, there were two other cases of saber injuries to the scalp at the Seminary Hospital. One of these men was a member of the 17th Connecticut, also of the Eleventh Corps.[44] The other was Private Thomas F. Bennett, 10th Virginia Cavalry, who was wounded on July 2nd and admitted to the hospital the following day.[45] Both soldiers eventually recovered.

Although it was primarily a Union First Corps hospital, occupied mainly by soldiers from the Third Division, there was also an undetermined number of Confederate wounded inside the Seminary as a result of the July 1st fighting. Certainly, some of Perrin's South Carolinians were cared for at this hospital since over 400 members of the brigade were wounded during the assault on Seminary Ridge.[46] According to Captain Louis Duncan, a few soldiers from Heth's Division received treatment there as well.[47]

A perusal of the case histories in *The Medical and Surgical History of the Civil War* reveals several Seminary patients who did not fight near the campus. Three soldiers from the 13th Georgia of Gordon's brigade, Early's division, were admitted to the hospital on July 1st. All three suffered from dangerous wounds to the rectum and pelvic region. In late July and early August, the Georgians were transferred to another facility. Of the trio, two survived, but 23-year-old Private Joseph S. Haden died on August 30, 1863, from chronic diarrhea and secondary hemorrhaging.[48]

Two additional cases involved soldiers from Rodes' Division. A private from the 30th North Carolina sustained an arm wound while fighting on Oak Ridge and a member of the 53rd North Carolina was struck in the scalp region during the action at the railroad cut. The latter wound proved fatal.[49]

Although very similar in organization to the Union medical department, the Confederate doctors faced a problem not often encountered by those in blue — the periodic shortage of hospital and medical supplies. To fill this deficiency, the Southerners used a variety of methods. Large quantities of pharmaceutical products were purchased abroad and delivered to Confederate ports through blockade-running ships. Supplies from the North were smuggled through the lines by enterprising purveyors. Private and state agencies also made sizable contributions throughout the conflict.

The Confederates had no qualms about seizing supplies and instruments from their opposite numbers when the opportunity arose. After the battle of Chancellorsville in early May of 1863, the Union surgeons who remained behind with the wounded asserted that Confederate surgeons took their instruments, making it impossible for them to render proper care to their patients.[50] Two months later, the medical personnel of the First Corps at the Seminary found themselves in the same predicament.

Worse, an order by General Meade issued on June 30th stipulated that only ammunition wagons and ambulances would be permitted to accompany the Union troops, in order to facilitate the rapid movement of the army. The medical and supply trains remained at Westminster, Maryland, about 25 miles from the field of conflict. As a result, tents, bedding, clothing, cooking utensils, and food were almost entirely lacking throughout the battle. Fortunately, special medicine wagons accompanied the divisional ambulance trains and thus provided a limited supply of anesthetics, dressings, drugs, and instruments. Unfortunately, the demand for these products far outstripped what was available.[51]

The Confederates extended their

confiscation efforts to the private sector. The July 14, 1863, issue of the *Adams Sentinel* asserted that local physicians would have rendered efficient aid to the army surgeons had it not been for the fact that the Rebels seized nearly all of their surgical instruments and medical stores.

Anesthetics were particularly prized. One loyal female citizen related that during the battle she walked past a number of Confederate soldiers with a bottle of chloroform wrapped in her apron. She was relieved to get through without being questioned "for next to food and money, there was nothing they were more rejoiced to obtain."[52]

A Confederate surgeon at the Seminary voiced a hope shared by many of his comrades when he wrote the following prayer on the margin of a copy of the General Synod Minutes for 1859: "Oh! this horrible war — it has saddened the hearts of so many both in the U.S. and C.S. O! Thou who controlleth the destiny of nations and individuals, give us peace and independence. Would that the North would stop this cruel war and let all parties return to their quiet homes and worship God under their own vine and fig tree."[53]

This heartfelt prayer would remain unanswered. As Union and Confederate medical teams labored tirelessly with limited resources to save lives and provide what comfort they could to those injured on the opening day of the battle, the two opposing commanders developed strategies for the renewal of hostilities.

By the early evening of July 1st, General George Meade had made the decision to concentrate his army and fight at Gettysburg. Leaving his Taneytown, Maryland, headquarters, the army commander reached Cemetery Hill near midnight, where he met his assembled generals. In the pre-dawn darkness, Meade surveyed the surrounding terrain on horseback. The Pennsylvanian was pleased with the defensive potential of the ground.

By noon of July 2nd, the entire Army of the Potomac, with the exception of the massive Sixth Corps, had reached the field. As no Confederate attack developed throughout the morning and early afternoon hours, Meade had the luxury of making his dispositions without interference. Gradually, the famous fishhook configuration of the Union line emerged: Culp's Hill formed the tip of the hook; Cemetery Hill, the rounded bend; Cemetery Ridge, the long shank, led to Little Round Top, which represented the eye.

Meade's watchful arrangements were severely compromised when politician-general Daniel Sickles impetuously shifted his entire Third Corps from its former position on Cemetery Ridge to occupy the high ground along the Emmitsburg Road nearly a half-mile in advance of the main line. This move isolated Sickles' men from the remainder of the army and endangered the southern flank of the Union line by leaving Little Round Top unoccupied. In the late afternoon, before Meade could rectify the situation, Confederate artillery thundered from Seminary Ridge, announcing the long-anticipated Southern attack.

General Robert E. Lee had fully intended to strike earlier, but his chief lieutenants were not in a cooperative mood. After some deliberation, Lee opted for an assault on the Union left flank near the Round Tops utilizing General Longstreet's fresh corps of veteran fighters. The attack was to precede en echelon northward to include Hill's corps, which would assail the center of the Union line. At the same time, Ewell was ordered to demonstrate against the Union right on Culp's and Cemetery Hills, with the discretion of converting his jab into a full-scale attack if an opportunity arose.

The plan started unraveling from the

outset as Longstreet spent hours of precious daylight in maneuvering his troops into position. The subsequent attacks by Longstreet and Hill were spirited, but lacked coordination. Nonetheless, Sickles' advanced line was smashed and the Confederates gained a toehold on the Union left through the desperate and bloody fighting which occurred at Devil's Den, the Wheatfield, and the Peach Orchard. Meade narrowly averted disaster as he, with the valuable assistance of General Winfield Scott Hancock, sent fresh troops to threatened sectors with an uncanny timeliness.

In the heat of battle, however, the Union commander stripped too many men from Culp's Hill as he struggled to shore up his endangered left flank. Ewell took advantage of this error, delaying his attack until just the right moment. By nightfall, Johnson's division had gained a lodgment on the southeast slope of the rugged hill by taking the trenches constructed there by Union troops.

Throughout the day's fighting, Captain Benjamin H. Smith's battery of four 3-inch rifles was positioned just south of the Seminary edifice. The guns opened fire at about 4 P.M. in concert with other Confederate batteries. George McFarland never forgot the frightening experience:

> The discharges of this battery were so heavy that they caused the building to tremble to its very foundation, and the window sash to rattle as though shaken by an earthquake. This sent many a pang not only through shattered limbs and aching heads, but through loyal hearts fully conscious of the fearful issues then trembling in the balance…. This battery proved to be one of the most efficient the Rebels had, and soon drew a heavy fire from the Union batteries posted on the opposite heights. This fire was particularly accurate, and disturbed the enemy; but it also put our hospital and its inmates into a very dangerous and critical

position. A perfect shower of shot and shell was hurled upon us….[54]

The nightmare ended at nightfall when the guns finally fell silent. After more than six hours of desperate combat, the result was inconclusive. The Union line was dented, but not broken. Although no clear victor emerged, the second day at Gettysburg ranked as one of the costliest engagements of the war. The killed and wounded of the two armies totaled about 15,000 officers and men. About three-fifths of these losses were incurred by the Union Second, Third, and Fifth Corps.[55] Although the Seminary was located within the enemy lines, a number of wounded from these organizations joined their comrades from the First and Eleventh Corps inside the hospital.

Among the first Union casualties to reach the Seminary Hospital on July 2nd was Corporal William H. Leach, Company F, 1st United States Sharpshooters. A contingent of about 100 of these elite riflemen had formed part of a reconnaissance ordered by General Sickles during the early afternoon to ascertain the strength and location of Confederate troops opposite the Third Corps. The Union force encountered three Alabama regiments in Pitzer's Woods and a fierce fire fight ensued. Leach was one of 19 sharpshooters hit by the Southerners. Two missiles entered the corporal's abdomen, fracturing one of the lower ribs and injuring both kidneys. For nearly three weeks afterwards, blood was observed in his urine. Though he eventually recovered, Leach was permanently disabled from limited flexion of the spinal column and occasional attacks of diarrhea.[56]

The 4th Michigan, a Fifth Corps regiment, played a prominent role in the swirling, see-saw battle for the Wheatfield. Near the final stages of the chaotic struggle, the fighting was often hand-to-hand.

Colonel Harrison Jeffords was shot and bayoneted to death as he attempted to rescue the regimental flag from a group of enemy soldiers.[57]

A less well-known casualty of this unit was Private Royal W. Hamlin, who fell senseless after a bullet struck him in the right ear and emerged at the base of the neck six inches from the point of entrance. The private was carried to the Seminary where he remained unconscious for two days. Hamlin suffered from chronic pain in the side of his head, and at one point, a piece of bone exited from the wound. He experienced difficulty moving his jaw and could not close his right eyelid. After his transfer from the Seminary, Hamlin received treatment at a series of general hospitals before he was finally released on September 13, 1864.[58]

Remarkably, others with similar injuries suffered virtually no adverse affects. A musket ball left a one-inch contusion upon the skull of the 20th Maine's Private Franklin Tree during his unit's legendary stand on Little Round Top. Following a brief stay at the Seminary and at Satterlee U.S. Hospital in Philadelphia, the hardy Maine soldier returned to duty in the fall.[59]

Considering the nature of these wounds, soldiers like Private Tree could count their blessings. While injuries of the head, face, and neck represented only about one-tenth of all gunshot wounds, in one study, over 80% of the corpses in a particular section of a battlefield had sustained hits in this region.[60]

In most instances, those who managed to survive these serious wounds suffered with symptoms far more severe than in Tree's case. Among the many wounded from Sickles' Third Corps was Private Edward Powers. As the 11th New Jersey fought just north of the famous Peach Orchard, a bullet crashed into Powers' forehead and lodged deep in his skull. The Jerseyman was removed to the Semi-

nary, but received no treatment for three days. Finally, the ball and fragments of bone were removed from the wound. It was recorded that pulsations of the patient's brain were clearly visible over a space an inch in diameter. Although he briefly returned to active duty, Powers reportedly suffered from headaches, dizziness, the inability to stoop, as well as impaired memory and intellect throughout his life.[61]

During the collapse of the Third Corps' advanced position, General Hancock dispersed various elements of his Second Corps to support Sickles. At one critical juncture, General Cadmus Wilcox's brigade of nearly 1,600 Alabamians rushed unopposed toward the center of the Union position on Cemetery Ridge. In desperation, Hancock ordered his nearest unit, the 262 soldiers of the 1st Minnesota, to countercharge the onrushing Confederates. The Minnesotans obeyed and rushed down the gentle slope towards the enemy. After fifteen minutes of combat, 215 of the regiment's officers and men had fallen, but the costly charge stalled Wilcox's attack long enough for other units to arrive, and the ridge remained in Union hands.[62]

Private Albert Sebers was struck twice during the fray, once in the left leg between the tibia and fibula, and then on the right side of his head. At the Seminary, a surgeon removed the first missile through an incision at the outer side of the knee. The leg swelled and considerable pus formed along the outside of the thigh. After the pus was drained, a gradual improvement took place. Later, a small piece of bone was removed from the cranium and small portions of brain exuded. By December, the wound was covered with scalp and hair. Sebers was subsequently assigned to the Veteran Reserve Corps, an organization comprised mainly of invalids.[63]

Farther to the south, two brigades of U.S. Regulars fought a determined rearguard action near the bloody Wheatfield. One volunteer recalled that the Regulars "moved off the field in admirable style, with well-aligned ranks, facing about at times to deliver their fire and check pursuit ... this action ... gave ample evidence of the fighting qualities, discipline, and steadiness under fire which make them the pattern and admiration of the entire army."[64]

Colonel Sidney Burbank's brigade held the advanced line during the withdrawal. Half of its officers were killed or wounded, and nearly half of its enlisted men became casualties. Private John Durkin received a bullet in the upper left thigh. The missile fractured the femur and remained buried in the leg. Later, at the Seminary, Assistant Surgeon William R. Ramsey extracted the ball by making a three-inch incision near the point of entrance. The wound suppurated freely for years and the damaged limb shrank four inches in length. Durkin became an inmate of

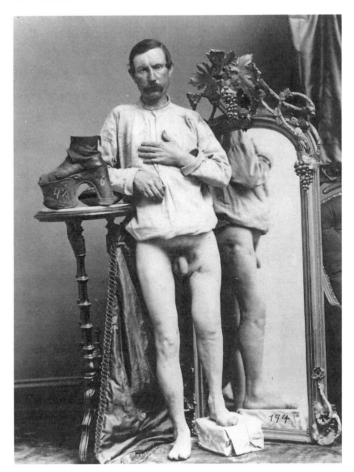

Private John Durkin, 11th U.S. Infantry, photographed at the Army Medical Museum in 1868. Note the scar on his upper left thigh and the special shoe designed to compensate for the shrunken length of the limb. Courtesy of NMHM.

the Old Soldiers' Home in Washington, and in 1868, he visited the Army Medical Museum and had his photograph taken.[65]

Fighting on the skirmish line could be just as dangerous. The 73rd Ohio was involved in sharp actions near the base of Cemetery Hill throughout the day. As testimony to the accurate fire of the Confederate snipers, 19-year-old Private Warren Miller sustained gunshots to his right shoulder, left forearm, and left side. The teenager was admitted to the Seminary Hospital the same day and remained there for three weeks. The bullet that entered his abdomen could not be located. The colon

was perforated resulting in the discharge of considerable pus and fecal matter. In early 1864, an examining physician declared Miller to be totally disabled.[66] Another member of Company B, Private George Nixon, fell with a mortal wound during the same action. His great-grandson would become president of the United States.[67]

The Confederates also contributed to the influx of wounded at the Seminary. Among the casualties admitted to the facility as a result of the second day's fighting were soldiers from General Ambrose Wright's Georgia brigade of A. P. Hill's corps. Near sunset, the Georgians surged up the slope of Cemetery Ridge south of the Copse of Trees and pierced the center of the Federal line. Wright's triumph was short-lived, however. A violent Union counterattack drove the Southerners back to Seminary Ridge with heavy losses.

The 48th Georgia suffered more casualties than any other regiment in the brigade, including 97 wounded.[68] During the retreat, enemy bullets hit Private Andrew J. Bowen on the right side of the neck and back, while a shell fragment struck him on the back of the head. His initial treatment consisted of cold water dressings with tonics and stimulants. The Georgian lost his appetite and became "very much disheartened and reduced."

Less than three weeks after his wounding, Bowen was stricken with erysipelas, a highly contagious strep infection. The principal symptom of this ailment was a characteristic rash accompanied by fever. The inflammation first appeared in Bowen's neck and back region, then spread to his face, completely closing the eyes. At one point, a serious hemorrhage developed from the neck wound and his pulse became faint. A local tincture of iodine was given as a curative agent. Gradually, Bowen's condition improved.[69]

Another providential recovery was made by a soldier of the 22nd Georgia. Private J. W. Brannon had been wounded by a minie ball, which entered a little above the left hip joint and passed out through the rectum. The 18-year-old suffered from intense pain in the pelvis, experienced difficulty in passing urine, and the openings of his wound discharged freely. Brannon also developed a case of diarrhea. Otherwise, it was noted, his health was good!

In addition to extra food, iron, quinine, acetate of lead, opium, and ipecac were administered. By the end of August, the young Georgian was able to walk, and his wound had nearly healed.[70] Unfortunately, the case of another member of the 22nd terminated fatally; the patient succumbed to a head wound in a Baltimore hospital following his treatment at the Seminary.[71]

Other cases at the hospital involving Confederates wounded on July 2nd included an artilleryman of the 1st Maryland Battery, who lost his left testicle as a result of a shell fragment injury; a private from the 51st Georgia, Semmes Brigade, who died later; and a 4th Alabama lieutenant. This officer stayed at the Seminary for a week during his initial convalescence from a wound of the large intestines.[72]

Like Colonel McFarland and the other patients inside the Seminary Hospital, the citizens of Gettysburg were apprehensive about the results of the second day's fighting. "We know not what the morrow will bring forth, and cannot even tell the issue of today," wrote a nervous Sallie Broadhead.[73] From a terse conversation with an officer serving on the staff of General Jubal Early, Sallie learned that the Union army held the best position. The Southerner assured her, however, that the Yankees could not hold it much longer. Although she now knew the advantage rested with the Army of the Potomac, Sallie posed an anxious question: "Can they keep it?"[74]

That same evening, General Meade queried his chief commanders on the same topic during a council of war held at his headquarters. Inside the cramped bedroom of the Lydia Leister home on Cemetery Ridge, the officers reached a momentous decision. The army would stay and fight it out from its present position, but maintain a defensive posture. Ironically, the first course of action approved by Meade was an offensive maneuver. At daybreak, the Twelfth Corps would launch an assault to drive Johnson's men from the base of Culp's Hill.

A mile away on Seminary Ridge, General Lee was equally determined. The Confederate chief had witnessed parts of the

July 2nd fighting from near the Seminary in company with Generals Hill and Heth. For much of the day, however, he sat alone on a stump intently observing the action through his field glass. Although one observer detected no visible signs of anxiety upon the countenance of his chief, Lee was greatly annoyed by the lack of "proper concert of action" in the execution of his battle plans.[75] In the evening, Henry Kyd Douglas visited the headquarters of both Lee and Ewell. "I was not encouraged by any appearance of cheerfulness at either place," recorded Douglas. He also observed that Lee was "not in good humor over the miscarriage of his plans and his orders."[76]

Despite the poor execution by his chief lieutenants, Lee realized that his veteran troops had nearly carried the day. As a result of this partial success, the general resolved to stay the course. His initial strategy for July 3rd called for an early morning attack on both Union flanks. Reinforced by the arrival of General George Pickett's fresh division, Longstreet was ordered to renew his assault on the Union left. Simultaneously, Ewell would attempt to follow up his late evening gains on Culp's Hill. To achieve this goal, General Johnson's attacking force was augmented by troops from Rodes' and Early's divisions. The stage was set for another bloody showdown.

At around 4:30 A.M. on the morning of July 3rd, over two dozen Union guns roared to life just south of Culp's Hill. For fifteen minutes the guns hurled hot iron at the seven Confederate brigades assembled near the wooded eminence. Throughout the bombardment, the 20th Connecticut held an advanced post to serve as spotters for the artillerists. It was a hazardous assignment. Occasionally, shells fell short through misjudgments of range or due to defective fuses.

Several casualties took place within the ranks of the 20th as a result of this friendly fire. A piece of shell hit Private Bradley Allen of Company I one inch above the right eyebrow. Afterwards, Allen was taken to the Seminary, where he was incoherent for five days.[77]

The Union commanders planned to follow up the artillery barrage with an infantry assault, but the Confederates mounted their attack first. For nearly seven hours, Ewell's troops struggled up the steep, rock-strewn slope of the hill to assail the entrenched enemy position. With minimal losses the Union infantrymen swept the area with a tremendous volume of fire. Despite the desperate odds, Johnson pressed the attack throughout the long morning and continued to feed additional units into the battle.

During the early morning action, Major Douglas guided two regiments into position on the lower portion of Culp's Hill. Henry rode into the smoke-filled woods and sent a line of skirmishers forward. As he directed the main force to the left with his drawn sword, a dozen or more Union riflemen sprang up from the trees several hundred yards up the slope.

Douglas later recalled the dramatic moment, "I fancied I could look down the barrels and I fancied also they were large enough to crawl into. There came little puffs of smoke, a rattle of small arms, the sensation of a tremendous blow and I sank forward on my horse."[78] Several nearby soldiers held the wounded staff officer on his horse and guided him down the hill. After being carried to the rear on a litter, Douglas was placed in an ambulance and transported several miles to the Henry Picking farm on the Hunterstown Road.

The wounded officer was placed on the floor in the parlor of the house, and during the course of the day, a half dozen surgeons examined him. Initially, the wound was thought to be serious. At the last instant, Henry had wheeled away from the gunmen. As a result, the ball had struck him in the back, ranged upwards through the left shoulder, and lodged near the clavicle. Although his left shoulder and arm were paralyzed, no major bone was fractured. Not only would he survive, but Douglas would also regain the full use of his limb after a proper recovery period. He later wrote a friend that carrying a hunk of Yankee lead inside his body was a small price to pay for his good fortune.[79] Perhaps the new hat had been a blessing rather than a curse.

From Henry's perspective, the final outcome of the battle contained no positive results. After a series of bloody repulses, the Southerners terminated their efforts to wrest Culp's Hill from the determined Union defenders. By 11 A.M., the firing subsided.

Meanwhile, the other end of the line remained silent throughout the morning. Due to a misunderstanding between Lee and Longstreet, the First Corps did not attack in concert with Ewell's troops, forcing Lee to revamp his plans.

The Confederate chief shifted the target area of the assault to the Union right-center, where Wright's Georgians had temporarily pierced the Union lines the previous evening. The attack was to be preceded by a concentrated bombardment of the Federal position by roughly 140 artillery pieces. Afterward, nearly 12,000 men would move across a mile of open ground in an effort to smash through the center of the Union line. Pickett's division would assault on the right or southern end of the line. Heth's division, under the command of General James J. Pettigrew, would advance to the left of the Virginians, while two brigades of Pender's division would follow in Pettigrew's wake.

Pickett's division consisted of three brigades totaling about 5,500 troops. Unlike his fellow brigade commanders, Lewis Armistead and Richard B. Garnett, 40-year-old James Lawson Kemper was not a

Major General James Kemper, CSA. Courtesy of MOLLUS, USAMHI.

soldier by profession. A successful lawyer and planter, Kemper had been serving his fourth term as Madison County's representative in the Virginia House of Delegates at the outbreak of the war.

Kemper had always possessed a keen interest in the military. While attending Washington College in Lexington, Virginia, young James received training at the nearby Virginia Military Institute. Like many of his fellow Civil War officers, he served in the Mexican War, but witnessed no combat action. In 1858, Kemper was appointed brigadier general of the Virginia Militia. Following Virginia's secession, the politician accepted a commission as colonel of the 7th Virginia.[80]

Described as a man of "fine bearing, fearlessness, dash ... impassioned eloquence ... good sense and high conception of duty," Kemper developed an affinity for command.[81] Throughout the first two years of the war, he received numerous accolades from his superiors. His boyhood friend, A. P. Hill, himself an aggressive fighter, remarked that Kemper possessed that "military quickness and intuition that prove the thorough soldier." General Longstreet praised him for his "marked skill and fearlessness." The dashing cavalier Jeb Stuart also cited James for his "good conduct, bravery, and coolness."[82]

Kemper's leadership acumen did not escape the notice of General Lee, who recommended his appointment to brigadier general. The promotion was approved by President Jefferson Davis on June 3, 1863.[83] As his troops assembled on Seminary Ridge near the Spangler farm, General Kemper might have briefly reflected on the significance of the date. Tomorrow, July 4th, would mark his 10th wedding anniversary.

Meanwhile, on the other end of the line, another general was anxious for the attack to commence. After skulking about for much of the previous day following his altercation with Ewell, Isaac Trimble begged Lee for a meaningful assignment. He was well aware of the fact that two division commanders in Hill's Corps had been wounded. At noon, the zealous officer received an order placing him in charge of the two brigades of Pender's Division that would participate in the assault. Finally, 10 months after his severe wounding at Second Manassas, Isaac would once again lead troops into combat.

As he rode in front of the assembled North Carolinians, Isaac announced in his bull voice, "I am a stranger to you and have been sent to command you in the absence of your wounded general, and will lead you upon Cemetery Ridge."[84] With the preparations complete, the Southern troops hunkered down to wait out the cannonade.

Shortly after 1 P.M., the painful silence was broken as the massed Confederate guns thundered into action. The Union gunners responded. The reverberations of nearly 250 guns shook the earth. The air vibrated with the scream of shells and the discords of their explosions. To Sallie Broadhead "it seemed as if the heavens and earth were crashing together." As she huddled in the cellar with her family, she reflected on the consequences of the terrible inferno:

> We knew that with every explosion, and the scream of each shell, human beings were hurried, through excruciating pain, into another world, and that many more were torn, and mangled, and lying in torment worse than death, and no one able to extend relief. The thought made me very sad, and feel that, if it was God's will, I would rather be taken away than remain to see the misery that would follow. Some thought this awful afternoon would never come to a close.[85]

For two hours, shot and shell rained down upon Cemetery Ridge. Although many of the Confederate projectiles passed harmlessly overhead, a number found their mark, especially during the initial stages of the bombardment. Corporal Timothy Fitzgerald of the 72nd New York was leisurely sitting on a fence when a solid shot struck the rail directly underneath him. Later, the dazed soldier received treatment at the Seminary Hospital for a wounded right thigh and bruised testicles.[86]

During the cannonade, the Southern infantrymen suffered even more severely than their Union counterparts. Losses were especially high within Kemper's brigade, which was positioned on the extreme right of the division line. Finally, at around 3 P.M., the fire slackened. The order to fall in was almost a welcome relief to the men who formed the assault force.

As the smoke slowly lifted like a curtain from the valley between the ridges, the

Confederate troops advanced towards the Union position with parade ground precision. Kemper's and Garnett's men formed the front of Pickett's line and Armistead followed closely in support.

As they neared the Emmitsburg Road, Pickett's ranks were decimated by the accurate salvos of the Union artillerists. After crossing the road, Kemper's troops passed to the south of the Nicholas Codori farmhouse and barn. As the line obliqued to the left and headed for the Copse of Trees, a brigade of Vermont troops swung around Kemper's exposed right flank and unleashed a devastating fire. Other infantry units pounded them from the front as the gunners blasted away with canister. Still, the shrinking line surged onward.

As the survivors approached to within one hundred yards of the enemy position, Kemper stood up in his stirrups and with his ringing, clarion voice, shouted, "There are the guns, boys, go for them!"[87] After firing a well-directed volley, the troops obediently charged into the maelstrom. The bold general presented a conspicuous target, and an instant later, a bullet drove into Kemper's groin. He tumbled backward from his sorrel into the arms of his orderly. At the time of his wounding, Kemper was close enough to observe the facial expressions of some of the enemy infantrymen, and he later wrote that he could identify the soldier who shot him.

A Federal officer and several enlisted men placed the fallen general on a blanket and started to carry him away. Suddenly, several Virginians fired into the group. They immediately rushed forward to reclaim the body and then quickly made for the rear.

Near the same time, General Garnett, who was also mounted, was killed by an artillery blast. Pushing through the chaotic mass of troops up ahead, Armistead led about 150 men over the stone wall on foot. He fell mortally wounded just inside the enemy lines. Any lingering pockets of resistance were soon dispersed by Union counterattacks.[88]

The Confederate troops on the other end of the mile-long line fared no better. As his brigades followed about 150 yards behind the first assault wave, Trimble noticed that Pettigrew's men "seemed to sink into the earth under the tempest of fire poured into them."[89] In response, Trimble accelerated the pace of his brigades. The North Carolinians rushed forward with a hearty shout. Turning to his aide, Major Charles Grogan, Isaac optimistically predicted, "I believe those fine fellows are going into the enemy's line."[90]

The attack was pinned down near the fence bordering the Emmitsburg Road by the incessant discharge of canister and musketry. As he rode forward into the fray to encourage the men, Isaac was struck in the left leg. His faithful mare, Jinny, was hit during the same volley. Nevertheless, both horse and rider remained by the fence as the troops rushed up the hill.

As the wounded officer looked on, the Confederate battle flags briefly mingled with the colors of the Union defenders on the top of the smoky ridge. In an instant, the Southerners came tumbling back; the volume of fire was simply too great to endure. Trimble's aides inquired if they should rally the men and renew the charge. Glancing to the right, the commander witnessed Pickett's troops moving to the rear in small squads. Realizing the futility of another offensive, Isaac remarked to Grogan, "No, Charley, the best thing these brave fellows can do, is to get out of this."[91]

As his shattered command sullenly retreated, Trimble guided his injured horse back to Seminary Ridge. Upon reaching the initial position, he dismounted and supervised the formation of a defensive line. Feeling faint from the loss of blood, Isaac turned the command over to General James Lane and sought medical assistance.

As he departed, Lane overheard Trimble remark, "If the troops I had the honor to command today couldn't take that position, all hell can't take it."[92]

Farther down the line, General Robert E. Lee rode out to meet his dejected troops. Noticing an officer being carried past on a litter, the commanding general inquired as to his identity. When informed that it was Kemper, Lee hastened to the side of his wounded friend.

"General Kemper, I hope you are not seriously wounded."

"I am struck in the groin and the ball has ranged upward. They tell me it is mortal."

"I hope it will not prove so bad as that. Is there anything I can do for you, General Kemper?"

"Yes, General Lee, do full justice to this division for its work today."

"I will," Lee promised, then walked away with his head bowed.[93]

The charge had started and ended in the space of about one hour. Only about one-half of the roughly 12,000 men who had formed the main assault force returned to Seminary Ridge unscathed. A Confederate officer, who viewed the assault from the cupola of the Lutheran Seminary, recorded sadly, "When the smoke of battle lifted, Pickett's Division had melted away; a few scattered, disorganized remnants were left on the field and drifted back to their own line."[94] In what was becoming a sickening pattern, more torn and bleeding bodies entered the Seminary Hospital.

In contrast to the orderly formations utilized during marches and upon the field of battle, bedlam reigned supreme in the crowded rooms and halls of this field hospital. Thus, one might find a Pennsylvania lieutenant lying beside a private from North Carolina. Death and suffering did not distinguish among rank, level of education, social position, or place of birth.

The casualties of the third day's battle only added to this heterogeneous mix. Private P. S. Bobbitt, 47th North Carolina, Pettigrew's Division, suffered from "a shot wound of the urethra." The ball passed completely through his pelvis and urine discharged entirely from the posterior wound. A catheter was attached, but blockages constantly developed. Bobbitt also suffered from diarrhea and a complete loss of appetite. His torment finally ended three and a half months later when he succumbed to exhaustion. It was a slow, painful, and incremental death.[95]

The bizarre case of Sergeant James T. Dowdy of the 28th Virginia had a more pleasant outcome. Dowdy was also shot through the body during the charge, but he did not go into shock and no hemorrhaging was detected. About 14 hours after the reception of the wound, a copious stool was passed by the patient at the Seminary. He heard something fall heavily to the bottom of the vessel. Suspecting it to be a ball, Dowdy requested the nurse to look carefully for it, whereupon a minie ball was found. Surgeon William H. Rulison noted that the ball was considerably battered, "showing that it had struck something before wounding the man."[96]

The Army of the Potomac incurred only about one-half the casualties of their Southern opponents on July 3rd, but this statistic offered little consolation to the unfortunate victims and their loved ones. One such example was Corporal Edward Jones of the 8th Ohio. His unit had played a prominent role in the repulse of "Pickett's Charge" by pouring a deadly flank fire into the ranks of Pettigrew's advancing troops.

During the action, Jones was shot in the forehead just above the nose. The missile emerged behind the left eye. In a semiconscious state, Jones was admitted to the Seminary. The wound proved mortal, and like his adversary, Private Bobbitt, Jones suffered an agonizingly slow death. The Buckeye soldier passed through a number of general hospitals before he finally returned to his home state at the end of the year. Despite the familiar surroundings, his condition worsened. Jones suffered from recurring head pain, drowsiness, paralysis of the right side, and the involuntary evacuation of urine and feces. During the middle of February, he lapsed into a deep coma. An emergency operation was performed to relieve pressure in the brain. Although Jones briefly regained consciousness, he died at the end of the month. An autopsy revealed marked congestion and inflammation near the wound.[97]

Corporal Jones and numerous others received little attention at the crowded field hospitals of Gettysburg. The overworked surgeons passed over both the slightly wounded and the near fatal cases. This triage system ensured that the surgeons' limited time and resources were devoted to those who had the best prospects of recovery.

As the medical teams of the respective armies labored unceasingly to examine and treat the growing backlog of patients, Robert E. Lee prepared his forces for an expected counterattack. This event never materialized. As so often occurred following a large battle, a severe thunderstorm rumbled through the area in the early evening. But as one observer noted, "It suffered greatly by comparison with that which filled our ears a few hours before."[98] The climax of the great battle had passed. Paradoxically, most of the participants and civilians had very little knowledge of the bigger picture as a result of their limited perspectives.

Sallie Broadhead expressed the anxiety and guarded optimism of Gettysburg's citizenry when she wrote, "Who is victorious, or with whom the advantage rests, no one here can tell. It would ease the horror if we knew our arms were successful....

We shall see tomorrow. It will be the 4th of July.... If it only ends the battle and drives them off it will be glorious, and I will rejoice."[99] In his memoirs, Henry Jacobs recalled that "it was only gradually that the magnitude of the battle dawned upon us.... A *Baltimore Sun* of Saturday [July 4] gave us the first connected account of the battle and information of those who had fallen."[100]

Throughout much of the battle, Martin Culler and Mahlon Horine were confined to the cellar of the John Winebrenner home on Baltimore Street. As the students and the members of the Winebrenner household huddled in their basement prison, Confederate riflemen occupied the upstairs rooms and kept up a lively exchange with Union snipers at the foot of Cemetery Hill. During the terrific cannonade, the house shook as shells shrieked overhead, and bullets crashed through the windows and doors above them.

At about 9 o'clock on Friday evening the beleaguered civilians received an invitation to attend a supper being prepared upstairs by a group of enemy soldiers. Having had very little to eat for the past two days, they readily accepted the kind offer. In a truly droll scene, the rugged, but chivalrous, Southerners served their hosts a bounteous feast of chicken, biscuits, tea, coffee, butter, honey, milk, and all the delicacies of the season. The soldiers and citizens conversed freely during the meal, but Culler concluded that "they knew no more of the outcome of the three day's battle than we did."[101]

Three hours later, the Confederates vacated the town. Under the cover of darkness, Lee consolidated his troops in preparation for a retreat. The new Confederate battle line extended two and a half miles along Oak and Seminary Ridges, the midpoint being located on the Seminary campus. An extensive series of breastworks and rifle pits were quickly constructed by the Southern soldiers.

Observing the frantic activity of the Confederates, the Union Seminary patients sensed that their comrades had prevailed. "For half an hour bedlam reigned in the neighborhood," recalled one officer. "Fences were torn down, outbuildings demolished, boardwalks knocked to pieces, and everything seized upon that could contribute to the formation of breastworks...."[102]

As the Confederates dug in, an unlikely Union "surgeon" was working behind the lines. Colonel Henry Morrow, 24th Michigan, had been wounded and captured on July 1st. The next day his wound was dressed by a Confederate surgeon, whom Morrow fortuitously discovered to be a master Mason, like himself. Because of their mutual brotherhood, the Union officer was permitted to remain in Gettysburg while other captives were marched away. Henry lodged at the home of Judge David Wills on the town square.

A day's rest restored the colonel's health to the point where he was able to venture outside. He witnessed Pickett's Charge from the steeple of the nearby courthouse and was nearly struck by a shell. Afterwards, Morrow learned that many of the First Corps wounded were still lying out in the open. Audaciously, Morrow approached Confederate General John B. Gordon and urged his assistance. Gordon courteously agreed to look into the matter. Shortly afterwards, he returned with the promise that a train

Colonel Henry A. Morrow, 24th Mich. Vols. Courtesy of Roger D. Hunt, USAMHI.

of ambulances would report to Morrow that evening. In preparation for his sortie, the colonel donned a green scarf provided by Mrs. Wills in imitation of a surgeon's insignia.

By nightfall, only two ambulances had arrived. Undeterred, the small band set out for McPherson's Ridge. The light of swinging lanterns and a half clouded moon revealed a macabre scene. The unburied dead were already swollen and blackened from exposure to the heat and humidity. Threading their way through the corpses, Morrow and his Confederate companions answered the plaintive moans and cries of the wounded, some of whom were in a state of delirium. Morrow continued his sad labors throughout much of the night. He always expressed his belief that General Gordon's "humane and Christian conduct ... was the means of saving the lives of many of the Federal wounded."[103] Lieutenant Henry Chancellor was among those relocated to the Seminary.

Colonel Morrow was not the only one who went to great lengths to assist the wounded. Throughout the battle, the ladies of Gettysburg provided food, beverages, and nursing care to injured soldiers from both armies. They also contributed their linen and muslin goods to supply lint and bandages for the various field hospitals. Robert McCreary, a prominent town lawyer, noted that the female citizenry attended to these self-imposed duties "with a devotion that never flagged" and no sacrifice was deemed too great.[104]

Some of these heroines put their own safety in jeopardy as they performed their acts of mercy. Elizabeth "Lizzie" Critzman, in her mid–40s at the time of the battle, conducted one of the leading boarding houses for students of Pennsylvania College. As throngs of Union soldiers rushed pell-mell through the streets of Gettysburg on July 1, Lizzie stood in front of her residence passing out refreshing drinks of water until bullets struck the door jambs close beside her. Later, she threw open her cellar doors and hid away the fugitives cut off from Cemetery Hill. Professor J. Howard Wert, a well-known writer, educator, and Civil War veteran, described another brave act of Miss Critzman's that directly impacted the wounded at the Seminary:

When fell the shades of evening ... she ascertained that the theological seminary and its adjacent grounds were crowded with wounded men lacking surgical attention. There was a scarcity of instruments, and the Confederate surgeons naturally were giving their care first to the wounds of their own army. She also learned that, while Dr. Robert Horner had one set of instruments in use in his volunteer labors of humanity at the College Church hospital, across the street from his residence, he also had an older set which he had concealed and thus preserved from the marauders who had invaded his office in search of supplies.

With this brave woman, to see the line of duty open before her was to act. Obtaining the instruments and concealing them in her clothing, she made her way to the seminary ... amid the campfires and roaming soldiery of the enemy, amid oath and jeer and coarse badinage, amid wounded men, stretched out in rows moaning with pain and calling out with hoarse iteration for "water-water-water."

She reached the seminary and there, finding one of the Union surgeons ... committed to him the burden she bore. I am told that it was with these very instruments, carried to the seminary by Miss Lizzie Critzman, the amputation upon brave Colonel George F. McFarland, of Harrisburg, was performed.[105]

On July 3rd, while McFarland was lying upon his bed in the southwest corner of the building's first floor, a solid shot crashed through a window, passed lengthwise over him, and lodged itself in a nearby partition, covering him with lime and fragments. If he had been sitting up, the stray round would surely have decapitated him. Lieutenant Hoffman recalled that George was taken away in a fainting condition.

As if that was not enough excitement for one day, the colonel was later placed upon a makeshift operating table and his right leg was amputated several inches below the knee by Surgeon Blakeslee. In a surgeon's certificate, Blakeslee testified that, "In the consequence of the enemy taking all of my instruments, medicines, and assistants, I was unable to amputate his limb until the third day, at which time extravasation had taken place to such an extent that sloughing took place, and union by granulation was the consequence, making recovery long protracted."[106]

It appears Surgeon Blakeslee was quite active on July 3rd. Perhaps he was the surgeon whom Lizzie Critzman met upon her entrance into the hospital. At the very least, it appears by his heightened activity that he had gained access to the instruments at some point during the day.

Another member of the 151st treated by Blakeslee was Private Diedrich Dasenbuck. On July 1st, Dasenbuck sustained injuries to his scalp from two bullet fragments. The largest projectile struck him an inch and a half behind the right ear and then lodged in the right cheek, while the other piece entered through the right side of the neck near the trapezius muscle. Apparently, the ball split upon impact with a hard surface just prior to striking the patient. Blakeslee was able to remove the smaller missile, a flattened piece of lead, through a button-hole incision above the middle of the right clavicle. The position of the larger section could not be located.[107]

On the same day, Sergeant Edwin Aylesworth, like McFarland, parted with his right leg. The fact that these three individuals were fortunate enough to receive primary care for their injuries in no way guaranteed their survival. They would not only need to recover from the initial shock of their operations, but would also need the strength to overcome the various postoperative infections that would inevitably appear.

On the morning of July 4th, the stillness of the battlefield was broken by the bands of the Union army. The sweet strains of the "Star-Spangled Banner," "Hail Columbia," and other national airs wafted across the valley to Seminary Ridge, providing a strange juxtaposition to the horrific scenes inside the hospital.[108]

In the midst of this impromptu concert, 21-year-old Corporal William G. Cunningham, 44th New York Volunteers, arrived at the Seminary. Two days earlier, a bullet had lodged in his skull, another had grazed his scalp, and yet another had slammed into his left shoulder. For five days Cunningham was unintelligible, and for nine days he could not utter a word.[109]

As a temporary escape from such sorrowful scenes, the inmates at the Seminary utilized the most ordinary of items to provide comic relief. When Jeremiah Hoffman discovered Mary Ziegler's church pennies in the pocket of a dress lying on his bunk, the patients on his floor sang out in unison, "hand 'em round!" The pennies were passed out for mementos and provided the men with "at least a few minutes fun."[110]

A longer lasting diversion was provided by the enemy soldiers stationed near the hospital throughout the 4th of July. A number of them entered the rooms to converse with the wounded. They also distributed water and flour biscuits. In reciprocation, the Union soldiers provided the Confederates with coffee beans. One delighted Southerner stated that it had been two years since he had last enjoyed the precious beverage!

A number of soldiers from the 1st South Carolina discussed the merits of secession with a group of Yankees. Hoffman admitted that the issue was debated from the Northern perspective with less "ill-feeling" than on other occasions. The Southerners readily made one concession — the Union army's position at Gettysburg equaled their own at Fredericksburg.

Two members of the 1st stated that they had deserted from Captain Abner Doubleday's battery of the 1st U.S. Artillery at Fort Sumter. They were quite amused to learn that they had defeated their old commander, now a major general, on July 1st.[111]

Lieutenant Hoffman recalled an amusing incident with a "long, lank, ignorant North Carolina mountaineer" who was "in continual fear of everybody and everything." The Southerner wished to desert, but was reluctant to do so because he thought the Pennsylvania Dutch were "a terrible people, who would be apt to kill him upon sight."[112]

Chuckling, the Pennsylvanian explained that the Dutch were a kindhearted, honest, and quiet people, mostly farmers. Although Hoffman thought he might have overstated his case, he certainly made an impression. Several days later, it was reported to him that the Tarheel was hiding in the lower part of the building and planned to steal off into the countryside.[113]

Meanwhile, the civilians of Gettysburg were not enjoying the company of the Rebels nearly as much as the Union patients inside the Seminary. For the fourth consecutive day, the residents of the western part of the borough were largely confined to their homes as the opposing pickets exchanged fire in the streets. Through his powerful glass, Henry Jacobs studied the Confederates near the Seminary. He was drawn to a group of sharpshooters positioned by a small barn. An "attitude of attention" was noted upon their countenances.[114]

It would mark the last time Henry observed armed enemy soldiers in Gettysburg. Throughout the evening and early morning hours, the Army of Northern Virginia sullenly pulled out from behind their works and commenced the long march back to Virginia. The torrential rains and muddy roads matched the somber mood of the dejected procession.

Between 6,000 to 7,000 of the wounded Confederates, roughly half of Lee's total tally, could not endure the jostling, bone-jarring trip in a rickety ambulance. They remained behind in the scattered field hospitals throughout the countryside.[115] Among those left to the mercy of their captors were Isaac Trimble, Henry Kyd Douglas, and James Kemper.

For the first time in a week, Sallie Broadhead went to bed feeling safe. Although anxious to start caring for the wounded, she decided to get a good night's rest and commence her efforts in the morning.[116]

As Sallie retired, a "delicate, fragile, and feeble-looking" lady in her late 40s picked her way through the darkness and debris of battle, becoming perhaps the first civilian to enter the Seminary Hospital following the battle. Ellen Orbison Harris, the secretary of the Philadelphia Ladies Aid Society and their "worker among the sol-

Mrs. Ellen Orbison Harris, the fearless secretary of the Philadelphia Ladies Aid Society. Courtesy of Centre County Library and Museum, Bellefonte, Pa.

diers," had departed from Washington early on July 3rd with a supply of chloroform and stimulants. Ellen left Baltimore on the morning of the 4th and reached Gettysburg by evening.[117]

George McFarland was among the soldiers comforted by Mrs. Harris that night. Kneeling by his side, she penned a hasty letter to Addie McFarland at home in McAlisterville, Pennsylvania. Besides offering her heartfelt sympathy and prayers, she assured the colonel's wife that her husband was doing well and had been strong enough to write his name on a slip of paper. The intrepid relief worker confided that she was too "steeped in sorrow and death" to celebrate the Union victory.[118]

Although she had witnessed the carnage on the Peninsula and at Antietam during the previous year, Harris was appalled by the state of affairs at Gettysburg:

> Am full of work and sorrow. The appearance of things here beggars all description. Our dead lie unburied, and our wounded neglected ... thousands of them are still naked and starving. God pity us!—pity us![119]

CHAPTER 7

The Hospital Period: July 5–September 1863

I have no more strength than a few drops of water.
All my bones are out of joint;
  my heart is like melted wax.
My strength has dried up like a broken clay pot,
  and my tongue sticks to the roof of my mouth.
You, God, have left me to die in the dirt.
                                    Psalm 22, verses 14–15.

Lieutenant Andrew Tucker clung to life long enough to learn of the Union triumph, which he had fought so hard to secure. On Sunday, July 5th, at 3 A.M., the young officer died. One of his comrades delivered a fitting eulogy, describing Andrew as "a friend I prized so highly; a patriot, who knowing his duty to his country, nobly performed it; a hero and a Christian, who suffered and died for his country without a murmur."[1]

Jeremiah Hoffman, who may have owed his life to Tucker's selflessness, vividly recalled his friend's burial in the Seminary garden:

> They roughly lined his grave with fence palings and buried him beside the Col. I was then lying on the bunk, and by lifting my head could see into the garden. I could not assist in the burial, but I could look on. They were holding the body

over the grave when the head slipped over the edge of the blanket and the lieutenant's beautiful, jet black hair dragged over the ground. The thought of his mother and sisters was called up, and surely it cannot be called unmanly that a few tears stole down my cheeks.[2]

Following the retreat of Lee's army, Union ambulance details combed the field of the first day's battle, searching among the swollen corpses for signs of life. Most of the wounded not discovered by Colonel Morrow and his party two days earlier were either located in remote locations or had been passed over for dead.

One wounded Iron Brigade soldier had crawled into the dense undergrowth that fringed the banks of Willoughby Run. Throughout the battle, the Westerner had remained hidden. Occasionally, he soaked his injured foot in the stream or gathered

Lieutenant Andrew G. Tucker, 142nd Pa. Vols. Courtesy of Alex Chamberlain, USAMHI.

missile and his sense of smell was entirely destroyed. Coates was reportedly in "a tolerably good condition, but restless."[5]

Not far from where the Wisconsin sergeant was discovered, a squad of Union soldiers detected the low moans of a severely wounded man they had thought was a corpse. Suffering with nearly the same ghastly wounds as Coates, Musician Michael Link also had spent the first few days of his permanent blindness alone and helpless. Oral tradition states that Michael's damaged eye sockets were eaten away by maggots as he lay on the battlefield. Barely alive, he, too, was carried to the Seminary.[6]

Sallie Broadhead awoke early and walked the short distance to the hospital. She remembered it as a beautiful morning and rejoiced at the restoration of her freedom. Her elation was short-lived. With

up loose cartridges from the ground. He watched intently as the Confederate rear guard passed near him during the withdrawal. As a rescue crew prepared to lift him up into an ambulance, the plucky soldier exclaimed, "Hold on a minute. I thought I saw one of the Johnnies skulking around over there. I want to pop him over before I go."[3]

The long ordeal of Sergeant Jefferson Coates also came to an end. "Wrapped in darkness, in the enemy's line, hungry, suffering, bleeding, friendless day and night," the sergeant somehow survived.[4] After being removed to the Seminary, his sightless eyes were cleansed and bandaged. A subsequent examination revealed that "the tunics of the right eye were hanging out and much tumefied, about as large as a black walnut, and covered with a mass of slough…. The left eye was shrunken, its contents evacuated, and the upper lid was overlapped by the lower." There was a profuse discharge of pus from both wounds. The optic nerves had been severed by the

Sergeant Francis Jefferson Coates, 7th Wisc. Vols., after his severe wounding at Gettysburg. Coates received the Medal of Honor for his gallant conduct on July 1, 1863. Courtesy of Edith Shefer, USAMHI.

every step she was reminded of the dreadful contest. The roads and surrounding fields were littered with dead horses, discarded weapons, and scattered accoutrements. Ripening fields of grain were trampled and large sections of fencing had been leveled. In the Seminary garden, the freshly turned soil and crude headboards marked the awful harvest of death.

Shaken, Sallie and an unidentified companion hesitated at the door. After a few long moments, they mustered their courage and walked inside. The scene was overwhelming. The nauseating stench of pus, gangrene, and human excrement permeated the air. Moans and cries for water arose from every room and hall. The sights were even worse: "hundreds of men wounded in every conceivable manner, some in the head and limbs, here an arm off and there a leg, and just inside a poor fellow with both legs shot away." After distributing her limited goods, Sallie felt utterly powerless to render any assistance of consequence. "I turned away and cried," she wrote despairingly.[7]

As shell-shocked residents emerged from their homes, they could barely recognize the once familiar surroundings. "[T]here were many sights too horrible for description," recalled Henry Jacobs. "Dead men lay in the streets from Wednesday till Saturday.... Hundreds of dead horses were scattered about.... They lay for weeks exposed to the July sun. When the wind blew from the south and west in the evenings, the stench was so overpowering that for a number of evenings all windows had to be closed.... The Union dead on the field of the first day's battle, were covered with only a few inches of soil. Portions of the body protruded, as the rain washed away the soil. The Confederate dead on the fields of the second and third days' fight were mostly buried in long trenches, made in haste and also very superficially covered."[8]

An article in the July 16th edition of the *Lutheran and Missionary* reported that "Gettysburg is now a vast hospital, and there is scarcely a house to be found that does not contain one or more wounded men. All the public buildings are given up to their use; the churches, courthouse, college, theological seminary, are filled with the wounded, whilst all around the town for miles in every direction, hospital camps have been improvised, and barns, stables, and dwellings have been deprived of their legitimate tenants and devoted to the use of the wounded and their attendants." The correspondent closed with a grim prediction: "Gettysburg will not soon recover from the blow it has received."[9]

Perhaps no pen more poignantly described the desolation than that of J. Howard Wert:

> The saddest, most pathetic sight in all the universe is a field of battle when the thunder of cannon has ceased.... When the splendor, the pomp and the circumstance of battle's magnificently stern array have gone, then the horrible and the ghastly only remain and remain in their most terrible forms.
>
> Hideous is the sorrowful appearance of the bloated, distorted, and blackened dead, so lately noble, stalwart men as they are packed together, side by side, some in blue and some gray. But yet more horrible is the agony of the wounded to whom speedy death would often be an unspeakable boon.... Days elapsed before the dead were all buried. Days elapsed before the wounded were all brought off the field. It was a gigantic task that confronted the willing hands that sought to alleviate their sufferings.[10]

In the aftermath of the conflict, thousands of patients still required their wounds to be dressed or a shattered and painful limb to be removed. These poor soldiers were found lying on the wet ground or upon bare floors in bloodied and soiled clothing. Although rations of hard tack and salted beef were distributed following the battle, the hot, nourishing delicacies so desperately craved by those suffering from shock and fatigue were almost nonexistent. One observer was deeply touched by the patience, fortitude, and quiet dignity displayed by the injured warriors.[11]

For a visitor from New York, the perfunctory burial efforts and the destitute condition of the wounded elicited a legitimate query. "I do not know who should be censured for such things, or how far any one should be," he wrote.[12]

It is a natural tendency to seek a scapegoat for unexplainable tragedies that are beyond the realm of human comprehension. The most likely target for the fiasco at Gettysburg was the Army Medical Department. In fact, one medical inspector of the U.S. Army conceded that "The period of ten days following the battle of Gettysburg was the occasion of the greatest amount of human suffering known to this nation since its birth."[13]

As did nearly all branches of the military, the Army Medical Department entered the war grossly unprepared. Its modest staff was made up of the Surgeon General and 98 surgeons and assistant surgeons. The department subsisted on a paltry annual budget of $241,000. Headed by rigidly conservative bureaucrats who resisted reform, the administration was handicapped by faulty organization and extreme frugality.[14]

The first major land battle of the war revealed the inadequacies of the medical corps. During the battle of First Bull Run, fought on July 21, 1861, panicked civilian ambulance drivers fled the field, leaving hundreds of wounded men to drag themselves back to Washington. One surgeon obstinately refused to admit soldiers into his hospital if they did not belong to his regiment, a prime example of the lack of overall direction.[15]

Fortunately for Union soldiers, William A. Hammond took over as Surgeon General in the spring of 1862. He immediately proposed a number of far-reaching reforms, including the organization of a special hospital and ambulance corps, an increase in field and executive personnel, administrative changes that would promote greater efficiency and patient care, and the establishment of a medical school in Washington, which would include a museum with pathological and surgical exhibits. In marked contrast to the parsimony of his predecessors, Hammond hiked expenditures to $11,594,000, a nearly five-fold increase from the previous fiscal year.

Just as importantly, the new chief began to infuse the ranks with brilliant innovators. Among the most talented of these appointees was Dr. Jonathan Letterman, who became medical director of the Army of the Potomac. The energetic 37-year-old developed an ambulance system that became a model for the world's armies for the next two generations, reorganized the medical supply system, and created an efficient field hospital organization. Under his direction, the medical department turned in credible performances at Fredericksburg and Chancellorsville.[16]

At the outset of the Gettysburg campaign, Letterman commanded a magnificent organization of 650 medical officers, 1,000 ambulances, and nearly 3,000 drivers and stretchermen.[17] Despite the increased manpower and advancements in field techniques, nothing could prepare the medical corps for the extreme conditions it faced at Gettysburg, where a number of external factors combined to greatly reduce its effectiveness.

The first detrimental event was the reduction in the number of medical supply wagons by General Joseph Hooker at the outset of the campaign to facilitate the rapid movement of the army. The situation was exacerbated by Meade when he detained the supply trains at Westminster. After much persuasion, the cautious commander permitted half the wagons to proceed to the front after the close of the fighting on July 3rd. Medical Purveyor Jeremiah Brinton arrived with the lead train the next evening. The remainder of the wagons did not reach Gettysburg until the 5th.[18]

"Without proper means, the Medical Department can no more take care of the wounded than the army can fight a battle without ammunition," recalled Letterman bitterly. The medical director pronounced that he would have rather risked the capture of the supplies than to have the wounded suffer from the lack of them. "Lost supplies can be replenished, but lives lost are gone forever," he added.[19]

However, it is unlikely that a crisis situation could have been averted even if the trains had been parked closer to the battlefield. It was simply a matter of logistics. The medical department could comfortably handle about 10,000 wounded. In the wake of the three-day battle, 21,000 men required some degree of care. The Army of the Potomac's surplus of some 4,500 patients could have been accommodated reasonably well, but the 6,000–7,000 Confederates not fit to travel stretched the resources of the department beyond its capacity.[20]

Most of the Southerners were left in primitive hospital camps south and west of the town. The surgeons who remained behind to care for them also faced acute shortages of food and supplies. One relief agency official remarked that "The terrible destitution of many of the Rebels will not bear description. It was too horrible for recital."[21]

The brigade hospitals of Pickett's division were located in the vicinity of Marsh Creek near the Fairfield Road. Following his severe wounding, General James Kemper was placed inside the home of William E. Myers, who operated the nearby mill owned by Francis Bream. A Confederate surgeon concluded that the general would soon die and ordered a coffin built for him.[22] One of Kemper's men, Sergeant David E. Johnston, reached the same conclusion. He did not believe that his commander would live through the night as "his sufferings were so great — almost beyond endurance."[23] General Lee sent his condolences to Kemper's wife and newspapers throughout the country carried stories of the general's death.

It was not until July 27th that the Gettysburg *Compiler* printed the following retraction: "Gen. Kemper, of the Confederate army, reported killed at Gettysburg, it is now stated, was only wounded, and is in a fair way to recover. He is lying at Bream's Mill, three miles from Gettysburg, and was shot through the breast the ball lodging in his back."[24]

Early on the morning of July 4th, Isaac Trimble's left leg was amputated by a team of surgeons headed by Dr. Hunter McGuire. Before the operation was performed, Trimble bawled out the doctors for not removing the limb following his wounding a year earlier. He pointed out, with a logic hard to dispute, that had they heeded this advise the bullet fired into his leg the previous day would surely have missed him.[25]

Several days later, Isaac was relocated to the home of Robert McCurdy on Chambersburg Street. Young Charles McCurdy recalled Trimble as being "a delightful and appreciative guest." Since the general displayed a fondness for children, Charles and his younger sisters were frequent visitors to his room and helped to relieve the tedium of his confinement.[26]

Henry Douglas' good fortune continued. As he convalesced in the parlor of Henry and Charlotte Picking's farmhouse, he was treated "with a delicacy and kindness that I shall never cease to be grateful for."[27] Douglas later proclaimed, "God, every and now and then, does make such people ... and breathes into them his spirit of Christian charity, beneficence, and unpretentious nobility, to let the world know to what a high plane he could lift up mankind." The major was a huge attraction for the couple's four children who referred to him as the "big Rebel."[28]

The primary concern of General George Meade was the pursuit of the Army of Northern Virginia. He barely paused to consider the plight of the thousands of wounded from both armies. On the evening of July 5th, the army commander wired Washington: "The enemy retired, under the cover of night and heavy rain, in the direction of Fairfield and Cashtown.... All my available cavalry are in pursuit.... My movement will be made at once on his flank.... I cannot delay to pick up the debris of battle."[29] Meade fully expected to fight another battle within a few days and thus deemed it prudent to carry away the greater portion of his surgeons, medical supplies, and ambulances.

In a marked divergence from other accounts, Jonathan Letterman wrote that "the greater portion of the surgical labor was performed before the army left." He also maintained that there was never a severe shortage of supplies or rations and that most of the wounded had been picked up from the battlefield in a timely manner. His chief complaint was the inadequacy of the railroad serving the town, the destruction of which effectively isolated Gettysburg from the outside world.[30] The medical director, like his commander, seemed to be looking ahead. In doing so, it appears he shaped an unrealistic assessment of the true state of affairs.

In his official report, Letterman explained that only 106 surgeons could remain behind since he anticipated that another battle would soon take place that

would likely result in an equal number of casualties. As a result, the ratio of doctors to patients at Gettysburg was about 1:150.[31] One of these surgeons bitterly declared that "the failure to furnish a sufficient number of medical officers ... cost the country more good men than did the charge of any rebel brigade on that severely contested field."[32]

The combination of the sheer volume of patients requiring care and transportation, along with supply difficulties and the rapid movement of the Army of the Potomac away from the battlefield, created an emergency situation that could not be immediately remedied by the medical department. Meade later admitted that the well-being of the wounded was in large measure dependent upon "extra assistance" from the private sector.[33]

Propitiously, help came from almost every quarter. For those who surveyed the carnage and human suffering caused by the battle, the universal quality of the disaster relief effort was truly uplifting. Medical Inspector Edward P. Vollum wrote that "benevolent societies, Sanitary and Christian Commissions, express companies, fire organizations, bands of generous people of all denominations, and individuals from great distances, all came forward with their offerings, sympathy, and personal services, forming a spectacle at once touching and magnificent, exceeding any similar outburst of sympathy and sacrifice ever witnessed."[34]

At the vanguard of this outpouring were two large and well-established relief organizations that had come into existence near the beginning of the war. Officially sanctioned in June of 1861, the United States Sanitary Commission was patterned after the British Sanitary Commission of the Crimean War. The leaders of the American movement were an eclectic mix of prominent New Yorkers: the Reverend Henry W. Bellows, a well-known Unitarian minister; the leaders of the Women's Central Association of Relief, which included in its membership many of the city's wealthiest and most influential families; and a coalition of noted physicians.

The primary mission of the group was to investigate sanitary conditions in army camps and hospitals and to provide items and services for the citizen soldier which the government could not provide. The commission was granted no legal powers nor did it receive any funding from the Federal budget. Many of its accomplishments were attributable to the energy and leadership of its executive secretary, Frederick Law Olmstead, the architect and superintendent of New York's Central Park.[35]

Of all the services the Sanitary Commission provided, none was more vital for the wounded at Gettysburg than its highly efficient commissary system. The agency functioned as a conduit for the myriad items collected by local aid societies throughout the North. Through experience, officials of the organization learned to anticipate the movements of the army in order that supply depots could be established at convenient locations.

Before rail service was restored to Gettysburg, the commission dispatched wagons laden with supplies from its base at Frederick. Two loads arrived even before the conflict had ended and other teams reached the field on the Monday following the battle. The next day, with the repair of rail lines to within one mile of the town, the commission shipped massive quantities of provisions in refrigerated cars from Philadelphia and Baltimore. Over 60 tons of perishable items were transported in this manner.

Even a cursory glance at the table of articles supplied by the agency during the 10-day period immediately following the battle reveals the breadth of the relief effort: 11,000 pounds of poultry and mutton, 12,900 loaves of bread, 8,500 dozens of eggs, 675 bushels of fresh garden vegetables, 116 boxes of lemons, 2,000 jars of jelly, 400 gallons of pickles, 850 pounds of coffee, 831 pounds of chocolate, 100 pounds of tobacco, over 4,000 bottles of liquor, 7,143 pairs of drawers, 10,424 shirts, 2,114 pillows, 2,300 sponges, 1,500 combs, 250 pounds of soap, 110 barrels of lint and bandages, 4,000 pairs of slippers, 1,200 crutches, etc. Delicacies like brandy peaches, Jamaica ginger, oysters, tamarinds, and comfort items, such as fans and mosquito netting, supplemented the list of staples.

President Bellows, who made a personal visit to Gettysburg, estimated the value of the goods distributed to be not less than $5,000 daily. A warehouse was established in the Fahnestock Brothers store at the northwest corner of Baltimore and West Middle Streets. In a brief time, all of the available shelf and counter space was occupied and the goods overflowed outside onto the sidewalks. Each morning the supply wagons of the division and corps hospitals lumbered up to the door to fill their requisite.[36] Meanwhile, just down the street, a similar scene could be viewed at the temporary depot of the United States Christian Commission, housed on the first floor of J. L. Schick's store overlooking the town square.[37]

This benevolent agency was organized in New York City in the fall of 1861 as an offshoot of the Young Men's Christian Association. According to the group's charter, its main concern was "the spiritual good of the soldiers of the army, and incidentally, their intellectual improvement and social and physical comfort." To achieve these goals, representatives known as "delegates" accompanied the army to organize religious meetings and to distribute Bibles, temperance letters, and tracts. The commission also provided stationery and postage so that soldiers could remain in touch with their loved ones.[38]

An ad placed in the *Lutheran and Mis-*

sionary described the ideal candidate for a delegate position: "The best talent is demanded, and the most glorious results promised. The wisdom and experience of our ablest men are needed. Ministers who can preach with power to audiences of thousands, will find ample scope for their talents.... More nurses are not wanted, though every man who goes as a delegate for the Commission, should willingly and heartily and skillfully nurse the sick and wounded when occasion serves, but men who can speak with power as well, and help the suffering are the men for the work. All expenses are paid by the Commission to and from the field, but no salaries allowed."[39]

Just as its sister agency, the Christian Commission tried to anticipate the locations of battles so that it could quickly provide needed supplies. When railroad service to Gettysburg resumed, the group's distribution system shifted into high gear. On July 7th, two commission agents on the scene wired Chairman George H. Stuart in Philadelphia: "Send all the stores of every kind possible. There is a great want of most kinds of hospital stores, shirts and drawers especially, and delicacies. Please publish; *the necessity is very great that everything should be hurried on.* The best route is by Baltimore. Sixty-three delegates arrived last night, and will go to work this morning."[40]

The response to this appeal was so great that additional space was required to store all of the donated goods. Eventually, over 300 delegates canvassed the field hospitals to provide spiritual guidance and physical comfort for the wounded of both armies.[41] Among the first group to arrive on the evening of July 5th was Charles H. Keener, the superintendent of an instructional institute for the blind, who recalled, "My first duty was to take baskets of provision to the Seminary, and finding them in want of nurses, I sat up all night with

two officers, who had suffered amputation."[42]

Unfortunately, Keener did not record the identities of these officers, but both Captain Brice Blair and Lieutenant Henry Chancellor underwent the knife on this date. Blair's left arm was removed near the shoulder by a junior surgeon after the chief surgeon declined to perform the operation because he deemed it hopeless.[43]

Chancellor had suffered with intense pain for four days before his shattered leg was removed above the knee joint. After the operation, he was placed in a recovery room with Colonel McFarland. An immediate bond developed between the two officers. George was moved by the youngster's "patient, cheerful, [and] hopeful manner," which "could not fail to elicit the admiration and win the sympathies of those around him."[44]

A friend of the family paid Henry a visit several days later and remarked that his fighting days were over. "Yes," replied the lieutenant, "I'm afraid they are, but I should like to have one crack at the rebels yet." He remarked with pride that "the rebels will not soon forget the drubbing they got here."[45]

This unflagging patriotism seemed to be universal. "The men, both sick and well, wounded and sound, are in excellent spirits. They look like heroes!" proclaimed Henry Bellows.[46] Another visitor exclaimed, "It is heart-rending to go as I did through these hospitals and witness the suffering and distress, and listen to the groans and exclamations of those in acute pain or upon whom operations were being performed.... Many have been shot in several places; and yet all without exception, I believe, are patient in their tribulation, and exult in their glorious victory achieved at so great a sacrifice."[47]

Eventually, Christian Commission delegates were assigned to serve at specific hospitals. Each day these individuals reported to the depot headquarters with a list of needed items. "A mother could not have been more anxious for the supply of her children than these men were to procure whatever would make comfortable the wounded in their particular district," wrote one official.[48]

The Reverend J. O. Sloan, "one of the most faithful and efficient" delegates, supervised the commission's operations at the Seminary. The surgeons there "spoke of him in the kindest and most affectionate manner, and wrought with him very pleasantly in the performance of their mutual labors."[49]

The vast contributions of the Sanitary and Christian Commission to the well-being of the wounded at Gettysburg did not go unnoticed. Medical Inspector John Cuyler wrote that "The promptness, energy, and great kindness uniformly exhibited by these benevolent associations doubtless helped to save the lives of many, and gladdened the hearts of thousands, who … will hold their good and noble deeds in grateful remembrance."[50] College President Dr. Henry Baugher also praised the services of both relief organizations:

> I regard the United States Christian Commission as one of the most useful and blessed agencies which the spirit of our Master has called into exercise in these last days. I have witnessed its zeal and enterprise in relieving the wounded and the dying; tireless in its labors, and unintimidated by danger. How many lives it saved, and how many precious souls it directed to the Lamb of God during and after the battle of Gettysburg, eternity only can reveal. How our poor wounded soldiers would have fared without its timely assistance, and that of its sister, the Sanitary Commission, we may well conjecture, when we consider that the immediate region occupied by the troops had been stripped of provisions, and the army supplies had not yet reached their destination.[51]

Sarah Broadhead echoed these sentiments: "The merciful work of the Sanitary and Christian Commissions, aided by private contributions, was to be seen at every hospital. Without the relief they furnished, thousands must have perished miserably, and thousands more have suffered from want of the delicacies, food, and clothing their agents distributed, before the Government even could bring assistance. They are God's blessed agencies for providing for the needy soldier."[52]

Although the timely response of the various relief agencies and aid societies had solved the initial supply crisis, severe shortages still remained. As late as July 9th, Medical Inspector Vollum wrote that "the demand for stationery, disinfectants, iodine, tincture of iron, and some other articles was so great and immediate, that I purchased them in Gettysburg…." He also telegraphed a U.S. Army Hospital in Baltimore to immediately send forth medical supplies and equipment.[53] An even greater dilemma was the lack of doctors and nurses on hand. Sadly, nearly three weeks would elapse before they were present in sufficient numbers to handle the staggering patient load.

Summoning her courage, Sallie Broadhead made a return trip to the Seminary with as much food as she could scrape together along with some old quilts and pillows. She was relieved to learn that sufficient quantities of provisions had begun to arrive. Medical attention was an entirely different matter, however.

Perceiving that most of the patients had still not had their wounds dressed, Sallie procured a basin of water and entered a room occupied by seven or eight wounded soldiers. One of the men directed her to a man lying on the floor who could not assist himself. Stooping over him, Sallie inquired about his wound. The patient pointed to his worm-infested leg.

Appalled, the volunteer nurse asked

The Seminary shortly after the battle. The camera angle is facing west. The rooms occupied by Colonel McFarland and Lieutenant Hoffman were located on the lower south side (left) of the building. The garden was located near the southeastern corner of the structure. Courtesy of ACHS.

to see a doctor. When one appeared, she demanded to know how the men came to be in such a condition. The somber response was that not enough surgeons and attendants had been detailed to care for the wounded and "that many would die from sheer lack of timely attendance." Learning that the man with the injured leg would be among this number, Sallie resolved to write his wife, but she feared it was too late for he was sinking rapidly. "I am becoming more used to sights of misery," she wrote in her diary entry for July 7th.[54]

The same shocking sights were beheld by the former residents of the Seminary as they returned from their exiles. On the Monday evening following the battle, the Ziegler family returned home after a depressing journey over the scene of the re-

cent conflict. "Oh, what a homecoming!" recalled Lydia. "Everything we owned was gone — not a bed to lie on, and not a change of clothing. Many things had been destroyed, and the rest had been converted to hospital purposes."[55] The feet of the family's four fat hogs were found lying in the pen. Miraculously, the Ziegler's two white cows had survived the battle, though they had been milked often during their absence.

The family put their own losses aside and focused on the care of the wounded. Lydia described the ordeal:

> It was a ghastly sight to see some of the men lying in pools of blood on the bare floor.... Nights and days were alike spent in trying to alleviate the suffering of the

wounded and dying. How often did I receive the dying message of a father or husband to send to his loved ones whom he would never again meet on earth! I shall ever hold in sweet memory the repeatedly uttered "God bless you, my girl!" from poor fellows after some little act of kindness had been shown them.[56]

Hugh Ziegler recalled that the building was so congested that even the hallways were occupied. Somehow, the doctors cleared out two of the rooms for the returning family. Mary Ziegler took charge of the kitchen and was hailed by the wounded and others connected with the hospital as "mother."[57]

Student Martin Culler experienced a less cordial welcome from a member of the medical staff:

> I found a Union surgeon in my room, and that he had been freely using everything as well as my bed. I told him he was entirely welcome so far, but as Seminary work was at an end, I must secure my bedding and place it in care of the steward. I advanced to remove the bedding, but he coolly informed me that I could not do so. Demanding an order from Gen. Meade, he said he had none; and when I attempted to remove the bedding, he tried to hold it. This of course aroused my blood, which compelled me to say: "Sir, if you do not release your hold I shall be driven to the necessity of throwing you upon the floor, and stomping you with my feet." This speech had its desired effect, though he was a stalwart man. He stepped back like a craven coward as he was.[58]

Like Culler, second-year student Henry C. Holloway returned to the building shortly after the battle to secure his personal effects. With the exception of some blank paper missing from his desk, he was amazed to discover that his belongings were untouched. Even the coat and leather shoes entrusted to him by his friend, Edmund J. Wolf, a college student

who had enlisted in the 26th Pennsylvania Emergency Militia, remained in the open cupboard where he had left them. For the most part, no wanton damage took place in the dorms.[59]

One Gettysburg civilian reported that during the Confederate occupation the general consensus among the town's residents was that "Dr. Krauth's and Schmucker's dwellings were not worth three cents."[60] Fortunately, this negative appraisal was much exaggerated.

When the Krauths returned to the campus on July 6th, the wounded were removed from their residence and taken to the main Seminary building. Much of the family's clothing, small furniture, beds, and bedding were soiled and bloodstained. The carpets were almost completely ruined and floor matting had to be carried out and burned.

Charles Krauth near the time of the battle. Courtesy of LTSG.

A number of items were missing, most notably, a silver tea service. The four-piece set had been given as a wedding gift to the couple in 1834 by Mrs. Krauth's parents. Harriet resigned herself to the fact that this highly prized heirloom was lost forever. Several days later, however, the couple observed a notice in the local paper submitted by the burgess of Waynesboro, Pennsylvania, which announced that Union cavalry had discovered the stolen silver in a wagon during the Confederate retreat and had requested that the items be returned to the owners if possible. Dr. Krauth promptly answered the ad and the service was returned to its proper place in the dining room.[61]

Charles estimated his losses at several hundred dollars. Much of the larger furniture and his extensive library sustained only minor damages. Upon reflection, the family rejoiced that so many of their possessions were salvageable and they gave thanks for the Union victory. During a service held after the battle, Krauth preached from the text found in Hebrews: "And took joyfully the spoiling of your goods."[62]

It would require a considerable effort to restore everything to its former condition, but Charles was far more concerned about the well-being of his family. On July 9th, he informed his aunt in Philadelphia that "Harriet & Sallie stood the trial wonderfully & Harriet is engaged at the house with her wonted energy." The professor also noted that their son, John, was at Harrisburg with the militia and was doing well.[63]

The remainder of the campus did not fare as well as the Krauth house. "Our grounds are completely desolated," wrote Dr. Krauth. "Intrenchments were thrown up between us and the Seminary. Dr. Schmucker is a much greater sufferer than some."[64]

Samuel must have been mortified by the condition in which he found his home

and the school that had consumed so much of his time and energy. "The injury to the property of the Institution is considerable," he wrote. "The house I occupy was most damaged.... Thirteen cannon balls or shells pierced the walls, and made holes several of which were from 2 to 3 feet in length and nearly as broad; window frames were shattered to pieces, sash broken and the greater part of the glass in the house destroyed. The fences around the yard and garden were nearly all leveled with the ground, as well as those around the entire Seminary lands."[65]

Upon entering his house, the professor received an even greater shock. The damage sustained to the interior was far greater than the incidental losses incurred by his colleague. Samuel discovered that "the archives of the Seminary were, like everything else in my house, broken open by the rebels, and the contents scattered promiscuously with my books, papers, letters, etc., over the floor...."[66] Much of the household furniture was destroyed and an oil portrait of Schmucker's father had been pierced and slit by a sharp object, probably a bayonet.[67]

Even Samuel's personal wardrobe had been confiscated, including a brand new broadcloth suit valued at $40. All told, Schmucker estimated that the damage to his personal property, real estate, and crops exceeded $3,000.[68] In comparing the damages to the Krauth and Schmucker dwellings, it appears likely that Schmucker's home was targeted for vandalism, perhaps as a result of his outspoken views on slavery.

As he sorted through the wreckage, the heartbroken professor made a discovery that perhaps restored his faith in the goodness of man. One of the vandals, apparently guided by his conscience, picked out a leather-bound Holy Bible from among the debris and carefully placed it back on a nearby bookcase. The Confederate soldier,

A modern view of the Schmucker house. The view is from the southwest. Author's collection. Inset: *A projectile from a 10-pounder Parrott rifle still embedded in the south wall of the structure. Author's collection.*

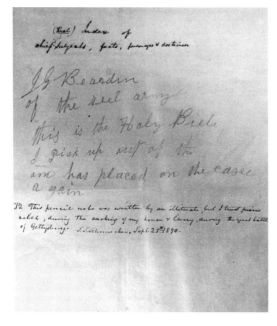

The inscription in the Schmucker Bible. Courtesy of the LTSG.

who signed his name as J. G. Beardin, scrawled a hasty note on one of the rear flyleaves of the Bible explaining his deed. Later, Schmucker added an annotation directly below: "This pencil note was written by an illiterate, but I trust pious rebel, during the sacking of my house & library, during the great battle of Gettysburg."[69]

In the midst of this personal turmoil, Schmucker displayed his compassion for others. Following the battle, he took in the displaced Slentz family, whose home would be uninhabitable for three months. The accommodations were very primitive, however. The Slentz family slept on the floor and subsisted on bread, butter, and molasses.[70]

Schmucker soon discovered that facilities associated with the Seminary had also been scarred by the battle and converted into hospitals. The Christ Lutheran

Church on Chambersburg Street contained over 150 wounded patients, primarily from the Second Division of the First Corps. Beds were improvised by laying boards on top of the pews and knapsacks served as pillows. On Sunday, July 12th, Dr. Baugher held a brief religious service in the church, during which five men died.[71]

Like the Seminary and Christ Lutheran, all of the buildings of Pennsylvania College housed wounded soldiers. Inside the main edifice were between 500 and 700 Confederates. One former student who visited the campus after the battle was "heart sickened at the devastation and ruin that surrounded the college" and by the sight of Rebel soldiers who "lay scattered about the floor in various states of filth and wounds."[72]

Student Michael Colver was also deeply touched. "All rooms, halls, and hallways were occupied with the poor deluded sons of the South," he recalled. "The moans, prayers, and shrieks of the wounded and dying were heard everywhere. Only a heart dispossessed of all feeling of humanity could refuse sympathy and help in such a time as that…. Students and citizens combined to act the part of the good Samaritan."[73]

Henry Bellows pointed out that "had it not been for the unwearied labors of the people of Gettysburg and the neighboring towns … the sufferings of these wounded men must, in thousands of cases, have ended in early death."[74] A dramatic event which took place at the Seminary on July 8th proved the validity of this statement.

After dressing wounds and distributing soup to the patients on the upper floors, Sarah Broadhead descended to the basement of the building. She was horrified by what she witnessed there. "Men, wounded in three and four places, not able to help themselves the least bit, lay almost swimming in water," she re-

called. Sallie and several other ladies secured some stretchers and evacuated nearly 100 men to the fourth story. Broadhead was drawn to one poor fellow who had both legs and one arm taken off. Many of these helpless patients would have surely perished in the subterranean flood had it not been for the quick action of Sallie and her companions. Later, the fatigued volunteer marveled that not long ago she "would have fainted had I seen as much blood as I have today."[75]

Conditions at the hospital slowly improved. A contingent of physicians and nurses from Washington arrived on the evening of July 7th. Miss Anna Burkhart, Miss Anna Whitson, and Miss Mary Evingham were stationed at the Seminary. These ladies were most likely members of the Army Nurse Corps headed by the indefatigable Dorthea Dix, who had gained international fame in the antebellum era by uncovering the appalling treatment of the mentally ill in asylums throughout the world. Near the beginning of the war, Miss Dix conceived of the concept of a corps of women nurses for the army, and with her characteristic drive, she quickly gained the approval of official Washington.

About 40 trained nurses from her corps labored in the field hospitals at Gettysburg. The celebrated philanthropist was also a frequent visitor at these facilities, attracting the attention of patients and staff alike.[76] She apparently became acquainted with Colonel McFarland, as the officer later wrote his wife that the superintendent of nurses sent him "two papers of Broma, a bottle of cologne, and a handkerchief" near the end of his stay at the hospital.[77]

Meanwhile, another group of volunteer nurses quietly performed their duties with little fanfare. On the Sunday following the battle, Father Francis Burlando, a priest at St. Joseph's Academy in Emmitsburg, Maryland, escorted 16 members of the Sisters of Charity, a convent of Catholic nurses, toward the battlefield in an omnibus and carriage. The vehicles were loaded with bandages, sponges, and other necessities.[78]

The Union pickets stationed along the Emmitsburg Road marveled at the odd spectacle. The Sisters wore plain black dresses with white aprons topped off by a large, butterfly-like white bonnet. One Union soldier compared the unusual headgear to a scoop shovel and considered it "the ugliest piece of furniture I ever saw."[79] Despite their odd appearance, the Sisters earned an enviable reputation among the leaders and soldiers of both armies for their consummate skill and impartial treatment of the wounded. Doctors always preferred them to other civilian nurses.

Father Burlando assigned small groups of the Sisters to serve at each of the major hospital sites, including the Lutheran Seminary. Soon, additional members of the order reached the scene from Emmitsburg and Baltimore, bolstering their number to about 40.[80]

One historian described the service of the devout nurses at Gettysburg as "one of the grandest exemplifications of Christian heroism ever displayed on the continent."[81] A wounded Pennsylvanian fondly recalled "should I live to be a hundred years old I will always hold them in grateful remembrance for the kind and loving attention that they gave us while we were under their care and keeping. I never see one of them wearing their peculiar garb but my mind goes back to the time when, wounded and sick and away from home and our own loved ones, they ministered to our every want as tenderly and cheerfully as our own mothers or wives or sisters could have done."[82]

The Patriot Daughters of Lancaster were yet another group of volunteer nurses who offered their services. The representatives of this civilian aid society had formulated no systematic plan of action, but soon agreed they would be most effective by functioning as a team at one hospital site. The decision was made easy for the women when they obtained lodging directly opposite Christ Lutheran Church.[83]

On July 10th, Sarah Broadhead was asked if she would be willing to care for three wounded soldiers in her home. The young housewife consented to the request. Nurses and other medical personnel were arriving in increasing numbers at the field hospitals and she wanted to spend less time away from her family.

Sallie's decision was reinforced when she visited the Seminary. Much to her delight, she discovered that nearly all of the patients had been provided with beds and clean clothing. However, Sallie missed many faces she had come to know, including the man whose wife she had written to earlier. She learned that a fellow nurse had stayed by his side until he died.[84]

A large percentage of the doctors and nurses at Gettysburg were volunteers like Sallie. Their contributions were certainly appreciated by Dr. Henry Janes, the man assigned by Dr. Letterman as chief surgeon of all field hospitals at Gettysburg. The 31-year-old Vermonter had earned a reputation as a skilled surgeon and a talented administrator.[85] He would need all of his ability to tackle the daunting task before him.

At the very least, his superior had left behind a well-organized system of hospital administration. Each army corps had in place a well-outlined chain of command for its medical personnel. Generally, the hospitals were set up to operate at the division level, in contrast to the earlier regimental system, to increase efficiency. The officers on duty at the various facilities adhered to a system that called for a division of labor according to ability and experience. The best surgeons comprised the team that performed primary operations.

The less skilled operators functioned as wound dressers. Others served in administrative roles, such as record-keeping and the supervision of food and medical supplies. A group of nurses and attendants assisted the officers.[86] Of course, due to the chaotic state of affairs at Gettysburg, this system did not always function exactly as intended.

Dr. Andrew Jackson Ward, the Surgeon in Chief of the First Corps, took charge of all of the organization's wounded, contained in seven hospitals. Born in New Milford, Pennsylvania, in 1824, Ward had graduated from the University of Pennsylvania in 1846. Shortly thereafter, he served in the Mexican War as an assistant surgeon. After returning home, he moved to Madison, Wisconsin, where he set up a private practice. The adventurous physician took extended vacations in California and Colorado during the gold rush. At the outbreak of the Civil War, he joined the 2nd Wisconsin as an assistant surgeon. Ward's rise through the ranks culminated in March of 1863, when he was promoted

Dr. Andrew J. Ward, Surgeon in Chief, First Army Corps. Courtesy of Marc J. Storch, USAMHI.

to supervise the First Corps surgeons.[87]

Ward's assistant, Dr. Henry Leaman, a Lancaster County, Pennsylvania, native, celebrated his 24th birthday on July 3, 1863. In the spring of 1856, Henry had entered the freshman class of Franklin & Marshall College, where he befriended an upper classman by the name of Henry Kyd Douglas. Leaman graduated as salutatorian in 1859, the same year that Jeremiah Hoffman entered the institution. After graduation, he taught briefly at the Paradise Academy in Lancaster, then read medicine under his uncle. In 1862, Leaman became a medical cadet at the Christian Street Hospital in Philadelphia. Meanwhile, he attended lectures at nearby Jefferson Medical College. His education would be greatly enhanced by the several weeks of practical experience he received at Gettysburg under the tutelage of Dr. Ward.[88]

On the morning of July 4th, his 28th birthday, Dr. Robert Loughran received an unusual "gift"—he was placed in charge of the Seminary Hospital. Loughran had graduated from Albany Medical College in 1857. He then practiced medicine for three years before being lured into politics. The physician had secured a seat in the state legislature as a Republican from Ulster County, New York, and served as chairman of the committee on Medical Societies and Colleges. Loughran had served as the surgeon of the 20th New York State Militia since the beginning of the war.[89] This trio of officers—Ward, Leaman, and Loughran—received the praise of both Union and Confederate patients alike.

The maximum patient load at the Seminary was probably reached on or about July 6th. On this date, Colonel McFarland noted that 173 wounded officers and men from his regiment alone had been collected at the site. As many as 600 patients might have been housed on the campus at this time.[90]

An amputation scene at Camp Letterman Hospital, Gettysburg, in August 1863. Courtesy of MOL-LUS, USAMHI.

Surgical work intensified throughout the week. Even under adverse conditions, a typical amputation required only about 12 minutes to complete.[91] Hugh Ziegler remembered that one of the large rooms at the Seminary was "used as a clinic, where many arms and legs were amputated and several times I was called on to carry one to the rear of the hospital and deposit with many others, that had been placed in a pile. There had been an accumulation of several days before they were taken away and buried: and the pile of arms and legs placed there like a pile of stove wood, would have filled a wagon bed."[92]

One of the limbs handled by Hugh might have been the left leg of Captain Daniel McMahon. The officer's thigh had been fractured so severely that it had to be removed nine inches from the hip.[93]

Dr. Loughran also removed the right thigh of Sergeant Abram Swart. The young man, who had previously worked as a farm hand, had plenty of time to worry over how he would support his mother and younger siblings minus one of his legs.[94] Other limbs on the growing pile included the right arm of cavalryman Lyman Shaw and the left leg of the 6th Wisconsin's Abe Fletcher.

The survival rate of those who underwent multiple amputations was quite low. Private Samuel Cramer, Company B, 142nd Pennsylvania, died on July 9th inside the Seminary following the removal of both his left arm and left thigh. Mr. and Mrs. Cramer lost two additional sons at Gettysburg. Adam and Enos Cramer, also members of the 142nd, both died as a result of wounds suffered on the opening day of the battle.[95]

A less common technique used to treat damaged arms and legs was known as "resection." In this less radical operation, the surgeon cut away the damaged portion of the bone and then reconnected the remaining parts. Although the limb was shortened by this procedure, it could still be used by the patient. The fractured right leg of 43-year-old Private Orrin Brown of the 147th New York underwent resection on July 6th at the Seminary.[96]

During the weeks following the battle, throngs of visitors crowded into Gettysburg. The newcomers were greeted by a blighted environment. Copious rains temporarily purified the fetid atmosphere and washed the blood from the rocks and vegetation, but the putrid odors of decaying animals and imperfectly buried corpses returned with the heat and humidity.[97]

The July 10th issue of the *Union County Star and Lewisburg Chronicle*, a Central Pennsylvania newspaper, reported, "Several of our citizens have been to visit the battlefield at Gettysburg. The little town is crowded and odious with decaying bodies and the marks of battle. Our wounded at first lacked aid and supplies, but nurses and doctors were pouring in by the score, and supplies by the ton. Visitors are impressed to bury horses and aid generally."[98]

The second invasion of Gettysburg consisted primarily of three classes of travelers: the altruistic individuals and groups that sought to relieve the human suffering; the sightseers, whose only purpose was to satisfy their morbid curiosities; and lastly, the thousands who poured in from every direction to nurse their loved ones or to locate the grave of a fallen hero.[99]

The influx of strangers severely tested the overwrought nerves of the town's citizenry, but most of the residents did all they could to assist the visitors, particularly those who had suffered a personal loss. Sallie Broadhead recorded that "the old story of the inability of a village of twenty-five hundred inhabitants, overrun and eaten out by two large armies, to accommodate from ten to twelve thousand visitors, is repeated almost hourly." The Broadhead home was filled to capacity for many days after the battle.

On July 12th, the lady whom Sallie had written nearly a week earlier knocked at her door and was given the sad news that her husband had died three days ago. Thanks to Sallie, the bereaved widow was able to locate the remains. "I hope I may never again be called upon to witness such a heartrending scene," wrote Broadhead.[100]

These melancholy events became commonplace, but no less sorrowful, for those who witnessed them. Lydia Ziegler somberly recalled that "So many pathetic scenes took place during those days." She recorded the details of one of them:

> I remember going into the yard, late in the afternoon, about a week after the battle, and finding there an old man supporting the head of a sweet faced old lady on his shoulder. I walked up to this couple and asked if I could be of any assistance, for I saw the old lady looked faint and weary. The answer came from the trembling lips of the old gentleman: "Mother's most tuckered out, but if we can find our boy Charlie, I guess she will be all right." After listening to the pitiful story told us of losing four sons in the War, and knowing their last son had been in the battle of Gettysburg, and walking all the twenty-one miles over the mountain from Chambersburg, since there was no other mode of travel for them, and carrying all this distance a satchel filled with dainties such as Charlie was fond of, we attempted to help them. And their son Charlie was found lying in one of the rooms of the third floor of the seminary building in a dying condition. The cries of that mother as she bent over the body of her boy were heartbreaking. For a short time consciousness returned to Charlie, and he knew his parents, who shortly after had at least some measure of

comfort in taking his dead body home for burial.[101]

Reaching the battlefield was a tricky proposition even for those with access to better means of transportation. After learning of her son's wounding, Margery Tucker, accompanied by her Baptist pastor and members of the University at Lewisburg faculty, headed south for Gettysburg to care for Andrew and other Union County soldiers in the various field hospitals. After a circuitous journey by way of Baltimore, the party reached the scene several days after Lieutenant Tucker's burial.

One can only imagine Mrs. Tucker's shock and grief upon discovering her son's shallow grave in the Seminary garden. On July 8th, Andrew's body was laid to rest on the peaceful slope of the Lewisburg Cemetery adjacent to the university he had attended a year earlier.[102]

Addie McFarland started for Gettysburg on the morning of July 7th after receiving the brief letter written for her husband by Mrs. Harris. She brought along her two small children, three-year-old John Horace, and little Emma, who had just turned one, as well as Dr. A. J. Fisher, a local physician. The party traveled the nine miles from McAlisterville to Mifflin by carriage and then took the train for Harrisburg. Beyond this point, all transportation was in a state of confusion. A determined Mrs. McFarland appealed to Governor Curtin for assistance and received a special pass to board a construction train. Since the bridge spanning the Susquehanna River between Columbia and Wrightsville had been destroyed during the invasion, the group crossed the waterway in a rowboat.

Finally, on July 10th or 11th, the McFarlands enjoyed a reunion inside the Seminary.[103] Sensing his wife's anxiety, the gritty colonel informed her, "I am sound of mind and of stomach and I do not in-

tend to die."[104] Addie and the children boarded with Lizzie Critzman during their stay in Gettysburg, but spent much of their time in the hospital. According to one witness, Addie not only nursed her wounded husband, "but found time to contribute many acts of kindness to the hundreds of wounded and dying soldiers of both armies, which lay in the Seminary."[105]

Sallie Broadhead received a very distinguished guest on July 17th. Governor Curtin paid a brief visit to see an old classmate who was helping to nurse the three wounded soldiers in the Broadhead home. Like the Governor, two of the soldiers hailed from Centre County. One of these men, Sergeant Elias Mingle of Company A, 148th Pennsylvania, was gradually sinking. His right knee had been shattered by a bullet on the second day of the fighting. Curtin spent several days touring the various field hospitals before returning to Harrisburg.[106]

By the time of the Governor's visit, the number of patients remaining in Gettysburg had declined considerably. As soon as rail communication with Gettysburg was restored, Dr. Janes commenced a mass evacuation of the wounded to Baltimore, Philadelphia, and other large cities. The general hospitals at these locations were better equipped to care for large numbers of patients and could provide specialized care.

Initially, the process was hampered by the lack of ambulances and the irregularity of the trains. The first groups of travelers boarded filthy box cars almost entirely void of provisions. A marked improvement took place after the government assumed military control of the line from Gettysburg to Hanover Junction. Under the supervision of Medical Inspector Vollum, the trains were placed on a regular schedule and each was placed in the charge of a medical officer. Each car was filled with a sufficient quantity of hay, water coolers, tin cups, bed pans, and urinals. Agents of the various benevolent agencies set up refreshments stations at the depot and along the route.

On July 9th alone, 2,073 patients were sent away, including 72 from the Seminary Hospital. By July 27th, the total number reached 16,125, leaving about 3,500 men in the various field hospitals. The vast majority of those remaining suffered with penetrating wounds of the head, chest, abdomen, or pelvis, or compound fractures of the limbs, and could not be transported.[107]

Among the first wave of departures from the Seminary Hospital were Lieutenant Jeremiah Hoffman, Musician Michael Link, and Sergeant Jefferson Coates. Hoffman received a leave of absence for 20 days from General Robert Schenck at Baltimore on July 10th. Three days later, he was back at his home in Schaefferstown, Pennsylvania.[108]

Both Link and Coates received follow-up care in Philadelphia. Upon his arrival, Coates was admitted to the Satterlee U.S. General Hospital. Throughout much of July, surgeons removed small pieces of bone from the wound entrance and exit. At one point, a thin plate of bone came out through the patient's nose. A profuse discharge of pus and a watery substance was noted during this period. Coates also suffered from "night sweats," for which he was given a solution of quinine and sulfuric acid.

Remarkably, by August 8th, the wound of entrance had healed and the exit area was rapidly closing. Near the end of September, the sergeant received his discharge. The attending surgeon recorded that after the insertion of artificial eyes there would be very little visible deformity.[109] Link's wounds also sealed up with a minimum of cosmetic damage, but on three separate occasions, a swelling "as large as a chicken egg" appeared over the

right eye socket before gradually disappearing over a six- to seven-week period.[110]

The evacuation operation continued at a steady rate through the middle of July, with numerous others leaving the Seminary. Private Diedrich Dasenbuck reached Turner's Lane Hospital in Philadelphia on July 11th. A week afterwards, the position of the larger foreign body that had struck him on July 1st was ascertained and it was removed through an incision in his right cheek. The ball was considerably battered and included in its folds a tuft of hair. A month later, Dasenbuck returned home.[111]

The Iron Brigade's Private John Shultz joined Dasenbuck at the Turner's Lane facility one day after the Pennsylvanian arrived there. After recuperating from his head wound, the Wisconsin soldier was reassigned to the Veteran Reserve Corps in early November.[112]

The better care afforded at the general hospitals did not always insure the survival of the patient. Throughout the early part of August, the severe leg wound of Corpo-

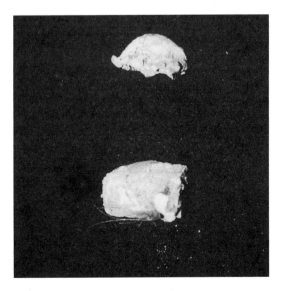

The projectiles extracted from the wounds of Diedrich Dasenbuck, 151st Pa. Vols. The smaller fragment was removed at the Seminary Hospital. Note the tuft of hair attached to the larger piece. Courtesy of NMHM.

ral Luke English exuded about four ounces of pus daily during his stay at a York, Pennsylvania, hospital. On November 4th, he was able to walk a short distance for the first time, but the wound still discharged considerably, indicating a severe infection. English died four years later in Oshkosh, Wisconsin, at the age of 25.[113]

The case of R. Dayton Harvey, 157th New York, also ended tragically. The patient was conveyed from the Seminary to Philadelphia's McClellan Hospital with a wound to the face region. There was total deafness in the left ear and Harvey's mental functions were impaired. The New Yorker died on October 31, 1864, from "inflammation of the brain."[114]

Not everyone traveled such great distances. On July 8th, Captain Brice Blair, accompanied by his black servant, Cato, arrived at the home of Peter Myers on West High Street, about a half-mile east of the Seminary. A number of other wounded soldiers, including Major Thomas Chamberlin, had also obtained lodging there. After about a week's stay, Blair departed for home on the morning of the 16th in company with his wife, son, and brother.

That same evening, the widow of Private John Thiele, 121st Pennsylvania, came to the Myers home seeking information on her husband, having learned of his death a few days earlier. She was told by his commanding officer, Captain James Ashworth, a patient at the residence, that her husband had died at the Seminary Hospital. Arriving there, Mrs. Thiele met Dr. Loughran, who treated her with great kindness and directed her to John's shallow grave.[115]

Mortality continued to thin the ranks of those who remained at the Seminary Hospital. From July 2nd to September 6, 1863, 68 patients, including two Confederates, died inside the building. One of the Confederate deaths was Corporal Alfred Eason, 33rd North Carolina. Eason expired on August 1st following the amputation of his right foot.[116]

A frequent cause of death in Civil War hospitals was secondary hemorrhaging, a profuse flow of blood from an infected wound when the arterial tissue disintegrated from the living tissue.[117] An illustrative example of this malady at the Seminary involved Private George W. Lundy of the 7th Michigan Cavalry. The 25-year-old trooper received a pistol-shot wound on July 3rd that entered below his left eye and emerged behind the ear. The missile passed very near the carotid artery and caused inflammation and ulceration in this region. During a forceful coughing spell, the artery ruptured and the patient bled to death.[118]

Even more common were the various post-operative infections or surgical "fevers," such as tetanus, erysipelas, hospital gangrene, and the deadly pyemia, a poisoning of the blood caused by the absorption of pus-producing microorganisms.[119] On July 10th, Sergeant Edwin Aylesworth died following his amputation a week earlier. His memory would continue to haunt Lieutenant J. Volney Pierce, who last saw him alive grievously wounded upon the field of battle. Six other members of the 147th died at the Seminary, including Private Orrin Brown, who was not able to recover after the resection of his leg.[120]

The mortality rate suffered by this regiment at the hospital was surpassed only by the 151st Pennsylvania, which lost eight men.[121] Among these casualties was Anson Miller, the multiply-wounded Freemason who received the tender care of his Confederate brothers during their occupation of Seminary Ridge. His remains were embalmed and shipped to relatives in Kinderbrook, New York, for interment. He was warmly remembered as "a mild, gentle, and honest man, a just friend and true soldier" who "died in the cause which his heart loved, … the nation's life and honor."[122]

Other fatal cases included the stout Abe Fletcher and Levi Stedman, who died on July 18th and 19th, respectively, far away from their Wisconsin homes. Five days later, Lyman Shaw, the cavalryman from Troy Mills, Illinois, passed away. The next day, Abram Swart gasped his last breath, leaving behind a grief-stricken mother and younger siblings in rural New York.

Several days before his death, Private Stedman sought the guidance of a visiting clergyman from Massachusetts. The pastor described the wounded soldier, toward whom he felt a special sympathy, as "an individual of a large and powerful frame" who had "the look of a man who had never known fear." While Levi displayed little concern over the mortal nature of his wounds, he expressed considerable anxiety about his spiritual welfare. The patient related to his new friend that during the long hours in the hospital he had contemplated his many sins against God and that he was in a state of great anxiety over his lack of religious education. The New England pastor explained to Stedman the fundamentals of the Christian faith and later performed the sacrament of Holy Baptism with the assistance of a surgeon and another soldier.

A medical attendant who was with Levi at the time of his death stated that he was sensible and peaceful to the end and that he frequently prayed that God would show him mercy for the sake of Jesus. "May we not hope that the repenting soldier, like the dying thief, was received that day into the paradise of God?" exclaimed the minister upon learning of his passing.[123]

Although his left leg was "dreadfully painful," George McFarland remained optimistic about his recovery.[124] Throughout the month of July, his beloved roommate also appeared "lively and hopeful" as his stump healed rapidly. Then, suddenly and unexpectedly, Henry Chancellor sank rapidly and died on August 6th.[125] It was a severe blow for the McFarlands as they had grown very fond of the young man. Since her arrival at the Seminary, Mrs. McFarland had lovingly nursed Henry. His elderly mother referred to Addie McFarland as "my darling lamented boy's valued friend." George wrote despairingly, "There was none whose death affected me more deeply."[126]

Major Thomas Chamberlin delivered a fitting eulogy when he made the following statement in his regimental history of the 150th Pennsylvania: "He had hardly passed the limits of boyhood, but in intelligence, courtesy, courage and all the traits which constitute a useful and efficient officer, he had few superiors."[127]

Chancellor's remains were embalmed and interred with military honors in the family vault at St. Peter's Church in Philadelphia. Colonel Langhorne Wister, the commander of the 150th, and Captain George W. Jones of Company B attended the ceremony. Both men had resided in Germantown with Henry prior to the war.[128] These mournful ceremonies cast a somber mood in cities and small rural communities throughout the country during the summer of 1863.

Besides the common afflictions, there were several deaths at the Seminary that took place under unusual circumstances. Despite the heavy case load of patients at Gettysburg, some physicians took the liberty of experimenting with new procedures. Surgeon Benjamin Howard, a proponent of the hermetic sealing of chest wounds, performed this operation on six soldiers with wounds in this region. The results were disappointing. All of the patients died shortly thereafter, including two who were sent to the Seminary to recuperate.[129]

During the Civil War, anesthetics were administered about 80,000 times. Overdoses were extremely rare, accounting for only 43 deaths. Chloroform was the most common substance because of its smaller bulk, speedy action, and nonflammable properties. However, if the patient was not carefully observed and inhaled too much of the sleep-inducing fumes, his heart could undergo paralysis.[130]

Surgeon C. S. Wood reported just such an occurrence in the amputation case of Private Samuel R. Green, 5th New Hampshire, at a field hospital on July 2nd. The doctor wrote that "out of the hundreds of cases in which I have administered chloroform this is the only one accompanied by any unpleasant symptoms; here the patient sunk under its use, was apparently dead, and respiration and circulation both ceased. But by the continual use for some ten or fifteen minutes of Marshall Hall's ready method he was restored and the operation was proceeded with. The cause was evidently inattention on the part of the operator." Green subsequently died at the Seminary on July 30th.[131]

As mortality and the evacuation process significantly decreased the number of patients at Gettysburg, medical authorities began to consolidate the remaining wounded into two major hospitals. The primary collection point was Camp Letterman, a large tent hospital established just outside of town along the York Pike near the railroad.

Much to the consternation of Dr. Schmucker, the Seminary was selected as an auxiliary site. In early August, several hundred patients from Christ Lutheran Church and the courthouse arrived there. Soon after Schmucker's return to the campus, he had called on Colonel Henry C. Alleman, the commander of the post, and received his positive assurance that the hospital would be cleared out in two weeks. When this period passed, the professor approached the medical board and was informed that the building would be vacated in time for the fall semester.[132]

Interestingly, one of the patients who arrived at the Seminary during the consolidation phase was Frederick A. Lehman, a 16-year-old student at the preparatory department of Pennsylvania College at the time of the battle. As the fighting raged near the campus on July 1st, Lehman, inspired by his unbounded patriotism, procured a musket from a fallen soldier and took his place in the ranks. The young student was captured near the close of the fighting, but was released upon the appeal of Lieutenant Charles P. Potts of the 151st Pennsylvania. After taking refuge in a house on Chambersburg Street, Lehman emerged on July 4th, only to be wounded in the right knee by a Confederate sharpshooter.[133]

Lehman was one of only two students of the College or Seminary known to have received a wound during the battle. Amos M. Whetstone, a 25-year-old Seminarian, was leisurely sitting on the porch of a

Amos M. Whetstone, Seminary student wounded during the battle. Courtesy of LTSG.

boarding house on Chambersburg Street when a stray bullet struck the fleshy part of his leg. Apparently, Whetstone's wound was not serious. He survived until 1894 and enjoyed a long pastoral career.[134]

Gradually, throughout late July and early August, the other hospitals were closed down. Private John Chase of the 5th Maine Battery was probably the most unique patient to arrive at the Seminary during this period. The First Corps artillerist remained unharmed during the first day's fighting near the Seminary, but the next day, while his unit was positioned on a small knoll between Culp's and Cemetery Hills, a premature discharge of one of the guns caused a shell to explode within a foot of him. The blast tore off his right arm at the elbow and destroyed his left eye. At least 48 shell fragments struck the Maine soldier, mainly in the face, throat, right breast, and right arm. Presumed dead, he was carried a short distance to the rear.

When Chase regained consciousness two days later, he discovered himself in a wagon load of corpses being carted away for burial. His painful moans attracted the attention of the driver. Afterwards, he was taken to a nearby field hospital and his wounds were finally dressed three days later. Against all odds, Chase survived. Perhaps no other man received as many wounds and lived to tell the story. During the first week of August, the 20-year-old private was moved to the Seminary, where he would continue his remarkable recovery.[135]

An order was also issued for the removal of the wounded from private residences. Sallie Broadhead pleaded with medical officers to allow her three adopted patients to remain under her care, but to no avail. The last soldier left her home on July 23rd. Two of the soldiers, Sergeant Elias Mingle and Sergeant George Leitzel, both of the 148th Pennsylvania, were moved a short distance to the Seminary. Although saddened by their departure, Sallie wrote afterwards, "A weight of care ... has been lifted off of our shoulders, and again we have our house to ourselves."[136] After undergoing the amputation of his right leg at the hospital, Sergeant Mingle died on July 31st.[137]

Hundreds of ministers visited Gettysburg after the battle to provide spiritual guidance for the wounded. The Reverend Franklin J. F. Schantz made two trips, the first from July 7th through the 9th, the other from July 22nd through the 27th. On the latter visit, he served as the agent for the distribution of donated goods from his three congregations in Eastern Pennsylvania. During his stay, Schantz lodged at the home of Dr. Frederick Schaeffer. The pastor spent many hours at his alma mater. On Saturday, July 25th, he recorded:

The Reverend Franklin Jacob Fogel Schantz, circa 1900–1905. Courtesy of FM.

In the afternoon I took hospital stores to the Theological Seminary and visited the many sick and wounded in the Building. I read Scripture Lessons and prayed with many of the men. What different scenes from those of the two years I spent as a student in the building. Many of the soldiers who had lost an arm or a leg told me that they still felt sensations in the parts separated from their bodies. I met a young soldier wounded and confined to bed who had lost the upper and lower set of artificial teeth. He had no tooth in his mouth and yet he was cheerful and managed to live. I was by the bedside of dying men who departed this life away from their homes and friends, thus no mother, no father, no sister or brother, no wife or children near to hear the last word of their beloved.[138]

At the request of the surgeon in chief, Schantz returned the following afternoon to conduct religious services. Upon his arrival, he was shocked to discover the doctor in his room with a party of men "drinking and singing negro melodies." Undaunted, Schantz took position near the stairway in the second hall of the building at the appointed time. The pastor recounted subsequent events:

> As the noise in the Surgeon's room had not ended, I sent a messenger to inform the Surgeon that I was ready to begin the Service. His reply, as repeated by the messenger, was, "I suppose that means that we are to stop our noise." Very soon after the messenger returned to me, the surgeon and his party came from the surgeon's room and passed me on a rush down the stairway and out of the Building. I was glad the noise of the carousers had ceased…. I preached to an audience which I did not see…. No thought entered my mind when I was a student in the Seminary … that six years later I would stand where I stood in July, 1863, and preach a sermon to sick and wounded soldiers occupying the same rooms which we had as our rooms in student years.[139]

Although Schantz did not reveal the identity of the carousing surgeon in his memoirs, it was quite possibly Dr. James Reily, 179th Pennsylvania Volunteers, who eventually took over for Dr. Loughran at the Seminary. In early September, George McFarland wrote of "some noisy, drunken attendants and doctors" who took part in "a general jolification — a regular drunk, in which rumor says all or nearly all were engaged, even many of the patients downstairs waiting for transportation…. Of course, they annoyed me, and mentioning it to Dr. Reily, he remarked, 'they felt jolly!' "Several days later, the colonel recorded, "There are some rowdies here with their chief Dr. R. who keep everyone awake with their revelries."[140]

Before leaving the Seminary, Schantz was introduced to a fellow graduate of Franklin and Marshall College, who had arrived at the facility four days earlier. The pastor instantly recognized Henry Kyd Douglas as he had attended his commencement exercises at the Lancaster, Pennsylvania, institution in 1858.[141]

During the third week of July, several high profile Confederate officers entered the Seminary Hospital. Major Douglas and Generals Kemper and Trimble were placed in separate rooms under heavy guard. When these celebrity officers began to attract considerable attention from curious visitors and southern sympathizers, the rules governing the conduct of the prisoners grew more stringent.[142]

Not surprisingly, the affable Douglas readily adapted to the trying circumstances. "I had nothing to complain of and no sympathy with those who looked for something unpleasant and found it," he wrote.[143] The Confederate officer was impressed by Dr. Ward's professionalism and he appreciated the "consideration and courtesy" the doctor extended to the enemy soldiers under his supervision.[144] Henry was delighted to discover that his dear friend, Dr. Harry Leaman, served as Ward's assistant, and he derived much pleasure from his frequent visits.

The convivial Douglas suffered no shortage of visitors, and they provided him with "not a little amusement and entertainment."[145] His first caller was the Reverend Dr. Philip Schaff of the Mercersburg Seminary. After some good-natured banter about Schaff's aged horse, the reverend shook his cane at the youngster and retorted that he was delighted to find Henry in a theological seminary, a place he should have come to more willingly. This ecclesiastical repartee was repeated with slight variations by every clergyman who visited the young officer.[146]

As usual, Douglas drew the attention of female admirers. While writing to Helen Boteler, a long-time love interest from his hometown, whom he affectionately referred to as "Miss Tippie," he was interrupted by a visit from several Baltimore ladies. Perhaps to arouse Tippie's jealousy, he described them as "most agreeable ... & pretty at that." The two ladies he perhaps admired the most — his mother and sister — passed through the lines to see him as well.[147]

Henry was certainly smitten with one of the Sisters of Charity who nursed at the hospital. He devoted considerable space in his memoirs to this comely Sister:

> She looked very young and was very capable; she touched my room so as to make me forget I was in prison; she made me delicate things to eat until I thought peacock brains would be no delicacy. She was from Mississippi and had a younger brother in the Confederate army. Her beauty was her only tinge of mortality — how fresh and beautiful she was! But her devotion to duty, her self-forgetfulness, her gentle manner must have made every man she met her friend and guardian.... There is no crown in Heaven too good for such an angel![148]

Douglas spent his days leisurely smoking, reading, and strolling through the wards. His favorite title during his confinement, Victor Hugo's *Les Miserables*, was brought to him by Samuel D. Schmucker, the professor's youngest son, who returned to Gettysburg following his brief military career as a sergeant in the 26th Pennsylvania Emergency Militia. The Southerner's room was adorned with luxury items such as dainty curtains and a comfortable chair sent to him by well-wishers.[149]

With friends as his keepers, security was bound to be lax in regards to Douglas. Few Civil War POWs enjoyed such a stimulating night life:

> Nearby lived two young ladies who were great favorites in the Hospital ... and on occasional nights, when Dr. Ward was conveniently absent or not visible, I would stroll with them to make visits in the town, the marks on the sleeve of my uninjured arm being artfully concealed by some little female headgear ... and marching between the sisters ... we generally landed at Duncan's and made an evening of it.[150]

Understandably, Henry was in no rush to leave Gettysburg. Near the end of July, he received a roommate, Colonel Robert Powell, the commander of the 5th Texas Infantry. After being wounded on July 2nd and confined at a crude field hospital near Little Round Top, Powell was whisked away by the Provost Marshall having been mistakenly identified as General James Longstreet.

Although the 37-year-old officer from Danville, Texas, had earned his living as an attorney and state legislator prior to the war, he was unable to convince the authorities of his true identity. Placed under heavy guard in a room at Pennsylvania College, Powell watched with great amusement as a large procession of townspeople filed past to get a glimpse of him. When

Longstreet was heard from in Virginia, the status of his counterfeit quickly subsided to that of his fellow prisoners.[151]

After his transfer to the Seminary, Powell was upstaged by the ever popular Douglas. With a tinge of jealousy, the colonel later wrote, "I was a Texan and credited with dining on negroes and unhappy unless I had killed a man every morning before breakfast."[152] Nevertheless, Powell was known for his "brave spirit and gentlemanly bearing," and he extracted considerable humor from the strange circumstances that surrounded him following his capture.[153]

The older officer was a witness to his younger companion's legendary charisma on several occasions. "The Major was charming and always successful in his efforts to entertain when ladies constituted the audience," he recalled.[154] But Douglas was not the only practitioner of this art. While visiting General Kemper one day, Powell watched admiringly as the Virginian turned the tables on a pair of loyal Northern ladies who delivered a well-rehearsed pro-Union speech by his bedside. The Texan related the general's cleverly disguised rebuttal:

> I was advised by a wicked glance of his eye that he intended to make a conquest of these zealous dames. His conversation was sparkling and brilliant. Woman, not war, was his theme. We forgot for the time that there was war and were in a land peopled by fairies, whose sole occupation was to minister to the afflicted. The ladies, forgetting their mission, personated his fairies, moved their seats nearer and, while one used her grateful fan to cool his fevered brow, the other bathed his parched and burning hands. His eyes sparkled with triumph as he quoted with feeling effect the lines of Scott, "Oh, woman, in our hours of ease."[155]

An odd proceeding took place in the same room on August 4th. Two ladies with Southern sympathies had just completed their visit and were about to leave. For some unexplained reason, the jumpy guards halted the women at the door and informed them that they would not be permitted to pass through. Powell recalled with much satisfaction that four Confederate officers had managed to keep an entire militia company in "a state of feverish agitation and anxiety."

Once again the Southerners swung into action. Powell attempted to remonstrate with the guard at the door, but was repelled with an explosion of profanity. Through the chaos, Kemper shouted from his cot, "Kill them! Kill them!" In mock compliance, the Texan brandished his pen knife. As the guard rushed down the hall for reinforcements, Powell slipped the knife to one of the ladies.

Shortly afterwards, a militia captain with a squad of men appeared on the scene. The offender was searched for weapons, and under the guard of a whole company was marched through the town to the railroad depot. It was Colonel Powell's last day in Gettysburg.[156]

On that same date, Major Douglas used his connections to have his transfer order countermanded. The officer realized he was merely delaying the inevitable, but he "did not again expect to be so well placed." He was correct. A short time later, Henry was transported to Baltimore and confined in West Buildings Hospital under stricter regulations.[157]

By contrast, Isaac Trimble did not enjoy his stay at the hospital. He would have been perfectly content to remain in his comfortable quarters at the McCurdy house. His removal was initiated by several neighbors who expressed their displeasure over the Southerner's preferential treatment.[158] Lincoln's former secretary of war, Simon Cameron, investigated the matter personally during a visit to Gettysburg on July 11th. Cameron telegraphed the president that Trimble was "living in comfort at the house of a rebel sympathizer in this town, while some of our wounded soldiers are still unattended."[159]

Against Isaac's repeated protests, he was moved to the Seminary on July 21st. The general was accompanied by his faithful orderly, "Frank," and his aide, Lieutenant Grogan, who had sustained a wound to his left thigh on July 3rd.[160] Although Trimble considered Dr. Ward "a gentleman" and conceded that he and his fellow prisoners were fairly treated, he felt nothing but contempt for the militiamen placed on guard duty at the hospital. "The Lt. of the Guard, Rice — a Penna. blackguard takes every occasion to vex us & circumscribe our privileges. May the chances of war put him some day in our power," wrote Isaac.[161]

But there is some evidence that Trimble invited trouble on his own. A week after his arrival, the indignant general had already become infamous. When Emily Souder, an independent nurse from Philadelphia, visited the Seminary she professed some curiosity to see the famous officer. She learned, however, that he could not be seen without a special permit. The hospital ward master told Emily that the general was "very fierce-looking." She also learned that Trimble received "a splendid dinner daily from the bounty of some sympathizer."[162]

According to one witness, the spoiled Southerner expected nothing less than royal treatment. Martha Ehler and the Patriot Daughters of Lancaster followed their patients from the College Church to the Seminary. In her published account of the group's experiences at Gettysburg, Ehler singled out Trimble for censure:

> For men like Gen. Trimble, I have no sympathy. Theirs was the infamy of inaugurating this wicked rebellion, and they should be the sufferers. Had any of our poor officers, in their Southern dungeons, dared to show half the audacity of this man, he would have been immediately shot; while Gen. Trimble would order the best of everything cooked, and if it did not please him, send it back to the kitchen. I was there one day when his dinner was returned; it consisted of nice fried ham and eggs, with mashed potatoes and onions, but it did not please him. Norris, who was the cook, asked me what he should do. I suggested letting him wait until his appetite improved, which was done; no other dinner was supplied.[163]

Isaac noted in his diary that he and his fellow prisoners received the kind attentions of several ladies from the South, who, much to his dismay, were ordered away on August 6th. This move was consistent with a general crackdown on Rebel sympathizers who provided their wounded with all kinds of delicacies while purposefully excluding the Union patients. Some even attempted to facilitate the escape of their soldiers by providing them with citizen's clothing.[164]

Despite these more stringent measures, conditions at the Seminary continued to improve with the passage of time. In early August, one observer asserted, "I have visited a great many hospitals, and must say that I have never seen anywhere the wounded are better treated in every respect, than they are in and about Gettysburg. They all appear cheerful and well satisfied."[165]

The grounds between the main building and the Krauth house were covered with tents, each one containing six beds. "I saw no distinction made between our own men and the rebels," wrote Martha Ehler. She described the enemy as "a poor, degraded, deluded set of men, much inferior in education and cleanliness to the Union soldiers, but many, be it said to their credit, are devout Christians...." The Lancaster volunteer nostalgically recalled "the white tents beneath the spreading branches of beautiful trees ... the snow-white bed, the little table on which were placed their Bibles and the cooling drink, and above all, the watchful care and kind attentions they received....["166]

Fannie Buehler visited the hospital tents every day and recalled that a cooking stove was taken to the woods behind the Seminary and "there we spent every day for weeks cooking and making 'nice things' for men who were suffering.... These men were from both armies, and were very grateful for all we did for them."[167]

Near the end of August, two members of the Committee of Maryland branch of the United States Christian Commission visited Gettysburg. The pair of inspectors reported the following concerning their visit to the Seminary Hospital:

> The arrangements of the hospital were good, and exhibited a degree of comfort beyond expectation. A number of ladies were in attendance, who were laboring faithfully in the performance of their Samaritan-like labors.... Their activity in preparing coffee and delicacies, and delivering them to the helpless subjects of their kind consideration and care, were witnessed with great satisfaction. Six to eight ladies were in attendance each day, and performed the service necessary in cooking and serving out the food they prepared.... The surgeons of the hospital, appeared to be humane and considerate in the treatment of their patients.[168]

The surgeons observed at this time were not the same staff that had labored there since the battle. During the middle of the month, an order was issued that called for all army surgeons to return to their units. This news was disappointing for many of the patients who still remained at Gettysburg. "This takes away Dr. Loughran, my surg[eon]," wrote Colonel McFarland. "He has been so faithful and so kind and I have such perfect confidence in him that I can scarcely let him go."[169]

To fill the void left by the army surgeons, the government contracted the services of nine civilian doctors to provide follow-up care at the Seminary Hospital. Among the contract surgeons were brothers Dr. Charles and Dr. Robert Horner, and Dr. Henry Huber, three long-time Gettysburg physicians.[170]

Medical Inspector Cuyler asserted, "As far as my observation extends, the medical officers of the army, and the citizen surgeons who were employed during the emergency, discharged their arduous duties with fidelity and ability. I never saw men work harder and complain less of the difficulties that surrounded them."[171]

Jonathan Letterman agreed in part. "The skill and devotion shown by the medical officers of this army were worthy of all commendation; they could not be surpassed," wrote the army's medical director. However, he did not hold the contract surgeons in nearly such high esteem. "No reliance can be placed on surgeons from civil life during or after a battle ... and the wounded men ... are much better satisfied to be attended by their own surgeons," wrote Letterman bluntly.[172]

McFarland's lament at losing Dr. Loughran adds validity to this statement. And although he wrote nothing negative concerning either Dr. Horner, he described Huber as "a kind but careless old man."[173] Of course, the army surgeons had been by no means infallible. The Christian Commission delegates inspecting the Seminary Hospital recorded the following incident:

> [A] man was heard to complain that he was so long recovering from the effects of an amputation that had taken place several weeks before. His stump would have been healed but for a spicula of bone which was working its way through the flesh. He complained of the inconvenience, and said the amputating surgeon had not been sufficiently careful in the removal of the pieces of bone before he

covered it with the flap and bound up the wound…. "If," said he, "the surgeon that took off my leg had scraped well the end of the bone, and taken off the sharp edge all round, I should have done much better. I am sure I would not now be suffering with the working of small pieces of bone through the flesh."[174]

Although the agents did not identify the patient by name, the case closely resembles that of Corporal John Crawford. It will be recalled that Crawford's right leg was amputated on July 2nd and that the operating surgeon had carelessly left a conical-shaped stump. On August 15th, the Wisconsin soldier came under the care of Acting Assistant Surgeon W. W. Welch,

A four-inch section of bone cut from Corporal Crawford's stump on February 2, 1864, at Newton University Hospital, Baltimore, Md. Courtesy of NMHM.

who reported: "[T]he stump was granulating slowly and there was a free discharge of healthy pus; but the flaps had sloughed, leaving the end of the femur bare." The surfaces of the bone were found to be very rough and surrounded with a wall of callus. After months of acute pain and two operations to remove portions of protruding bone, the stump finally healed up "with a good cushion" by the end of the following March. This was nearly nine months after the initial operation![175]

McFarland was also experiencing difficulty with his wounds. His diary entry for August 18th read in part: "I am still confined as closely as ever, my stump about ⅔ healed over, and my left leg is still suppurating badly. The wound has become less, but when is it going to heal up? God only knows. It has been very painful for the past three weeks and is now."[176]

Meanwhile, a short distance away, Samuel Schmucker addressed the members of the Board of Directors assembled at his home. The anxious chairman advised the group that "as the officers in charge have

A four-and-one-half-inch section of bone removed from the stump of Corporal John Crawford, 6th Wisc. Vols., by forcible traction on October 30, 1863, at Camp Letterman Hospital. Courtesy of NMHM.

recently been changed and sundry evidences seem to indicate a desire on the part of the authorities to make themselves at ease in the possession of the eligible and healthy Seminary edifice, I recommend that a communication be addressed to the supreme medical authority at Washington urging the reasons why the interests of the Seminary should be unnecessarily sacrificed to the convenience of these medical officials."[177]

Accordingly, a committee was formed "to urge upon the medical authorities there the desirableness and the importance of vacating the building as soon as possible."[178] A separate committee was organized to undertake repairs as soon as the hospital had been cleared out, while another prepared to seek compensation from the government for damages sustained to the institution's property. It was also resolved that the Board would solicit contributions from associated ministers and churches. Another measure stipulated that the students would be compensated for any losses they incurred during the battle.[179]

As Dr. Henry Janes came under increasing fire from Seminary officials, he was also forced to investigate an allegation that there was much sickness at the hospital "owing to the proximity of bodies imperfectly buried." Janes acknowledged that a considerable number of Confederates had been buried in a single trench immediately to the rear of the building. However, these bodies had already been exhumed and removed to another location. He also noted the existence of several scattered graves in the wooded grove, but these were located too far away to pose a health risk to the patients.[180] A number of the soldiers' remains, such as Andrew Tucker's, had been previously claimed by family members.

The doctor also pointed out that as of August 28th, ten unwounded sick men resided at the hospital. Several of these soldiers had been transferred to the Seminary when other hospitals were broken up. By this point, 150 wounded soldiers—109 Union and 41 Confederate — occupied the building. Janes concluded by stating that Dr. Reily, the current surgeon in charge, conducted his hospital admirably.[181]

Not all of the bodies were recovered. In 1909, a worker digging a trench on the west side of the Seminary woods discovered a coffin containing the remains of a Union soldier, along with part of his coat, several buttons, a comb and a mirror.[182] Also, a former Confederate soldier from Scales' Brigade wrote, "Have visited Gettysburg twice since the war, hoping to find the grave of a brother killed the 1st day and buried in a marked grave in the woods near the Seminary. My search was unsuccessful, and he sleeps in an unknown grave."[183]

The concerns about the healthiness of the hospital at this time seem irrelevant as Dr. Janes had already commenced removing the patients. Whether this action was taken as a result of the pressure exerted by the Seminary committee or by Janes' own design is not entirely clear.

Isaac Trimble described his departure on August 20th: "Taken to Baltimore in a miserable rough burden lime-car and laid on straw. Stood the trip well & placed in Hospital, Lexington St., clean and comfortable."[184] General Kemper had been removed two days earlier.[185]

Eventually, most of the wounded Southern officers were taken to the remote prison at Johnson's Island on Lake Erie near Sandusky, Ohio. Depending on individual circumstances, these prisoners were paroled or exchanged at various times throughout the war.

A mass evacuation of the Seminary Hospital began in early September. On the first day of the month, Colonel McFarland recorded, "Today the rebs go, tomorrow the 'one-armed' and the next day the 'one-legged' Union men. 60 or 70 were to go today but could not get off. So by Monday [September 7th] the whole thing may be cleared out."[186]

Some of the patients suffering with compound fractures were removed to nearby Camp Letterman. Among the "one-legged" Union soldiers was Corporal John Crawford, who arrived at the General Hospital on September 2nd.[187] Another soldier taken there was 48-year-old Private James McGeehen, 107th Pennsylvania. After being shot in the right leg on July 1st and losing a considerable amount of blood, the patient had been conveyed to the Seminary, where he remained until September 4th. On this date, his wound suppurated profusely. Thus, it was deemed expedient to place him under canvas at Camp Letterman rather than risk transporting him any farther.[188]

That same day, Private John Chase, the artilleryman who had been left for dead, departed for Philadelphia.[189] His remaining years would be almost as eventful as his war experiences.

Sergeant Jose Lifflith, 104th New York, a 26-year-old resident of Geneseo, had the sad distinction of being the last recorded death at the Seminary Hospital when he passed away on September 6th.[190] By this time, McFarland reported, "The work of clearing out the Hospital still continues though it goes slowly on account of so many being bad. Still nearly all are gone, not a half dozen left." The next day he proclaimed, "I am at last alone — so far as wounded are concerned — in this large building."[191]

The colonel certainly did not plan it this way. His wife and children had left for home on the last day of August, and George had planned to follow them a week later. Much to his disappointment, his wounds did not cooperate, and his stay was prolonged. Two soldiers recovering from illness, Privates Nicholas Kizer and Benjamin Carr of the 149th Pennsylvania, served as nurses for McFarland, while Mary Ziegler cooked his meals.

During his protracted stay, George met a number of Seminary students. He recruited recent graduate Mahlon Horine to serve as an associate principal at his academy in McAlisterville. McFarland described his young associate as a ripe scholar and a good teacher who possessed "all the qualities and virtues which adorn a gentleman and a Christian."[192]

George also met both professors prior to his departure. During a visit on September 3rd, Dr. Krauth told the colonel he could stay in the building as long as he pleased. A few days later, McFarland wrote his wife, "Dr. Schmucker, Pres. of the Seminary has been to see me twice. He is very pleasant and said if I remained 2 or even 3 weeks it would make no difference — he would teach me Theology."[193] As inviting as this offer might have been for the intellectual and religious officer, he longed for home and his loved ones.

When McFarland departed Gettysburg on September 16th, a memorable chapter in the history of the Lutheran Seminary came to a close. Samuel Schmucker must have breathed a sigh of relief; he finally had his building back! However, any feelings of elation would have been quickly tempered by the sobering reality that a considerable amount of work was needed to get the institution up and running again.

Perhaps the thoughts of all those connected with the Seminary during the summer of 1863 were best expressed by Sarah Broadhead when she wrote retrospectively: "Had anyone suggested such sights as within the bound of possibility, I would have thought it madness."[194]

Epilogue

You are true to your name,
*   and you lead me along the right paths.*
I may walk through valleys as dark as death,
*   but I won't be afraid.*
You are with me,
*   and your shepherd's rod makes me feel safe.*
                                    Psalm 23, verses 3–4

The day after Colonel George McFarland vacated the Lutheran Seminary, the following notice appeared in the *Lutheran and Missionary:*

> Lutheran Theological
> Seminary, Gettysburg, Pa.
>
> The fall session of this institution will commence on Thursday the 24th of Sept., 10 o'clock A.M., at which time it is desired that all applicants for admission should be present.—S. S. Schmucker, Chairman of the Faculty[1]

During the academic year following the battle, twenty-three students attended the school. On August 8, 1864, Samuel Schmucker delivered the encouraging news to the Board that these scholars "exhibited a laudable desire to adorn their Christian profession with a consistent conduct" and that the health of the institution was "more than usually good."[2]

Schmucker was a busy man throughout this period. On top of his regular duties, he headed the committee that was established to initiate the clean-up and repairs on the campus. The operation was hampered by the shortage of building materials and skilled laborers. As a result, the professor personally supervised much of the work. The Board later commended him for his "fidelity, diligence and sound judgment."[3]

All of the necessary work was completed by the summer of 1864. The shell-damaged northeast corner of the main edifice was rebuilt, and all three buildings were thoroughly cleaned and repainted. Landscape jobs included grading, grass seeding, and the repair and construction of fencing.

The entire project was financed almost entirely through an ambitious fund-raising campaign that netted $4,210.69. Of this amount, $2,346.18 was expended for repairs at the Seminary. The balance was used to pay for damages sustained at the College. The Government eventually awarded the Seminary a payment of $660 as compensation for the fence rails used as fuel during the hospital period and as rent for the occupancy of the buildings.[4]

On November 19, 1863, two months after the Seminary resumed operations, the school closed for the day to observe the dedication of the Soldiers' National Cemetery. As many as 20,000 people attended the ceremonies, including most of Gettysburg's citizens.

Hugh Ziegler recalled running alongside as President Abraham Lincoln rode up Baltimore Street towards the cemetery. Another youngster, Robert McClean, remembered that the assembled crowd was so dense that it became difficult to breath and several spectators fainted as a result.[5]

Daniel Skelly put the event in proper historical perspective when he noted that the war had been raging for over two years and there seemed to be no end in sight. In the audience were many who had lost a loved one as a result of the bloodshed. "Could there be much applause from such an audience?" he asked rhetorically.[6] The benediction was delivered by Reverend Baugher, who was still grieving over the loss of his son. The next day, the last of the wounded left Camp Letterman, and the hospital period officially came to a close.

The following summer, the residents of Gettysburg experienced another scare during the first anniversary of the great battle. Near the end of June 1864, in a desperate attempt to break the Union siege around Petersburg, Virginia, Robert E. Lee sent a 10,000-man force commanded by General Jubal Early down the Shenandoah Valley to threaten Washington. Reinforcements from the Army of the Potomac arrived just in time to save the capital from capture. Early's force recrossed the Potomac River and escaped back into Virginia on July 14th.

Two weeks later, however, two brigades of Confederate cavalry galloped into Chambersburg and levied a large ransom on the citizens in reprisal for the destruction of private property in Virginia. When these demands were not met, the inhabitants were evacuated and the town was torched.

Mindful of their proximity to that Franklin County community, and with the events of the preceding summer still fresh in their minds, Gettysburg residents reacted quickly to the startling news. Merchants concealed or sent off their goods. Numerous students at the higher learning institutions departed for home. Classes at the Seminary were interrupted once again.

Nine days after the incident, Schmucker wrote that "studies were continued as long as any considerable number of students remained." But since many of the scholars had sent off their books when the enemy was reported to be nearby, "the recitations & regular studies have been terminated for a fortnight past."[7] The summer session closed two weeks earlier than planned.

During the crisis, Dr. Charles Schaeffer, the instructor of German language and theology at the College and Seminary, departed Gettysburg for Philadelphia to accept a position with a rival seminary. He later explained his decision: "The expected Rebel raid, after the burning of Chambersburg, led me, like most of the citizens and all the merchants, to pack up and temporarily send away a portion of my goods. I was so discouraged by this latter circumstance, that when at the recent meeting of the Board of the new Seminary, I was requested to move at once to the city, I readily embraced the opportunity to withdraw from this exposed border region."[8]

Finally, during the spring session of the Seminary in 1865, Robert E. Lee surrendered his army to Ulysses S. Grant at Appomattox Courthouse. In May, the last major Confederate field army capitulated in North Carolina. The news was warmly received throughout the North, particularly in Gettysburg, where the price of the war would be reflected upon by the nation for generations to come.

Just as the concentric rings from a stone tossed into a pond slowly radiate away from the common axis, the men, women and children who met on Seminary Ridge during and after the battle drifted apart following their interactional experience.

In the fall of 1864, the man who had steered the Seminary through its infancy and rebuilt it following the battle, stepped down as chairman of the faculty after nearly four decades of service. Samuel S. Schmucker cited his advanced age, his desire to spend more time writing, and the dissension that had torn the Lutheran church as primary factors in reaching the decision.[9]

As a professor he had shared in the education of about 400 ministers. During his 38-year tenure, the number of practicing Lutherans in the United States had grown from 40,000 to 300,000 and the number of pastors had increased from 180 to 1,600.[10] In his letter of resignation, he hoped his successor, James A. Brown, the man who had fled South Carolina at the outbreak of the Civil War, "would carry on the work to which my life has been devoted, in the same liberal spirit in which this institution was founded and has been thus far conducted...."[11]

Schmucker was widely considered the "very life and formative power" of the Gettysburg Seminary and the reaction to his resignation was immediate. "His life has been only one of activity and usefulness, few men accomplishing more good for the church and the general welfare of society," wrote one reporter. Another proclaimed that Samuel had "won the affectionate esteem and confidence of the whole church ... he has done more than any man living, to make the American Lutheran church

Samuel Schmucker near the end of his life. Courtesy of LTSG.

known, and favorably to the whole religious world."[12]

Following his retirement, Schmucker moved with his wife and daughter to a home on Chambersburg Street. Besides his writing prolifically, Schmucker became active in civic affairs. He was one of the founders of the Evergreen Cemetery, serving many years as a board member and as its president from 1864 to 1865. He was also elected vice-president of the Gettysburg Battlefield Memorial Association, the group which purchased lands that became the nucleus of the Gettysburg National Military Park.

Samuel fell victim to a heart attack on July 26, 1873. Following funeral services at Christ Lutheran Church, he was laid to rest beside his beloved Catherine in the Evergreen Cemetery. His legacy—chief founder of the Seminary and College, leader in the ecumenical and abolition movements, and author of over forty publications on theology, church history, and philosophy — makes him one of the most important figures in American Lutheranism.[13]

Dr. Charles Philip Krauth continued to teach at the Seminary following Schmucker's resignation. Three years later, he became the first professor to die while in the service of the Seminary. The Board of Trustees expressed their "exulted admiration of his unaffected piety ... his entire consecration of his talents and influence to the welfare of the Seminary" and "his faithful and conscientious discharge of duty." Krauth devoted nearly 50 years of his life to the ministry and his service at the College and Seminary spanned over three decades.[14]

Emanuel and Mary Ziegler remained employed at the Seminary until 1874, when they relocated to Philadelphia.[15] In his last report as chairman of the faculty, Dr. Schmucker wrote that Mary "is not only most popular among the students, but exhibits a commendable spirit of accommodation & care of the premises."[16]

Hugh Ziegler moved with his parents to Philadelphia, but his sense of adventure soon led him westward. He eventually settled on a farm near Newkirk, Oklahoma. One year before his death in 1934, he wrote two stirring accounts of his experiences as a youngster in Gettysburg.[17]

On July 4, 1872, Lydia Ziegler married Richard Henry Clare, who had graduated from the Seminary in the spring. They served various parishes in Pennsylvania and New Jersey until Richard's death in 1905. Of their five children, three were graduates of the Gettysburg Lutheran Seminary and lifelong pastors. In an interesting coincidence, one of these ministers, Robert, married Ada McLinn, a great-niece of Colonel George McFarland. Lydia died on April 11, 1915.[18]

The Broadheads also moved away from Gettysburg following the war. The family returned to Sallie's native New Jersey, where Joseph sold coal for a living. After her husband's death in 1903, Sallie spent most of her final seven years with her daughter Mary's family. She was buried in Pleasantville, New Jersey. Long after her death, Sarah "Sallie" Broadhead gained national prominence when documentary filmmaker Ken Burns used excerpts from her diary in the making of his popular PBS production, *The Civil War*.[19]

The battle had a profound impact upon Henry Eyster Jacobs. He later recalled, "The experiences of that week of danger, the sorrowful scenes before me, the closer contact with death and the eternal world; the great need realized of consolation from a source higher than this world, and an intimate association on the battlefield with members of various churches and delegates of the Christian Commission, all deepened my conviction, and inspired me with a desire to devote myself to the ministry."[20]

Jacobs signed on as a delegate with the Christian Commission in 1864. After completing his studies at the Gettysburg Seminary and at Muhlenberg College, he taught at Pennsylvania College for 13 years. Much of the remainder of his life was spent at the Lutheran Theological Seminary in Philadelphia, where he served successively as professor, dean, and president. In addition to his extensive memoirs, Jacobs authored numerous books on Christian theology and history.[21]

Martin Luther Culler joined the Christian Commission with Henry Jacobs following the completion of his studies at the Seminary. Though his first scheduled service was canceled by the appearance of an enemy army in 1863, Martin had the opportunity to preach many sermons during his nearly 50-year ministerial career. He received the degree of Doctor of

Divinity from Susquehanna University in 1906. Culler also served as a director of the Gettysburg Seminary and as a trustee of Susquehanna.[22] He was considered "a Christian gentleman in the highest sense of that term."[23]

The Reverend Franklin J. F. Schantz continued to preach until his death in 1907. Like Culler, he devoted a half-century of his life to the ministry.[24]

Dr. Henry Leaman profited from his on-the-job training at the Seminary Hospital. After completing his studies at Jefferson Medical College the following spring, he served as an assistant surgeon in hospitals at Beaufort and Hilton Head, South Carolina. Leaving the government service in May 1865, Henry opened a private practice in Philadelphia. He also made the rounds as a visiting physician at Charity Hospital and at the Northern Home for Friendless Children. For ten years, Dr. Leaman volunteered as the vaccine physician for the city. He was also selected as Assistant Dean of Anatomy at his alma mater.

A specialist in the fields of obstetrics and gynecology, he presented a scientific instrument to the Philadelphia Medical Society in 1885. The "parturiometer" measured the effective force of the uterus during childbirth.

Henry's wife, whom he married in 1884, died seven years later, leaving him alone to raise their three-year-old daughter. Near the end of his life, Leaman told a friend, "When I came to Philadelphia I had but one purpose: to become a good physician, in order to be useful to men. Not having the qualifications for making money, I made good service to others my leading thought."[25]

Leaman's old friend Henry Kyd Douglas arrived at Johnson's Island prison on Lake Erie on September 29, 1863, his 23rd birthday. Douglas described the inhospitable environment as "just the place to convert visitors to the theological belief

Dr. Henry Leaman. Courtesy of FM.

of the Norwegian that Hell has torments of cold instead of heat."[26] Fortunately, Henry's stay there was relatively short. He was exchanged and released in the spring of 1864.

Rejoining the Army of Northern Virginia, Douglas rose to the rank of colonel and was assigned to brigade command during the final months of the war. His unit led the failed assault on Fort Steadman at Petersburg, Virginia, in what would be the last serious offensive mounted by Lee's army. Assigned as the rear guard during the evacuation of the city, Douglas was wounded twice on the retreat to Appomattox in early April 1865. His brigade was the last to surrender there and the last to stack arms.

Henry's adventures were not quite over. Returning to Shepherdstown, the former officer decided to have the Gettysburg ball removed from his shoulder, and then at the suggestion of a young lady, he accompanied her to a local photographic studio to have his picture taken. Two weeks later, this seemingly innocent act led to his arrest for treason for wearing a Confederate uniform during the session. His legal situation became further complicated when an unreliable witness linked him to Lincoln's assassination. Ultimately cleared of the charge, Douglas was set free in the fall.

With the war finally behind him, Douglas eventually settled in Hagerstown and returned to the practice of law, which he continued until the end of his life. He became a leading figure in the legal, political, and military circles of Maryland. In 1892, he was appointed adjutant general of Maryland. During the Spanish American War, President William McKinley offered him the position of assistant adjutant general of the United States Army, but Henry declined the post due to his poor health.

Besides his memoirs, Douglas wrote a series of articles for newspapers and magazines, most of which memorialized the beloved Stonewall Jackson. A gifted orator, Douglas was in great demand for speaking engagements and memorial ceremonies in both the North and South.

Douglas never married. He could not bring himself to attend the wedding of his sweetheart, Helen "Tippie" Boteler, in 1866, because he felt as if she was being "transferred away" from him. Helen's daughter confirmed that Henry had once been in love with her mother and that the two remained close friends until the end. For Henry, the end came on December 18, 1903, after a long bout with tuberculosis. His stirring war memoir was finally published in 1940. It is one of the most colorful and dramatic personal histories of the Civil War.[27]

Colonel Robert Powell, Douglas' former roommate at the Seminary, remained incarcerated at Johnson's Island until January 1865. After his parole, he took command of the Texas Brigade, which he led

A sketch of Henry Kyd Douglas in his later years. Courtesy of FM.

until the surrender at Appomattox Court House.

Powell then returned to Texas and lived there for 17 years. In 1882, he moved to St. Louis, Missouri. He died of pneumonia there on January 15, 1916, at age 90. One of his prized possessions was a tattered battle flag of the 5th Texas.[28]

Isaac Trimble continued to be an uncooperative prisoner after landing at the notorious prison on Lake Erie's Sandusky Bay. In January 1864 he submitted a long list of grievances to the prison commandant, chiefly concerning the poor quality and inadequate supplies of water, food, and firewood. He also pointed out that prisoners were being fired upon by the guards for trivial offenses, and he protested that Southern officers were required to perform the humiliating work of digging sinks, removing privies, and loading garbage.

The general was held in high regard

by the other captives for his leadership and for the courtesy he extended to less fortunate inmates. Conversely, Secretary of War Edwin M. Stanton considered him "the most dangerous rebel in our hands," a strange allegation considering Isaac's age and physical condition. As a result, Trimble languished in captivity as Southern fortunes waned on the battlefield.[29]

The failure of a bizarre rescue plot in September 1864 by Confederate operatives based in Canada resulted in the transfer of a number of high-ranking officers from Johnson's Island. Trimble was among those shipped off to Fort Warren in Boston Harbor. He was finally released in early March of 1865, but by the time he reported for duty, the end was near at hand.[30]

Isaac returned to Baltimore and settled back into civilian life as an engineer. Unlike many of his former comrades, who mellowed over time, Trimble remained defiant and unrepentant until the end of his life. He never tired of speculating over and writing about the lost opportunities at Gettysburg. Leading figures from the Confederacy, including Jefferson Davis and Wade Hampton, frequently visited his Ravenshurst estate. Isaac's great-grandniece recalled that he often experienced a recurrent nightmare of Pickett's Charge, after which he awoke emitting the Rebel yell at the top of his lungs.

After his second wife passed away in 1879, Trimble traveled extensively. While visiting relatives in Ohio in December 1887, he contracted a severe cold which developed into pneumonia. The old general succumbed to the illness on January 2, 1888, nearly 25 years after the battle that continually haunted his memories. His last words were, "Keep steady; keep steady!"[31]

James Kemper was the only member of the quartet of Southern officers not to be shipped to the dreary prison in Ohio. Less than a month after his transfer from the Seminary Hospital, the Virginian was ex-

changed for Union General Charles K. Graham. A joyous reunion with his family ensued in Madison, Virginia. Kemper attempted a return to active duty the following spring, but he was still too weak from his near fatal wound. Instead, he was placed in command of the reserve forces of Virginia. James received a promotion to major general on September 19, 1864.

After the war, Kemper resumed his law practice and his life as a planter. Tragedy struck in 1870 when his wife died less than a month after childbirth. Belle Kemper was 33 years old. James was devastated, but he could not grieve long; he had six children to support.

Once again, he was drawn to politics. After campaigning for Horace Greely in the 1872 Presidential Election, Kemper was selected as the candidate of the Conservative Party in the Virginia 1873 gubernatorial race. The party's platform accepted the abolition of slavery and urged the speedy restoration of the Union, but emphasized states' rights. Kemper advocated public education, defended the civil rights of blacks, and sought to improve race relations.

The old general won a landslide victory at the polls, but the honeymoon was short-lived. As governor he drew harsh criticism for vetoing a bill that would have aided conservative whites in Petersburg at the expense of the predominately Republican city council, which had been elected by the black majority. Kemper received national acclaim for his bold statesmanship, but many Southerners accused him of deserting the "white man's party."[32]

Kemper was never one to back down from any of his principles. Long after the war, he defended his allegiance to the Confederacy in a letter to a Northern correspondent:

> Be convinced, Sir, that a man who pours out his blood for a cause, exhibits a lofty and sacred devotion to principle which characterizes none but noble minds, and

which, even if it were prompted by error of judgment or education ought to command the respect of all honorable men.[33]

Kemper's poor health forced him to retire from public service after one term as governor. Much of the remainder of his life was spent on a 350-acre farm, known as "Walnut Hill," in Orange County, Virginia. In his final days, James was plagued by illness and financial difficulties. On Sunday, April 7, 1895, Kemper passed away at age 71. The Richmond *Dispatch* proclaimed, "Virginia never had a more loving son, nor one that served her from more unselfish purposes."[34]

Kemper's grandson, named in his honor, graduated from the U.S. Naval Academy in 1932. He was killed in action at Guadalcanal on November 13, 1942.[35]

Many of the Union patients at the Seminary Hospital never returned to active duty. Following his protracted stay at the facility, George McFarland was confined to his bed for over 42 weeks. The students of the McAlisterville Academy gathered by his bedside for recitals. George's war injuries crippled him for life and were a constant source of excruciating pain. His stump was slow to heal and over 50 pieces of splintered bone surfaced from his shattered left ankle.

Despite his handicap, McFarland pressed forward with his characteristic energy and willpower. In November 1864, he converted his academy into one of the first Soldiers' Orphans' Schools in Pennsylvania. Three years later, Governor John W. Geary appointed him as superintendent of the state-wide system. Following his move to Harrisburg, McFarland entered into a partnership in a large nursery and greenhouse operation. He also edited and published a weekly newspaper.

The former officer made several trips to Gettysburg following the war. He met Isaac Trimble there during a reunion of veterans who had participated in the opening day of the battle. As president of the 151st Pennsylvania's survivors' association, McFarland delivered the main oration at the monument dedication ceremony in 1888. He died three years later after coming down with pneumonia.[36] The Harrisburg *Star Independent* proclaimed that "As an educator and a soldier George F. McFarland will always bear an honorable place in Pennsylvania history."[37]

Captain Brice Blair returned home to Shade Gap, Pennsylvania, and following a lengthy recovery period, he returned to his business ventures. He also served as the town postmaster for about five years. Blair was eventually fitted with an artificial left arm. The old soldier was a great favorite of the employees of Blair's Stationary. He died of heart disease in 1890 at age 69.[38]

All amputees faced a difficult adjustment period, but for those who could not wear prosthetic devices, life was even more challenging. For many years, Daniel McMahon complained of tenderness in his stump, especially over its outer edge. He attempted to wear an artificial limb on several occasions, but the devices caused him too much pain. One wonders how Mary, his new bride, adapted to these difficult circumstances. The couple had no children during their long marriage.

Incredibly, Captain McMahon remained in the service following the amputation of his left leg. After a 60-day leave, he was assigned to detached duty in Alexandria, Virginia. Daniel received an honorable discharge from the army on June 23, 1864. Soon afterwards, he relocated to Washington, D.C., to begin a job with the Pension Office. McMahon, like Captain Blair, died from heart disease. He was 49 years old.[39]

Sergeant Francis Coates, only nineteen, and Michael Link, in his early twenties, faced greater obstacles than most disabled veterans as they struggled to adapt to a world of darkness. The parallel experiences of these two young men continued after their discharge from Philadelphia area hospitals. Both learned to read through the Braille system and received vocational training at the Philadelphia Institute for the Blind. Both developed into talented musicians. Coates learned the piano; Link played the French horn, violin, and accordion.[40]

In January of 1866, upon the recommendation of his former commander, William W. Robinson, Coates applied to the Federal government for the Medal of Honor, which he received in June. That same year, he returned to his hometown of Boscobel, Wisconsin. Less than a year later, he married Rachel Susanna Drew. Their marriage was blessed with two sons and three daughters. Through the Homestead Act, Francis acquired two tracts of land in Saline County, Nebraska. He moved his growing family there and took up farming.

Captain Daniel McMahon, 20th N.Y. State Militia (80th N.Y. Vols.). Courtesy of Seward R. Osborne, USAMHI.

It was noted that "His energy of body, mind and will were very great. He wrought on his farm and passed from place to place with almost as much accuracy as many who have both eyes can do, often taking care of his large stock without any assistance." Besides being self-sufficient, the veteran was warmly remembered for his benevolence: "Through his liberality, the sheriff was kept from many a door, many a table and wardrobe filled, and many a heart made happy."[41]

Although he overcame the limitations of his blindness, Coates suffered lingering pain from an abdominal wound that he had received at Fredericksburg. In January of 1880, he contracted pneumonia and died 10 days later. His family testified that his death was directly related to his old battle wounds. Sergeant Francis Jefferson Coates, Medal of Honor recipient and devoted family man, was 36 years old at the time of his death.[42]

Michael Link returned to Reading, Pennsylvania, and built two 3-story brick homes in the city. He also opened a shop where he cane-seated chairs. Michael seldom discussed his war-time experiences, but he never missed a Memorial Day celebration. He was a great favorite among other veterans for his jovial personality. Link died after an attack of paralysis on July 12, 1889, two months shy of his 50th birthday. His often repeated request that the three comrades who carried him out of harm's way should act as his pall bearers was carried out.[43]

Following his return to Augusta, Maine, ex-artillerist John Chase was married and eventually fathered seven children. Despite lingering medical problems from his multiple wounds, he lived to be 71. During his lifetime, the former soldier received 47 patents for various inventions, among which were an improvement to the hoop skirt and one for a new flying machine in 1909. John also served briefly as a guide at the Gettysburg Cyclorama painting. He was an early participant in the Florida land boom near the end of the 19th century. Chase died in St. Petersburg on November 28, 1914.[44]

Jeremiah Hoffman was promoted to captain of his company while lying in the Seminary Hospital, but he never returned to the field. He received an honorable discharge on November 21, 1863. Hoffman's injured right leg shrank in length and in thickness and could not bear any weight. The functions of the hip joint were almost entirely destroyed. Nearly two years after his wounding at Gettysburg, it was determined through a special examination that Jeremiah's disability was "permanent in character" and "total in degree."

Subsequently, Hoffman studied law and was admitted to practice in Lebanon County on January 4, 1866. A staunch Democrat, he also became active in local politics. Tragically, Hoffman died on July 29, 1867, at the age of 25 from the injuries he sustained after being thrown out of his carriage. The Reverend Darius Gerhard, historian of the class of 1862, Franklin and Marshall College, lamented, "Had he lived

to years of maturity there is no doubt that he would have attained a commanding social and professional position."[45] It was a strange way to die for a man who had survived the horrors of Fredericksburg and Gettysburg.

During the fall of 1868, Springs Avenue was constructed through the southern portion of the Seminary campus. This avenue carried travelers to a small rail line which trekked westward across Willoughby Run to the Springs Hotel, a magnificent four-story resort hotel that opened for business on June 28, 1869. During the heyday of the resort in the late 19th century, guests came from all along the eastern seaboard to partake of the luxurious surroundings.[46]

As a result of this popularity, the Seminary became an easily recognized tourist attraction. The building was mentioned in most of the early guidebooks devoted to the battle. In his 1886 handbook, J. Howard Wert provided comprehensive coverage of the Seminary's importance both during and after the battle, including the hospital period:

> After the battle it was for many weary weeks a hospital ... from every room of which resounded the groans of agony and pain. Within its walls Federals and Confederates were impartially nursed by tender hands to a new lease of life, whilst there many brave men breathed their last, far from their loved ones amid northern hills, or on western prairie, or on sunny southern plain.[47]

During the 1880s many Union regimental organizations erected monuments on the battlefield to mark the positions where they fought. Veterans from both armies frequently visited Gettysburg and fought the battle over on much more friendly terms. This interest was heightened during the 25th anniversary in 1888.

Seven years later, the United States Congress authorized and created the

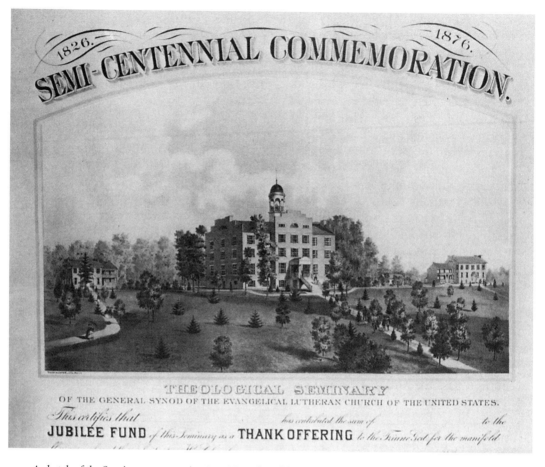

A sketch of the Seminary campus in 1876. Note the additions to the professors' homes. Courtesy of LTSG.

Gettysburg National Military Park. Over the years many improvements have been made to the park lands, including the construction of roads to facilitate visitor traffic.

Seminary Avenue was constructed during the summer of 1895. This avenue ran directly behind the three buildings on the campus and connected the Chambersburg Pike with the Fairfield or Hagerstown Road. The new road followed the course of an old lane which had been carved out during the first years of the institution. The required land was sold to the government for the nominal sum of $100. The name of the avenue was later changed to "West Confederate Avenue," and in 1999, simply to "Seminary Ridge." This public road has

provided millions of visitors with an up-close view of the historic campus.[48]

The Seminary played an active role in the celebration of the 50th anniversary of the battle in 1913. From June 29th to July 6th, approximately 55,000 veterans, both Union and Confederate, encamped on the old grounds and enjoyed the festivities as guests of the Commonwealth of Pennsylvania. At least 10,000 visitors came to witness the celebration. President Woodrow Wilson and 11 state governors participated in the formal exercises.

The Seminary served as the headquarters of the special guests of the Pennsylvania Commission. Together with the College, the institution entertained a total of 527 guests during the week. Among the dignitaries hosted by the Seminary were Lewis A. Grant, commander of the famed First Vermont Brigade; General Evander M. Law, who led a brigade in Hood's division of Longstreet's corps during the battle; Virginia Governor William H. Mann, who was also a Civil War vet; as well as descendants of Generals Meade, Longstreet, Hill, and Pickett.[49]

The Seminary was compensated by the state for the lodging it provided during the reunion. From these funds a semi-circular portico with six Doric columns was erected on the west side of the main edifice to commemorate the 50th anniversary. This addition converted the former rear of the structure into the main entrance.[50]

Interestingly, six weeks after the conclusion of the reunion, Mother Nature wreaked havoc on the famous cupola of the Seminary. On the evening of August 18th, a severe thunderstorm accompanied by high winds, hail, and torrential downpours touched down on Gettysburg. A bolt of lightning struck the cupola, and set it ablaze. The metal floor of the cupola together with the building's slate roof and the quick response of the Gettysburg Fire Department, prevented the further spread of the fire. Unfortunately, the historic structure, from which officers of both armies had surveyed the action a half-century earlier, was entirely destroyed.[51]

The mishap delayed the start of the fall semester by one week while repairs were being made. The Gettysburg *Compiler* of August 27, 1913, reported that the cupola would be rebuilt as a replica of the original so that "the old building will be preserved as it has always been known and remembered."[52]

The end of the war period ushered in a period of steady growth for the Gettysburg Seminary. The curriculum was expanded and the teaching force enlarged to four professors. After a sluggish period in the years immediately following the war,

attendance steadily increased throughout the remainder of the century, peaking at 74 in 1894.[53]

Propitiously, that same year, the cornerstone for a new administration building was laid a short distance south of the main edifice. Known today as Valentine Hall, the spacious French Renaissance structure was completed in the spring of 1895 at a cost of about $50,000. Up until this time, the original building had housed all of the institutions needed components: lecture halls, the library, the chapel, and dorm rooms. Now the older building was completely remodeled to serve as dormitory space. Also, by the end of the century, two additional professor homes had been built, additions placed on the original residences, and additional acreage purchased.[54]

This physical expansion continued throughout the first half of the 20th century. The most notable projects included a refectory or dining hall in 1910; the Church of the Abiding Presence, the school's first separate chapel, in 1942; and five years later, a new library, now known as the Abdel Ross Wentz Library.[55]

Following World War II, the student population spiked sharply upwards. Attendance passed the century mark for the first time during the 1948-1949 session. This growth continued steadily through the 1950s. Unlike past students, many of the new scholars were married. The directors of the Seminary recommended the construction of an apartment dormitory to better accommodate married students and to help alleviate the developing housing crisis. This project was completed in 1952 on the southwestern portion of the campus.

By this time the original building was referred to as "the Dormitory," which became simply "Old Dorm." The name was appropriate. During the 120 years of its existence, over 2,000 students had resided there.[56] However, the grand structure was

Lutheran Theological Seminary
Gettysburg, Pa.
Copyright by W.H. Tipton 1925.

showing signs of its age. As early as 1948, school administrators pointed out the need for a "complete remodeling of the old Dormitory so as to make the appointments within this old landmark worthy of the other facilities and the general standing of the Seminary."[57]

With limited financial resources, the Board of Directors decided that the construction of a new facility would be more cost-efficient. By 1954, Old Dorm was declared unsafe for occupancy. Three years earlier, President Abdel Ross Wentz had reported that the building would require "radical changes inside or else be completely removed."[58]

After the structure was vacated, the deterioration accelerated. At a Board meeting in May of 1957, the property committee offered two possible courses of action. First, the building could be removed and the area landscaped at a cost of $6,500. The other possibility required making temporary repairs to the structure until a lease agreement could be arranged with an interested party. Any preservation effort hinged on the financial support of concerned individuals and civic groups. Although the majority of board members favored removal, it was recommended that no action be taken until the next meeting in the fall.[59]

The possible demise of Old Dorm touched off a storm of protest. A letter to the editor of *The Gettysburg Times* from representatives of the Gettysburg Civil War Round Table and the Gettysburg Licensed Battlefield Guide Association expressed the sentiments of many:

> The loss of this priceless shrine would not only be tragic but would expose the citizens of Gettysburg to serious criticism…. History has endowed Old Dorm

with every right to live and be cared for. From its cupola the actions of great armies were prescribed…. The destiny of our nation is in some way connected with that cupola. The building provided a haven for countless wounded. Its walls and rooms are enshrined with memories. The history of a church and the history of the Civil War are drastically and intimately related to this old dormitory. A million tourists each year ask about Old Dorm on Seminary Ridge. Will they inquire someday what has become of it?[60]

Dr. Harry F. Baughman, the Seminary president, responded by stating, "I am on the side of those who would retain this building if it is possible and practical to do so. And I welcome any constructive and tangible proposal looking in this direction."[61]

The future of Old Dorm was the main topic of discussion at the November 14, 1957, Board meeting. A citizen's committee represented by Dr. Wilbur Tilberg, Dean Emeritus of Gettysburg College; Dr. Frederick Tilberg, Historian, Gettysburg National Military Park; and William G. Weaver, former mayor of Gettysburg, proposed that the building be made available to the Adams County Historical Society. They asked that the Board postpone any final action for another year to give them time to solicit funds for repairs. A lengthy petition endorsed by the Pennsylvania Historical and Museum Commission and by the National Trust for Historical Preservation was also presented. With some opposition, the Board agreed. Finally, on May 5, 1959, the Seminary's executive committee agreed to the terms of a lease that preserved the building as a historical site to serve as a repository for historical documents and artifacts relating to Adams County.[62]

Opposite: An aerial view of the Seminary campus in 1925. The new administration building is in the center of the image. Old Dorm is located just to the right. Author's collection.

A modern view of Old Dorm viewed from the west. All that remains of the Peace Portico is the concrete base. Author's collection.

It was discovered that the stringent regulatory codes established for dormitory space did not apply in full to the intended future use of the structure, considerably reducing the estimated restoration costs. Fire-proofing and safety upgrades began immediately, and the basic structure was stabilized. In 1966, a large grant funded an exterior renovation project. The building was sandblasted, bricks pointed, walls waterproofed, and woodwork repainted. Interior improvements, including a complete rewiring of the electrical system, were also completed. The building, now known as Schmucker Hall, was placed on the National Register of Historic Places in 1974.[63]

The growth of the Seminary continues. The size of the campus has expanded to 52 acres since the original 20-acre purchase in 1830. The number of buildings has increased to two dozen from the three that existed during the battle. As of 2001, the institution boasts a faculty of eighteen and a student population of two hundred men and women, as compared to the one professor and eight students present on inauguration day in 1826. The Lutheran Theological Seminary at Gettysburg now offers five degree programs and runs the Lutheran Center for Theology and Public Life in Washington, D.C. As of this writing, there are over 2,300 living graduates of the school.[64]

Learning from the previous crisis, Seminary officials are now trying to balance growth with preservation. Accordingly, on April 29, 1999, the Seminary Ridge Historic Preservation Foundation was incorporated as a Pennsylvania nonprofit corporation. The purpose of the foundation is to restore, preserve, and maintain the historic Civil War properties, architecture, and other legacies related to Seminary Ridge while providing educational and interpretive programs for the benefit of the public. Future plans include the establishment of a visitor center with exhibits and artifacts, a self-guided walking tour, and educational symposiums.[65]

To implement these objectives, The Commonwealth of Pennsylvania awarded the group a one-time planning grant of $250,000. At the check presentation ceremony, held on May 23, 1999, State Treasurer Barbara Hafer remarked, "There are few places in America with the historical significance of Gettysburg. In particular, the ground we stand on today. As you know, these historic buildings and this hallowed ground are forever linked to one of the most compelling and formative events in our nation's history. This spot is just as significant to the Battle of Gettysburg as Cemetery Ridge or Little Round Top.... But for too long, Seminary legacies and its powerful stories have been a well-kept secret — and these buildings have been deteriorating for lack of funds to properly preserve them all."[66]

"We are pleased that the state has joined with us in leading the stewardship effort ...", commented Seminary President and Foundation Trustee Darold Beekmann. "The importance of Seminary Ridge in American culture certainly involves knowledge about the battle itself, but it also extends to the monumental moral and cultural issues giving rise to the Civil War — issues such as slavery. The consequences of this great conflict continue to permeate our society today and deserve further exploration if we are to truly understand the American identity," he added.[67]

The price of establishing and refining our national identity was symbolized by the tragic events which occurred on the campus of the Lutheran Theological Seminary during the summer of 1863. The current slogan of the institution — "Bearing witness at the crossroads of history and hope" — embodies its proud past and its promising future.

No pen can write out those histories—no heart can enter into and be made fully to partake of those varied and unmingled sorrows, which identify so many thousand hearts, with the hills and fields, the rocky places, the swamps, the houses and barns around the lines of that terrible battle. Like the roll of the prophet, it must be written within and without, with lamentations and mourning and woe.

— Reverend Andrew B. Cross,
United States Christian Commission

Patient Deaths in the Lutheran Seminary Hospital

Name	Company/Regiment	Nature of Wound	Date of Death
Allen, Cpl. Thomas D.	A, 151st PA	unknown	unknown
Allen, Pvt. Morgan L.	C, 147th NY	left thigh	7/21
Aylesworth, Sgt. Edwin	G, 147th NY	right thigh	7/10
Barnes, Sgt. J. Edward	E, 126th NY	both thighs	7/12
Barnum, Cpl. William H.	K, 7th WI	bowels	7/16
Beechert, Pvt. Reuben	E, 151st PA	left arm	7/26
Brandstetter, Pvt. Charles	A, 2nd WI	left side	7/08
Briggs, Sgt. Jasper C.	G, 73rd OH	unknown	unknown
Brown, Pvt. Orrin	A, 147th NY	right leg	7/14
Bull, Cpl. Frank M.	D, 7th WI	thigh & ankle	7/09
Butler, Pvt. M.	I, 50th GA	unknown	8/01
Carlin, Pvt. Sylvan A.	A, 70th NY	head	7/21
Carpenter, Pvt. Samuel	E, 147th NY	unknown	7/10
Chancellor, Lt. Henry	B, 150th PA	left thigh	8/05
Christy, Cpl. John T.	F, 2nd WI	right foot	7/12
Clark, Pvt. Samuel J.	F, 126th NY	unknown	7/16
Cogswell, Cpl. Amos	F, 76th NY	right side	7/13
Contoil, Pvt. John	G, 6th US	lungs	7/05
Cowells, Pvt. John B.	E, 108th NY	disease	8/03
Cramer, Pvt. Samuel	B, 142nd PA	left arm & thigh	7/09
Cummins, Col. Robert	142nd PA	lungs	7/02
Day, Pvt. Charles E.	D, 94th NY	typhoid	8/12
Day, Pvt. Daniel	G, 126th NY	left thigh	7/20
Eason, Cpl. Alfred	E, 33rd NC	right foot	8/01
Fletcher, Cpl. Abram	K, 6th WI	left thigh	7/18
Garrison, Pvt. Mortimer	B, 126th NY	right leg	7/18
Grace, Lt. Newell	H, 24th MI	abdomen	7/03
Green, Pvt. Samuel R.	A, 5th NH	leg	7/30
Jones, Cpl. Joseph	A, 142nd PA	unknown	7/17
King, Pvt. George C.	C, 126th NY	unknown	7/05
Lamphear, Pvt. George	E, 76th NY	right lung	7/22
Lifflith, Sgt. Jose	D, 104th NY	leg	9/06
Livengood, Pvt. George	H, 151st PA	unknown	7/08

Name	Company/Regiment	Nature of Wound	Date of Death
Lohr, Pvt. George	D, 142nd PA	back, right arm	7/31
Lundy, Pvt. George	F, 7th MI Cav.	head	7/15
Lutz, Cpl. Cyrus	K, 151st PA	left leg	7/09
McCafferty, Sgt. William	C, 121st PA	back, left leg	7/12
McConnell, Pvt. George	I, 84th NY	left arm, lungs	7/08
Miller, Pvt. Anson	I, 151st, PA	left thigh, both knees	8/01
Miller, Pvt. Henry	B, 147th NY	right thigh	8/03
Miller, Pvt. Wilson	G, 90th PA	bowels	7/06
Mingle, Sgt. Elias	A, 148th PA	right leg	7/31
Morton, Pvt. Henry K.	F, 147th NY	left hand & wrist	7/25
Neelan, Pvt. Isaac	B, 14th VT	unknown	7/17
Palmer, Pvt. Mason	D, 24th MI	right arm	7/14
Ross, Sgt. Alexander	E, 140th NY	lung	7/09
Ruff, Pvt. Charles	D, 24th MI	arm & chest	7/22
Sain, Sgt. George W.	C, 7th WI	right hip	7/19
Schaefer, Pvt. George	A, 39th NY	knee	7/24
Schenck, Lt. William P.	D, 147th NY	shoulder	7/27
Scott, Pvt. John	D, 2nd WI	unknown	8/05
Sennott, Lt. John	A, 13th VT	forehead	7/16
Shaw, Pvt. Lyman A.	D, 12th IL	leg & both arms	7/24
Sherman, Lt. Jacob	E, 126th NY	left side	7/26
Siegfried, Pvt. Adam K.	H, 151st PA	unknown	7/03
Stamm, Pvt. William S.	G, 151st PA	right thigh	8/02
Stedman, Pvt. Levi	I, 6th WI	right lung	7/19
Straight, Pvt. John B.	E, 7th WI	head	7/22
Swart, Cpl. Abram	I, 20th NYSM	right thigh	7/25
Thiele, Pvt. John	I, 121st PA	left foot	7/12
Torango, Pvt. Louis	E, 76th NY	left thigh	7/22
Tripp, Pvt. David W.	A, 121st PA	unknown	7/06
Tucker, Lt. Andrew G.	E, 142nd PA	right arm & back	7/05
Upham, Cpl. Silas S.	G, 19th IN	unknown	7/13
Weber, Pvt. Henry M.	H, 151st PA	unknown	7/06
Wells, Pvt. John P.	E, 104th NY	left arm	7/20
White, Pvt. Henry C.	E, 16th VT	leg	7/14
White, Pvt. Pliny F.	E, 14th VT	right arm	8/05

The primary sources for this list are as follows: List of Deaths in Seminary Hospital, July 9 to August 7, 1863, Medical Registers 558 and 562, Seminary Hospital: Gettysburg, Pa., National Archives, Washington, D.C.; Busey, *These Honored Dead*; and the case histories from Barnes, *Medical and Surgical History of the Civil War.*

List of Surgeons and Medical Officers, Lutheran Seminary Hospital

Bache, Richard M.	surgeon on the staff of Maj. Gen. John F. Reynolds
Blakeslee, Amos C.	surgeon, 151st Pennsylvania
Fuller, Charles	civilian contract surgeon
Haines, Abraham	assistant surgeon, 19th Indiana
Horner, Charles	civilian contract surgeon
Horner, Robert	civilian contract surgeon
Huber, Henry S.	civilian contract surgeon
Jacobs, John N.	civilian contract surgeon
Janes, Henry	chief surgeon, Gettysburg area field hospitals
Kauffman, Jonas	assistant surgeon, 151st Pennsylvania
Leaman, Henry	civilian contract surgeon
Loughran, Robert	20th NYSM, surgeon in chief, Seminary Hospital, July 4–August 17, 1863
McCaffery, John B.	civilian contract surgeon
New, George W.	7th Indiana, surgeon in chief, First Division, First Army Corps
Osborne, William F.	assistant surgeon, 11th Pennsylvania
Ramsey, William R.	assistant surgeon
Reily, James R.	179 Pennsylvania, surgeon in chief, Seminary Hospital, August 17–September 8, 1863
Rulison, William H.	surgeon, 9th New York
Underwood, Warren	assistant surgeon, 151st Pennsylvania
Ward, Andrew J.	2nd Wisconsin, surgeon in chief, First Army Corps
Welch, W. W.	civilian contract surgeon

The primary sources for this list are as follows: List of the Medical Contract Physicians in Seminary Hospital at Gettysburg, Pa., Medical Registers 558 and 562, Seminary Hospital: Gettysburg, Pa., National Archives, Washington, D.C.; Barnes, *Medical and Surgical History of the Civil War;* and Coco, *A Vast Sea of Misery.* This list is not presented as a complete roster of medical officers who served at the Seminary Hospital. I have only included those whose presence at the facility either during or after the battle could be verified by official documents or other reliable sources.

Notes

Introduction

1. Michael A. Dreese, "The Saga of Andrew Gregg Tucker," *Bucknell World,* Vol. 26, no. 6 (November 1998), p. 21.

2. Lydia Catherine Ziegler Clare, "A Gettysburg Girl's Story of the Great Battle," circa 1900, Adams County Historical Society, Gettysburg, Pa. (hereafter cited as ACHS).

3. Gregory A. Coco, *A Vast Sea of Misery: A History and Guide to the Union and Confederate Field Hospitals at Gettysburg, July 1–November 20, 1863* (Gettysburg: Thomas Publications, 1988), p. 6.

Prologue

1. This excerpt and all subsequent quotes from the Bible are derived from the Contemporary English Version.

2. Diary of George F. McFarland, entry for June 28, 1866, Dr. Charles L. Eater, Jr., Collection.

3. John W. Busey and David G. Martin, *Regimental Strengths and Losses at Gettysburg* (Hightstown, N.J.: Longstreet House, 1994), p. 264.

4. Michael A. Dreese, *An Imperishable Fame: The Civil War Experience of George Fisher McFarland* (Mifflintown, Pa.: Juniata County Historical Society, 1997), pp. 9–10.

5. McFarland Diary, June 28, 1866.

6. *Ibid.,* June 28, 1866.

7. Varina Davis Brown, *A Colonel at Gettysburg and Spotsylvania* (Columbia, S.C.: The State Company, 1931; reprint edition, Baltimore, Md.: Butternut and Blue, 1991), p. 84.

8. Michael A. Dreese, *The 151st Pennsylvania Volunteers at Gettysburg: Like Ripe Ap-* ples in a Storm (Jefferson, N.C.: McFarland & Co., 2000), pp. 87–88.

9. McFarland Diary, June 29, 1866.

10. Dreese, *An Imperishable Fame,* pp. 142, 143, 146–148.

11. McFarland Diary, June 29, 1866.

12. Undated Newspaper Clipping, "Re-union of First Day's Fight," George McFarland Papers, J. Horace McFarland Collection, Pennsylvania State Archives, Harrisburg, Pa. (hereafter cited as PSA).

13. "Re-union of First Day's Fight," George McFarland Papers, PSA.

14. Gerald A. Patterson, *Debris of Battle: The Wounded of Gettysburg* (Mechanicsburg, Pa.: Stackpole Books, 1997), pp. 137–141; William Starr Myers, ed., "The Civil War Diary of General Isaac Ridgeway Trimble," *Maryland Historical Magazine,* Vol. XVII, no. 1 (March 1922), pp. 12–13.

15. "Re-union of First Day's Fight," George McFarland Papers, PSA.

16. John P. Nicholson, ed., *Pennsylvania at Gettysburg: Ceremonies at the Dedication of the Monuments Erected by the Commonwealth of Pennsylvania to Mark the Positions of the Pennsylvania Commands Engaged in the Battle,* 3 vols. (Harrisburg, Pa.: Wm. Stanley Ray, State Printer, 1914), Vol. 2, p. 770.

Chapter 1

1. Abdel Ross Wentz, *Gettysburg Lutheran Theological Seminary, 1826–1965,* 2 vols. (Harrisburg, Pa.: The Evangelical Press, 1965), Vol. 1, pp. 96–97; Samuel Simon Schmucker to "My dearest wife," March 3, 1826, Lutheran Theological Seminary File, ACHS.

2. Wentz, *Gettysburg Lutheran Theological Seminary,* Vol. 1, p. 98.

3. Mary Cecilia Kendlehart, "Our Village and its Future," Civilian Files, ACHS.

4. Henry E. Horn, ed., *Memoirs of Henry Eyster Jacobs,* 3 vols. (Huntingdon, Pa.: Church Management Service, Inc., 1974), Vol. 1, p. 8. Henry Jacobs was born in Gettysburg on November 10, 1844. He was the son of Dr. Michael Jacobs, a professor at Pennsylvania College during the Civil War. Henry entered the freshman class of his father's school in the fall of 1857, just prior to his 13th birthday, and graduated with the class of 1862. Wentz, *Gettysburg Lutheran Theological Seminary,* Vol. 2, p. 62.

5. Samuel Simon Schmucker to "My dearest wife," March 3, 1826, Lutheran Theological Seminary File, ACHS.

6. Undated newspaper clipping, Lutheran Theological Seminary File, ACHS.

7. A. Roger Gobbel with Donald N. and Elaine C. Matthews, *On the Glorious Hill: A Short History in Word and Picture of the Lutheran Theological Seminary at Gettysburg* (Lancaster, Pa.: Pridemark Press/Copy Print, 1990), p. 10.

8. Wentz, *Gettysburg Lutheran Theological Seminary,* Vol. 1, pp. 2, 5, 9–10.

9. George Wolfgang Forell, *Martin Luther,* Microsoft Encarta Encyclopedia 99, 1993–1998, Microsoft Corporation. According to this source, Lutheranism is the largest Protestant denomination in the world, with about 80 million members.

10. Wentz, *Gettysburg Lutheran Theological Seminary,* Vol. 1, p. 90.

11. *Ibid.,* pp. 85–86, 89. In 1797, the Hartwick Seminary commenced operations in Central New York State, making it the oldest Lutheran seminary in America. However, the school's remote location severely limited its sphere of influence. *Ibid.,* p. 69.

12. *Ibid.,* p. 87.

13. *Ibid.,* p. 99.

14. Gobbel, Matthews, and Matthews, *On the Glorious Hill,* p. 1.

15. Abdel Ross Wentz, *Pioneer in Christian Unity: Samuel Simon Schmucker* (Philadelphia: Fortress Press, 1967), pp. 1–17, 32–33, 61, 78; E. S. Breidenbaugh, ed., *The Pennsylvania College Book, 1832–1882* (Philadelphia: Lutheran Publication Society, 1882), pp. 154–157; Wentz, *Gettysburg Lutheran Theological Seminary,* Vol. 1, pp. 104–107; Gobbel, Matthews, and Matthews, *On the Glorious Hill,* pp. 12, 15, 25; Mark Oldenburg, "Happy Birthday, Samuel!: College Founder Samuel Simon Schmucker Celebrates his 200th Birthday," *Gettysburg,* Volume 90, no. 3 (Summer 1999), pp. 12–13.

16. Wentz, *Pioneer in Christian Unity,* p. 151.

17. Wentz, *Gettysburg Lutheran Theological Seminary,* Vol. 1, pp. 101, 147.

18. *Ibid.,* Vol. 1, p. 100.

19. Benjamin Oehrle to "My dear parents in the Lord," December 21, 1826, Manuscript Collection, Abdel Ross Wentz Library, Lutheran Theological Seminary at Gettysburg (hereafter referred to as LTSG).

20. Wentz, *Pioneer in Christian Unity,* pp. 145, 151.

21. Horn, *Memoirs of Henry Eyster Jacobs,* Vol. 1, p. 68.

22. Wentz, *Gettysburg Lutheran Theological Seminary,* Vol. 1, p. 130.

23. *Ibid.,* p. 141.

24. Breidenbaugh, *The Pennsylvania College Book,* pp. 95–97.

25. Wentz, *Gettysburg Lutheran Theological Seminary,* Vol. 1, pp. 150–152; William A. Frassanito, *Early Photography at Gettysburg* (Gettysburg: Thomas Publications, 1995), p. 68.

26. Wentz, *Gettysburg Lutheran Theological Seminary,* Vol. 1, p. 152.

27. Gettysburg *Compiler,* August 10, 1830.

28. Gettysburg *Compiler,* December 7, 1830.

29. Wentz, *Gettysburg Lutheran Theological Seminary,* Vol. 1, pp. 153–155; Gobbel, Matthews, and Matthews, *On the Glorious Hill,* pp. 18, 20; Coco, *A Vast Sea of Misery,* p. 6.

30. Letter printed in *Lutheran Observer,* Vol. II (October 1, 1832), p. 36.

31. Wentz, *Gettysburg Lutheran Theological Seminary,* Vol. 1, p. 156. A third professor's home was constructed on the campus in 1875 just south of present-day Springs Avenue. The structure became known as the Wolf House for its first occupant, Dr. Edmund J. Wolf. *Ibid.,* p. 239.

32. *Ibid.,* pp. 156–157; Gobbel, Matthews, and Matthews, *On the Glorious Hill,* p. 59. The path was filled with the residual tanbark from local leather industries. The tannin-rich bark of certain tree species was used to convert animal hides into leather. A number of leather-making facilities operated in Gettysburg to support the burgeoning carriage industry. It was customary in Gettysburg to use the bark remaining in the pits after processing as a paving material for walks. Horn, *Memoirs of Henry Eyster Jacobs,* Vol. 1, p. 67.

33. Gobbel, Matthews, and Matthews, *On the Glorious Hill,* pp. 20, 52.

34. Samuel Simon Schmucher, Report to Board of Directors, April 16, 1861, Abdel Ross Wentz Library, LTSG.

35. Wentz, *Pioneer in Christian Unity,* pp. 151–152.

36. Horn, *Memoirs of Henry Eyster Jacobs,* Vol. 1, p. 68.

37. Gobbel, Matthews, and Matthews, *On the Glorious Hill,* p. 64; Wentz, *Gettysburg Lutheran Theological Seminary,* Vol. 1, p. 158.

38. *Lutheran Observer,* Vol. I (January 16, 1832), p. 177.

39. Letter printed in *Lutheran Observer,* Vol. I (January 2, 1832), p. 174.

40. Wentz, *Gettysburg Lutheran Theological Seminary,* Vol. 1, p. 159, Vol. 2, p. iv.

41. Gobbel, Matthews, and Matthews, *On the Glorious Hill,* p. 4.

42. *Ibid.,* pp. 64, 66.

43. *Ibid.,* p. 70.

44. *Ibid.,* p. 73; Wentz, *Gettysburg Lutheran Theological Seminary,* Vol. 1, p. 189.

45. Wentz, *Gettysburg Lutheran Theological Seminary,* Vol. 1, p. 161.

46. *Ibid.,* pp. 188, 193; Oldenburg, "Happy Birthday, Samuel!" pp. 14–15; Gobbel, Matthews, and Matthews, *On the Glorious Hill,* pp. 23–26. For a thorough discussion of this controversy, see Wentz, *A Pioneer in Christian Unity,* pp. 195–242.

47. Wentz, *A Pioneer in Christian Unity,* p. 342.

48. Wentz, *Gettysburg Lutheran Theological Seminary,* Vol. 1, p. 391; Horn, *Memoirs of Henry Eyster Jacobs,* Vol. 1, p. 37.

49. Wentz, *Gettysburg Lutheran Theological Seminary,* Vol. 1, pp. 393–394.

50. *Franklin and Marshall College Obituary Record,* no. 11 (June 1907), Vol. 2, part 7, pp. 187–188; "Recollections of Visitations at Gettysburg After the Great Battle in July, 1863" by the Reverend F.J.F. Schantz, in Ralph S. Shay, ed., *Reflections on the Battle of Gettysburg* (The Lebanon County Historical Society, 1963), Vol. 13, no. 6, pp. 276–277, 285.

Chapter 2

1. William M. Artz to Mr. David Artz, May 14, 1861, Abdel Ross Wentz Library, LTSG.

2. Wentz, *Gettysburg Lutheran Theological Seminary,* Vol. 2, p. 1.

3. Mark M. Boatner III, *The Civil War Dictionary* (New York: David McKay, 1988), p. 598.

4. Wentz, *Gettysburg Lutheran Theological Seminary,* Vol. 2, pp. 46–47, 50, 51, 53. Interestingly, the 20th North Carolina was part of Alfred Iverson's Brigade, which sustained heavy casualties on the opening day of fighting at Gettysburg on July 1, 1863, within sight of the Lutheran Theological Seminary. Louis Bikle was not at the battle, however, as his enlistment commenced on November 13, 1863. Frassanito, *Early Photography at Gettysburg,* p. 383.

5. Wentz, *Gettysburg Lutheran Theological Seminary,* Vol. 2, pp. 1–57.

6. *Ibid.,* pp. 11–63. One of these soldiers, Cyrus S. Hoffa, died in combat while serving with the Union cavalry in 1865. In addition, two Union veterans entered the Seminary in 1863 following stints in nine-months units: Junius Remensnyder saw action at Antietam, Fredericksburg, and Chancellorsville as a member of the 131st Pennsylvania, while William Cornman, 130th Pennsylvania, received a wound at the battle of Fredericksburg in December of 1862.

7. John Chester Miller, *The Wolf by the Ears: Thomas Jefferson and Slavery* (New York: The Free Press, 1974), pp. 2, 3, 130.

8. *Ibid.,* pp. xi–xii, 2–3, 17, 47, 96, 131, 142, 168, 226.

9. *Ibid.,* p. 39.

10. Samuel Schmucker to "My dearest love," September 12, 1826, Manuscript Collection, Musselman Library, Gettysburg College.

11. Oldenburg, "Happy Birthday, Samuel!" pp. 12–13; Samuel Schmucker to "My dearest love," September 12, 1826, Manuscript Collection, Musselman Library, Gettysburg College.

12. Wentz, *Pioneer in Christian Unity,* p. 323.

13. Oldenburg, "Happy Birthday, Samuel!" p. 12.

14. Wentz, *Pioneer in Christian Unity,* p. 325.

15. Breidenbaugh, *The Pennsylvania College Book,* p. 157.

16. Wentz, *Pioneer in Christian Unity,* p. 318.

17. *Ibid.,* pp. 321–322.

18. Wentz, *Gettysburg Lutheran Theological Seminary,* Vol. 1, pp. 203–204; Wentz, *Pioneer in Christian Unity,* pp. 324–325.

19. Schmucker's unpublished manuscript was printed in its entirety with comments by Professor Mark Oldenburg in the Summer 1999 issue of the *Seminary Ridge Review.*

20. Samuel D. Schmucker, quoted in P. Anstadt, *Life and Times of Reverend S. S. Schmucker* (York, Pa.: P. Anstadt and Sons, 1896), p. 293.

21. Abdel Ross Wentz, "A Biography of the Schmucker House," *Lutheran Theological Seminary Bulletin: Gettysburg, Pennsylvania,* Vol. XXXVI, no. 2 (April 1956), pp. 10–11.

22. Stanley Appelbaum, ed., *Great Speeches: Abraham Lincoln, with Historical Notes by John Grafton* (Mineola, New York: Dover Publications, 1991), pp. 24–25, 35.

23. *Ibid.*, p. 61.

24. Wentz, *Gettysburg Lutheran Theological Seminary*, Vol. 1, pp. 202, 396–398; Horn, *Memoirs of Henry Eyster Jacobs*, Vol. 1, pp. 82–83.

25. *Lutheran and Missionary*, Philadelphia, Pa., October 31, 1861.

26. Wentz, *Gettysburg Lutheran Theological Seminary*, Vol. 1, p. 204.

27. Newspaper Clipping in Scrapbook of Samuel Simon Schmucker, Abdel Ross Wentz Library, LTSG.

28. Samuel Simon Schmucker, Report to the Board of Directors, August 11, 1862, Abdel Ross Wentz Library, LTSG.

Chapter 3

1. Eric A. Campbell, "The Aftermath and Recovery of Gettysburg," Part 1, *The Gettysburg Magazine*, no. 11 (July 1994), p. 102.

2. *Ibid.*, pp. 102–103; Horn, *Memoirs of Henry Eyster Jacobs*, Vol. 1, p. 8. The three newspapers were as follows: *The Adams Sentinel, The Star and Banner,* and the *Compiler.*

3. Frassanito, *Early Photography at Gettysburg*, pp. 2–4; Campbell, "The Aftermath and Recovery of Gettysburg," pp. 102–103.

4. Campbell, "The Aftermath and Recovery of Gettysburg," p. 102; Horn, *Memoirs of Henry Eyster Jacobs*, Vol. 1, p. 8.

5. Frassanito, *Early Photography at Gettysburg*, pp. 108–109; Horn, *Memoirs of Henry Eyster Jacobs*, Vol. 1, p. 9.

6. Tillie Pierce Alleman, *At Gettysburg or What a Girl Saw and Heard of the Battle* (New York: W. Lake Borland, 1889; reprint edition, Baltimore, Md.: Butternut and Blue, 1987), pp. 10–11.

7. Frassanito, *Early Photography at Gettysburg*, pp. 109–110; Robert L. Bloom, "We Never Expected a Battle: The Civilians at Gettysburg, 1863," *Pennsylvania History*, No. 55 (October 1988), pp. 163–164.

8. Michael Colver, "Reminiscences of the Battle of Gettysburg," The *Spectrum*, (Pennsylvania College Yearbook, 1902), p. 179.

9. Horn, *Memoirs of Henry Eyster Jacobs*, Vol. 1, p. 47.

10. *Ibid.*, Vol. 1, p. 49.

11. *Ibid.*, Vol. 1, pp. 47–49; Boatner, *The Civil War Dictionary*, p. 814.

12. Boatner, *The Civil War Dictionary*, pp. 136–140; 432.

13. Edwin B. Coddington, *The Gettysburg Campaign: A Study in Command* (New York: Charles Scribner's Sons, 1968), pp. 8–9.

14. *Ibid.*, pp. 11–12, 86–91; Douglas Southall Freeman, *Lee's Lieutenants*, 3 vols. (New York: Charles Scribner's Sons, 1944), Vol. 3, pp. 20–28; Wilbur S. Nye, *Here Come the Rebels!* (Baton Rouge: Louisiana State University Press, 1965), pp. 137, 147.

15. Robert McClean, "A Boy in Gettysburg—1863," Gettysburg *Compiler*, June 30, 1909.

16. Alleman, *At Gettysburg*, p. 20.

17. Lydia Catherine Ziegler Clare, "A Gettysburg Girl's Story of the Great Battle," ACHS.

18. 1860 Census Report, Gettysburg, Adams County, Pennsylvania. Emanuel Ziegler was listed as a 26-year-old lace weaver with no real estate, while Mary's age was listed as 25. Besides Hugh and Lydia, the other Ziegler children living in the Seminary at the time were most likely: William C., Jacob L., and George E.

19. Sarah M. Broadhead, *The Diary of a Lady of Gettysburg, Pennsylvania, From June 15 to July 15, 1863* (Gettysburg, Pa.: Privately printed, 1864), p. 5.

20. Clair P. Lyons to Adams County Historical Society, May 12, 1992, Civilians File, ACHS; Clair P. Lyons to Author, December 4, 2000. Mr. Lyons is the great-grandson of Sarah Broadhead. In numerous previous accounts it has been written that Sarah was a school teacher and Joseph was an engineer. According to Mr. Lyons, whose father spoke often of his grandmother, these statements are not true.

21. Broadhead, *The Diary of a Lady*, pp. 3, 6.

22. *Ibid.*, pp. 6–7; Nye, *Here Come the Rebels!* pp. 267–268, 271.

23. Horn, *Memoirs of Henry Eyster Jacobs*, Vol. 1, p. 1.

24. Bloom, "We Never Expected a Battle," p. 165.

25. Wentz, *Gettysburg Lutheran Theological Seminary*, Vol. 1, p. 204; Wentz, *Pioneer in Christian Unity*, pp. 326–327, 329. The informant was Dr. George Diehl, a Lutheran pastor in Frederick, Maryland. Diehl related the details of the incident in the January 1874 issue of the *Evangelical Review*.

26. Catherine Mary White Foster, "The Story of the Battle by a Citizen Whose Home was Pierced by Flying Shells: Some of the Things the People of the Town Went Through and What They Were Called Upon to Suffer," Gettysburg *Compiler*, June 29, 1904.

27. Horn, *Memoirs of Henry Eyster Jacobs*, Vol. 1, p. 70. Dr. Schaeffer arrived in Gettysburg in 1856, and taught German language and literature at the College and was inaugurated as the German Theological Professor at the Seminary. He was a leader in the conservative Lutheran movement. Wentz, *Gettysburg Lutheran Theological Seminary*, Vol. 1, p. 395.

28. *Ibid.*, pp. 212–213; Samuel Schmucker, Report of the Chairman of the Faculty, August 11, 1863, Abdel Ross Wentz Library, LTSG; Samuel G. Hefelbower, *History of Gettysburg College, 1832–1932* (Gettysburg: Gettysburg College, 1932), p. 203.

29. *The War of the Rebellion: A Compilation of the Official Records of the Union and Confederate Armies*, 79 vols. in 128 parts (Washington, D.C.: Government Printing Office, 1880–1901), Series 1, Vol. 27, Part 3, pp. 136, 145 (hereafter cited as *OR*).

30. Breidenbaugh, *The Pennsylvania College Book*, p. 420.

31. *Ibid.*, pp. 420–421.

32. Wentz, *Gettysburg Lutheran Theological Seminary*, Vol. 1, p. 206; Hefelbower, *History of Gettysburg College*, p. 185; Henry M. M. Richards, *Pennsylvania's Emergency Men at Gettysburg*, Papers Read Before the Soldiers' and Sailors' Historical Society of Rhode Island, February 1895, copy in 26th Pennsylvania Emergency Militia File, ACHS.

33. Klinefelter graduated from the Seminary in 1864. He retired from the pulpit in 1899 after a successful ministerial career, and died on July 28, 1903. Adam Stump, "Report of the Committee on the Death of the Rev. Frederick Klinefelter," in *Seventy-Ninth Annual Convention of the West Pennsylvania Synod* (Philadelphia: Lutheran Publication Society, 1903), pp. 51–53.

34. Breidenbaugh, *The Pennsylvania College Book*, p. 421.

35. *Ibid.*, pp. 421–422; Richards, *Pennsylvania's Emergency Men at Gettysburg*, pp. 5–6; Nicholson, *Pennsylvania at Gettysburg*, Vol. 2, pp. 785–786; Nye, *Here Come the Rebels!* pp. 158–159.

36. Nicholson, *Pennsylvania at Gettysburg*, Vol. 2, p. 784; Wilbur S. Nye, "The First Battle of Gettysburg," *Civil War Times Illustrated*, Vol. 4, no. 5 (August 1965), p. 13; Richards, *Pennsylvania's Emergency Men at Gettysburg*, pp. 7–8; Breidenbaugh, *The Pennsylvania College Book*, pp. 422–423.

37. *OR*, Vol. 27, Part 3, p. 914.

38. Douglas Craig Haines, "Lee's Advance Along the Cashtown Road," *The Gettysburg Magazine*, no. 23 (July 2000), p. 12; *OR*, Vol. 27, Part 2, pp. 464–465.

39. *OR*, Vol. 27, Part 2, p. 465.

40. Hefelbower, *History of Gettysburg College*, p. 189.

41. Broadhead, *The Diary of a Lady*, p. 7.

42. Richards, *Pennsylvania's Emergency Men at Gettysburg*, p. 9.

43. *Ibid.*, p. 9; Nicholson, *Pennsylvania at Gettysburg*, Vol. 2, p. 784.

44. Breidenbaugh, *The Pennsylvania College Book*, p. 423; Richards, *Pennsylvania's Emergency Men at Gettysburg*, p. 9; Nye, "The First Battle at Gettysburg," pp. 14–15.

45. Hefelbower, *History of Gettysburg College*, p. 193.

46. Breidenbaugh, *The Pennsylvania College Book*, p. 424.

47. Frank M. Myers, *The Comanches: A History of White's Battalion, Virginia Cavalry, Laurel Brigade, Hampton's Division, A. N. V., C. S. A.* (Baltimore, Md.: Kelly, Pieta & Co., 1871; reprint edition, Gaithersburg, Md.: Butternut, 1987), pp. 192–193.

48. Richards, *Pennsylvania's Emergency Men at Gettysburg*, pp. 10–11.

49. Hefelbower, *History of Gettysburg College*, p. 193.

50. Diary of Henry Wirt Shriver, quoted in Nye, "The First Battle of Gettysburg," p. 16.

51. Hefelbower, *History of Gettysburg College*, pp. 193–194; Breidenbaugh, *The Pennsylvania College Book*, p. 424.

52. Richards, *Pennsylvania's Emergency Men at Gettysburg*, p. 11.

53. Diary of Henry Wirt Shriver, quoted in Nye, "The First Battle at Gettysburg," p. 16.

54. Richards, *Pennsylvania's Emergency Men at Gettysburg*, pp. 11–12.

55. Nicholson, *Pennsylvania at Gettysburg*, Vol. 2, p. 786; Richards, *Pennsylvania's Emergency Men at Gettysburg*, p. 12.

56. Nicholson, *Pennsylvania at Gettysburg*, Vol. 2, p. 787; Breidenbaugh, *The Pennsylvania College Book*, p. 425; Hefelbower, *History of Gettysburg College*, pp. 195–196.

57. Diary of Henry Wirt Shriver, quoted in Nye, "The First Battle at Gettysburg," p. 18.

58. Hefelbower, *History of Gettysburg College*, p. 194.

59. Diary of Henry Wirt Shriver, quoted in Nye, "The First Battle at Gettysburg," pp. 17–18.

60. Frederick Klinefelter, quoted in Nye, "The First Battle at Gettysburg," p. 17.

61. Richards, *Pennsylvania's Emergency Men at Gettysburg*, pp. 15–19.

62. Breidenbaugh, *The Pennsylvania College Book*, p. 425; Nicholson, *Pennsylvania at Gettysburg*, Vol. 2, pp. 783, 788–789.

63. Richards, *Pennsylvania's Emergency Men at Gettysburg*, p. 5. Richards would have been more correct to assert that the 26th was the first *organized* body of troops to oppose Lee's invasion of the commonwealth. A contingent of about 40 men from Captain William H. Boyd's Company C, 1st New York Cavalry, contested the advance of General Albert Jenkins' Confederate cavalry the entire distance from Williamsport, Maryland, to Chambersburg. During a skirmish near Greencastle,

Pennsylvania, on June 22, 1863, Corporal William F. Rihl was shot in the face and died shortly thereafter. He earned the distinction of being the first Union soldier killed north of the Mason-Dixon Line during the Gettysburg Campaign. Coddington, *The Gettysburg Campaign*, p. 162; Nye, *Here Come the Rebels!* pp. 245–246.

64. Jubal Early, *Autobiographical Sketch and Narrative of the War Between the States* (Philadelphia: J. B. Lippincott Co., 1912), pp. 257–258.

65. Abstract of Meeting Minutes of the Board of Directors, Lutheran Theological Seminary, Gettysburg, Pa., August 11, 1863, Abdel Ross Wentz Library, LTSG.

66. Alleman, *At Gettysburg*, p. 16.

67. Broadhead, *The Diary of a Lady*, p. 8.

68. Robert McClean, "A Boy in Gettysburg—1863," Gettysburg *Compiler*, June 30, 1909.

69. Michael Jacobs, *Notes on the Rebel Invasion of Maryland and Pennsylvania and the Battle of Gettysburg* (Philadelphia, J. B. Lippincott, Co., 1864), p. 15.

70. Myers, *The Comanches*, p. 193.

71. Lydia Ziegler Clare, "A Gettysburg Girl's Story of the Great Battle," ACHS.

72. Broadhead, *The Diary of a Lady*, p. 9.

73. Jacobs, *Notes on the Rebel Invasion*, pp. 16–18; Bloom, "We Never Expected a Battle," pp. 166–167; Coddington, *The Gettysburg Campaign*, pp. 168–169, 647; Robert McClean, "A Boy in Gettysburg—1863," Gettysburg *Compiler*, June 30, 1909; *OR*, Vol. 27, Part 2, p. 465.

74. Jacobs, *Notes on the Rebel Invasion*, p. 17; Horn, *Memoirs of Henry Eyster Jacobs*, Vol. 1, p. 52; *OR*, Vol. 27, Part 2, p. 465.

75. Broadhead, *The Diary of a Lady*, p. 9.

76. Nye, *Here Come the Rebels!* p. 277.

77. *Lutheran and Missionary*, Philadelphia, Pa., July 9, 1863.

78. Horn, *Memoirs of Henry Eyster Jacobs*, Vol. 1, p. 52.

79. Jennie Croll, "Days of Dread: A Woman's Story of Her Life on a Battlefield," copy in Civilian Files, ACHS.

Chapter 4

1. Coddington, *The Gettysburg Campaign*, p. 172–175; Haines, "Lee's Advance Along the Cashtown Road," pp. 7, 15.

2. Gary W. Gallagher, ed., *Fighting for the Confederacy: The Personal Recollections of General Edward Porter Alexander* (Chapel Hill: University of North Carolina Press, 1989), p. 222.

3. *Ibid.*, p. 222.

4. J. F. J. Caldwell, *The History of a Brigade of South Carolinians Known First as "Gregg's," and Subsequently as "McGowan's Brigade"* (Philadelphia: King & Baird, 1866; reprint edition, Dayton, Ohio: Press of Morningside Bookshop, 1974), p. 95.

5. Abner Perrin to Governor Bonham, July 29, 1863, *The Mississippi Valley Historical Review*, (March 1938), p. 521.

6. Spencer Glasgow Welch, *A Confederate Surgeon's Letters to His Wife* (New York: Neale; reprint edition, Marietta, Ga.: Continental, 1954), p. 58.

7. Larry Tagg, *The Generals of Gettysburg* (Campbell, Ca.: Savas Publishing Company, 1998), p. 328; William M. Grace, *Isaac Ridgeway Trimble, The Indefatigable and Courageous* (Masters thesis, Virginia Polytechnic Institute, 1984), p. 26.

8. Henry Kyd Douglas, *I Rode with Stonewall* (Chapel Hill: The University of North Carolina Press, 1940; reprint edition, Atlanta, Ga.: Mockingbird Books, 1976), pp. 132, 207.

9. Myers, "The Civil War Diary of General Isaac Ridgeway Trimble," pp. 14–15.

10. Boatner, *The Civil War Dictionary*, p. 849; Stewart Sifakis, *Who Was Who in the Civil War*, 2 vols. (New York: Facts On File, 1988), Vol. 2, p. 284; Ezra J. Warner, *Generals in Gray* (Baton Rouge: Louisiana State University Press, 1959), p. 310.

11. Douglas, *I Rode with Stonewall*, p. 132.

12. Myers, "The Civil War Diary of General Isaac Ridgeway Trimble," pp. 5–6.

13. *Ibid.*, p. 9; Boatner, *The Civil War Dictionary*, p. 849.

14. Isaac Trimble to John Bachelder, February 8, 1883, in David L. and Audrey J. Ladd, eds., *The Bachelder Papers: Gettysburg in Their Own Words*, 3 vols. (Dayton, Ohio: Morningside, 1994–1995), Vol. 2, pp. 922–923.

15. Isaac Trimble, in R. A. Brock, ed., *Southern Historical Society Papers*, 52 vols. (Richmond, Va.: Southern Historical Society, 1876–1952), Vol. 26, pp. 118–121.

16. Isaac Trimble to John Bachelder, February 8, 1883, in Ladd and Ladd, *The Bachelder Papers*, Vol. 2, pp. 926–927.

17. Douglas, *I Rode with Stonewall*, p. 235.

18. Fletcher M. Green, "The Author and His Book," in Douglas, *I Rode with Stonewall*, p. 340.

19. Letter of Recommendation, Principal of Shepherdstown Classical School to the President of Franklin & Marshall College, September 8, 1856, Archives and Special Collections Department, Shadek-Fackenthal Library, Franklin & Marshall College, Lancaster, Pa.

20. Samuel H. Ranck, ed., *Franklin and Marshall College Obituary Record*, 3 vols. (Lancaster, Pa.: The Franklin and Marshall College Alumni Association, 1904), Vol. 2, p. 113.

21. Douglas, *I Rode with Stonewall*, pp. 16–17.

22. *Ibid.*, p. 17.

23. Douglas, *I Rode with Stonewall*, pp. 50–54, 153–154; Ranck, *Franklin and Marshall College Obituary Record*, Vol. 2, p. 114.

24. Douglas, *I Rode with Stonewall*, pp. 199–200, 212–219.

25. *OR*, Vol. 25, Part 1, pp. 1008, 1015.

26. Douglas, *I Rode with Stonewall*, pp. 154, 204–205, 352.

27. *Ibid.*, pp. 177–179, 234–235.

28. Coddington, *The Gettysburg Campaign*, pp. 180–181. The spy was Henry Thomas Harrison. For more information on this dramatic incident, see, James O. Hall, "Hunting the Spy Harrison," *Civil War Times Illustrated*, Vol. 24, no. 10 (February 1986) and Tony Trimble, "Harrison: Spying for Longstreet at Gettysburg," *The Gettysburg Magazine*, no. 17 (July 1997).

29. Issac Trimble, in Brock, *Southern Historical Society Papers*, Vol. 26, p. 121. This quote was according to Trimble's recollections.

30. Horn, *Memoirs of Henry Eyster Jacobs*, Vol. 1, p. 53; Bloom, "We Never Expected a Battle," p. 169; Jacobs, *Notes on the Rebel Invasion*, p. 21.

31. The following account was related by Martin Luther Culler in "Interesting Incidents Connected with the Battle of Gettysburg," Gettysburg *Compiler*, July 19, 1911. In the article, Culler does not identify his companion by name, but from clues in the article and an examination of Wentz, *Gettysburg Lutheran Theological Seminary*, Vol. 2, pp. 57–59, it is apparent that the individual was Washington Van Buren Gotwald. Gotwald entered the Seminary in 1861 after graduating from Pennsylvania College the previous year. He was born in York Springs, Pennsylvania, on November 10, 1836. Upon his graduation from the Seminary, he served as a pastor in the Emmitsburg charge from 1863 to 1866. Culler, a native of Jefferson, Maryland, was three years younger than Gotwald and a year behind him in the Seminary. He, too, was a graduate of Pennsylvania College. Martin joined the Christian Commission after completing his studies at the Seminary. He was ordained in 1865 and preached for nearly four decades in Pennsylvania, Maryland, and West Virginia. He also served as a director of the Gettysburg Lutheran Seminary and a trustee of Susquehanna University in Selinsgrove, Pennsylvania. *Ibid.*, pp. 57, 59.

32. Martin Luther Culler, "Interesting Incidents Connected with the Battle of Gettysburg," Gettysburg *Compiler*, July 19, 1911.

33. Daniel A. Skelly, *A Boy's Experiences During the Battle of Gettysburg* (Privately printed, 1932), p. 10, copy in Civilians File, ACHS.

34. Broadhead, *The Diary of a Lady*, p. 8.

35. *Ibid.*, pp. 11.

36. Coddington, *The Gettysburg Campaign*, p. 209; Tagg, *The Generals of Gettysburg*, p. 1.

37. *OR*, Vol. 27, Part 3, p. 61.

38. Coddington, *The Gettysburg Campaign*, pp. 225–233

39. D. Scott Hartwig, "Guts and Good Leadership: The Action at the Railroad Cut, July 1, 1863, *The Gettysburg Magazine*, no. 1 (July 1989), p. 5; Jeffry D. Wert, *A Brotherhood of Valor: The Common Soldiers of the Stonewall Brigade, C. S. A., and the Iron Brigade, U. S. A.* (New York: Simon & Schuster, 1999), pp. 188–189.

40. James L. McLean, *Cutler's Brigade at Gettysburg* (Baltimore: Butternut and Blue, 1994), pp. 1–15; R. L. Murray, *First on the Field: Cortland's 76th and Oswego's 147th New York State Volunteer Regiments at Gettysburg* (Wolcott, N.Y.: Benedum Books, 1998), pp. 2–3.

41. Dreese, *An Imperishable Fame*, p. 75.

42. Brown, *A Colonel at Gettysburg and Spotsylvania*, p. 84.

43. Dreese, "The Saga of Andrew Gregg Tucker, p. 20.

44. Michael A. Dreese, "Ordeal in the Lutheran Theological Seminary: The Recollections of First Lt. Jeremiah Hoffman, 142nd Pennsylvania Volunteers, *The Gettysburg Magazine*, no. 23 (July 2000), p. 102.

45. Biographical Sketch of Robert P. Cummins, George McFarland Papers, J. Horace McFarland Collection, PSA; Richard Sturtz, Somerset Historical Center, to Author, July 25, 1997.

46. Nicholson, *Pennsylvania at Gettysburg*, Vol. 2, p. 695; Barbara M. Croner, *A Sergeant's Story: Civil War Diary of Jacob J. Zorn, 1862–1865* (Apollo, Pa.: Closson Press, 1999), p. 37; Samuel P. Bates, *History of Pennsylvania Volunteers: 1861–1865*, 5 vols. (Harrisburg, Pa.: B. Singerly, 1869–1871), Vol. 4, p. 465; *OR*, Vol. 25, Part 1, p. 294.

47. Dreese, "The Saga of Andrew Gregg Tucker," p. 20.

48. *Ibid.*, p. 20.

49. *OR*, Vol. 21, p. 139.

50. *OR*, Vol. 25, Part 2, pp. 10, 12, 69–70.

51. Richard E. Matthews, *The 149th Pennsylvania Volunteer Infantry Unit in the Civil War* (Jefferson, N.C.: McFarland & Company, 1994), pp. 1–6; Thomas Chamberlin, *History of*

the One Hundred and Fiftieth Regiment Pennsylvania Volunteers (Philadelphia: F. McManus, Jr. & Co., Printers, 1905; reprint edition, Baltimore, Md.: Butternut and Blue, 1986), pp. 16–18, 32–35.

52. Obituary of Brice Blair, *The Huntingdon Monitor,* March 27, 1890; Biographical Sketch of Brice Blair, George McFarland Papers, J. Horace McFarland Collection, PSA; "Hon. T. A. Appleby Writes on Annals of Common People," *Huntingdon Daily News,* February 4, 1929.

53. Biographical Sketch of Henry Chancellor, Jr., George McFarland Papers, J. Horace McFarland Collection, PSA.

54. Ibid.

55. Dreese, *Like Ripe Apples in a Storm,* p. 23.

56. Dreese, *An Imperishable Fame,* pp. 6–7, 38.

57. *Ibid.,* pp. 96–100.

58. Seward Osborne, *Holding the Left at Gettysburg: The 20th New York State Militia on July 1, 1863* (Hightstown, N.J.: 1990), pp. 1–3.

59. *Ibid.,* pp. 4–5.

60. Pension and Military Service Records of Abram W. Swart, National Archives, Washington, D.C.; 1850 and 1860 Census, Saugerties, N.Y.; 20th New York State Militia Descriptive Book, Seward Osborne Collection.

61. Pension and Military Service Records of Daniel McMahon, National Archives, Washington, D.C.; Officer Biographical Information: 20th New York State Militia, Seward Osborne Collection.

62. Murray, *First on the Field,* p. 1.

63. Lucius Fairchild, quoted in Coddington, *The Gettysburg Campaign,* p. 35.

64. *Ibid.,* p. 35.

65. David G. Martin, *Gettysburg July 1* (Conshohocken, Pa.: Combined Books, 1995), pp. 24–25.

66. Richard S. Shue, *Morning at Willoughby Run* (Gettysburg: Thomas Publications, 1998), pp. 28–30.

67. Jacobs, *Notes on the Rebel Invasion,* p. 21.

68. Broadhead, *The Diary of a Lady,* p. 11.

69. Horn, *Memoirs of Henry Eyster Jacobs,* Vol. 1, p. 53.

70. Martin, *Gettysburg July 1,* pp. 27, 41–42.

71. *OR,* Vol. 27, Part 1, p. 923.

72. Alleman, *At Gettysburg,* p. 28.

73. Martin, *Gettysburg July 1,* p. 42.

74. William L. Heermance, 6th New York Cavalry, quoted in Marshall D. Krolick, "Gettysburg: The First Day, July 1, 1863," *Blue & Gray Magazine,* Vol. 5, issue 2 (November 1987), p. 23.

75. *OR,* Vol. 27, Part 1, pp. 923, 927.

76. Martin, *Gettysburg July 1,* pp. 43–46; Gary Kross, "Fight Like the Devil to Hold Your Own," *Blue & Gray Magazine,* Vol. 7, issue 3 (February 1995), pp. 9–10, 12; Edward G. Longacre, *The Cavalry at Gettysburg* (Lincoln: University of Nebraska Press, 1986), pp. 182–183.

77. Lydia Ziegler Clare, "A Gettysburg Girl's Story of the Great Battle," Civilian Files, ACHS.

78. Hugh M. Ziegler, "Lincoln's Gettysburg Address," May 13, 1933, Civilian Files, ACHS.

79. Kross, "Fight Like the Devil to Hold Your Own," pp. 10, 12; Longacre, *The Cavalry at Gettysburg,* pp. 182–183.

80. *OR,* Vol. 27, Part 1, pp. 923–924.

81. Quoted in Martin, *Gettysburg July 1,* p. 47.

82. Henry Heth, "Letter from Major General Henry Heth of A. P. Hill's Corps, A. N. V.," in Brock, *Southern Historical Society Papers,* Vol. 4, p. 157.

83. Lydia Ziegler Clare, "A Gettysburg Girl's Story of the Great Battle," Civilian Files, ACHS.

84. Horn, *Memoirs of Henry Eyster Jacobs,* Vol. 1, p. 54.

85. Daniel Skelly, *A Boy's Experiences During the Battle of Gettysburg,* p. 10.

Chapter 5

1. Horn, *Memoirs of Henry Eyster Jacobs,* Vol. 1, p. 46. While Dr. Muhlenberg did not serve in the military during the Civil War, his brother, Lieutenant Edward Muhlenberg, commanded the artillery brigade of the Twelfth Army Corps, which fought on and near Culp's Hill during the Battle of Gettysburg.

2. *OR,* Vol. 27, Part 3, p. 416.

3. Chamberlin, *History of the One Hundred and Fiftieth Regiment Pennsylvania Volunteers,* p. 117; McLean, *Cutler's Brigade at Gettysburg,* p. 52.

4. *OR,* Vol. 27, Part 1, p. 244; Martin, *Gettysburg July 1,* pp. 90–94; Dreese, *Like Ripe Apples in a Storm,* pp. 32–33.

5. Haines, "Lee's Advance Along the Cashtown Road," p. 24; Martin, *Gettysburg July 1,* pp. 59–61.

6. John L. Mayre, "The First Gun at Gettysburg," *Civil War Regiments,* Vol. 1, no. 1, p. 30.

7. Coddington, *The Gettysburg Campaign,* pp. 194–195, 281.

8. Lydia Ziegler Clare, "A Gettysburg Girl's Story of the Great Battle," Civilian Files, ACHS.

9. Hugh M. Ziegler, "Reminiscence of Hugh M. Ziegler of the Battle of Gettysburg Which Occurred on the First, Second, and Third Days of July, 1863," Civilian Files, ACHS.

10. Aaron Brainard Jerome to Winfield Scott Hancock, October 18, 1865, in Ladd and Ladd, *The Bachelder Papers*, Vol. 1, p. 201; Colonel Bill Cameron, "The Signal Corps at Gettysburg," *The Gettysburg Magazine*, no. 3 (July 1990), p. 9.

11. *OR*, Vol. 27, Part 1, p. 930.

12. Frassanito, *Early Photography at Gettysburg*, pp. 58–59; Shue, *Morning at Willoughby Run*, p. 37; "Local Woman Fled with Mother to Seminary Here," *The Gettysburg Times*, 75th anniversary edition, July 1938.

13. Frassanito, *Early Photography at Gettysburg*, pp. 59–60.

14. Timothy H. Smith, *The Story of Lee's Headquarters, Gettysburg, Pennsylvania* (Gettysburg: Thomas Publications, 1995), p. 4.

15. Aaron Brainard Jerome to Winfield Scott Hancock, October 18, 1865, in Ladd and Ladd, *The Bachelder Papers*, Vol. 1, p. 201.

16. *OR*, Vol. 27, Part 1, p. 927.

17. Lydia Ziegler Clare, "A Gettysburg Girl's Story of the Great Battle," Civilian Files, ACHS.

18. Hugh M. Ziegler, "Lincoln's Gettysburg Address," May 13, 1933, Civilian Files, ACHS; Hugh M. Ziegler, "Reminiscence of Hugh M. Ziegler of the Battle of Gettysburg Which Occurred on the First, Second, and Third Days of July, 1863," Civilian Files, ACHS.

19. *OR*, Vol. 27, Part 1, p. 927.

20. *Ibid.*, p. 927.

21. Thomas Day, "Opening the Battle: A Cavalryman's Recollections of the First Day's Fight at Gettysburg," *The National Tribune*, July 30, 1903.

22. John W. Busey, *These Honored Dead* (Hightstown, N.J.: Longstreet House, 1996), p. 29.

23. Hugh M. Ziegler, "Lincoln's Gettysburg Address," May 13, 1933, Civilian Files, ACHS.

24. Broadhead, *The Diary of a Lady*, pp. 11–12.

25. Martin Luther Culler, "Interesting Incidents Connected with the Battle of Gettysburg," Gettysburg *Compiler*, July 19, 1911.

26. Hefelbower, *History of Gettysburg College*, p. 205.

27. Colver, "Reminiscences of the Battle of Gettysburg," p. 179.

28. *Ibid.*, p. 179.

29. Daniel Skelly, *A Boy's Experiences During the Battle of Gettysburg*, p. 11.

30. Aaron Brainard Jerome to Winfield Scott Hancock, October 18, 1865, in Ladd and Ladd, *The Bachelder Papers*, Vol. 1, p. 201.

31. Tagg, *The Generals of Gettysburg*, p. 9.

32. Chamberlin, *History of the One Hundred and Fiftieth Regiment Pennsylvania Volunteers*, p. 111.

33. Tagg, *The Generals of Gettysburg*, p. 9.

34. Aaron Brainard Jerome to Winfield Scott Hancock, October 18, 1865, in Ladd and Ladd, *The Bachelder Papers*, Vol. 1, p. 201.

35. John W. De Peyster, *Decisive Conflicts of the Late Civil War* (New York: MacDonald & Co., 1867), p. 153. Some controversy exists as to where the initial meeting between Buford and Reynolds took place—at the Seminary, or on McPherson's Ridge. Historian Richard Shue carefully weighed all of the available evidence and concluded that it took place at the Seminary. See Shue, *Morning at Willoughby Run*, pp. 216–217.

36. Michael A. Riley, *"For God's Sake, Forward!" Gen. John F. Reynolds, USA* (Gettysburg: Farnsworth House, 1995), pp. 47–48.

37. L. Patrick Nelson, "Reynolds and the Decision to Fight," *The Gettysburg Magazine*, no. 23 (July 2000), p. 43.

38. Riley, *For God's Sake, Forward!* p. 48.

39. Robert McClean, "A Boy in Gettysburg—1863," Gettysburg *Compiler*, June 30, 1909.

40. Riley, *For God's Sake, Forward!* p. 48; McLean, *Cutler's Brigade at Gettysburg*, pp. 54, 57.

41. Horn, *Memoirs of Henry Eyster Jacobs*, Vol. 1, p. 55.

42. McLean, *Cutler's Brigade at Gettysburg*, p. 57.

43. Lydia Ziegler Clare, "A Gettysburg Girl's Story of the Great Battle," Civilian Files, ACHS.

44. Theodore B. Gates, *The Ulster Guard and the War of the Rebellion* (New York: Benjamin H. Tyrrel, Printer, 1879), p. 425.

45. "Local Woman Fled with Mother to Seminary Here," *The Gettysburg Times*, 75th anniversary edition, July 1938.

46. Riley, *For God's Sake, Forward!* pp. 49, 51; Martin, *Gettysburg July 1*, pp. 102–108, 140–141.

47. Busey and Martin, *Regimental Strengths and Losses at Gettysburg*, p. 239.

48. Joseph K. Barnes, ed., *The Medical and Surgical History of the Civil War*, 12 vols. (Washington, D.C.: Government Printing Office, 1870; reprint edition, Wilmington, N.C.: Broadfoot Publishing Company, 1990–1991), Vol. 11, p. 74. Under the direction of Surgeon General William A. Hammond, detailed case reports were submitted for each hospital patient. These individual histories were

categorized, analyzed, and later published as the above cited work. At times the dates given for a soldier's wounding appear to be in error. These inaccuracies are understandable considering the confusion which existed at the field hospitals. In such instances, I chose the date the soldier's unit was most heavily engaged. More accurate and detailed records of the patient's condition and treatment were usually kept after his evacuation to a general hospital. Hammond also initiated the practice of collecting specimens in the field, which led to the establishment of the Army Medical Museum in Washington, D.C., known today as the National Museum of Health and Medicine, Armed Forces Institute of Pathology.

49. Riley, *For God's Sake, Forward!*" p. 51.

50. Martin, *Gettysburg July 1,* pp. 156–161.

51. Lydia Ziegler Clare, "A Gettysburg Girl's Story of the Great Battle," Civilian Files, ACHS.

52. New York Monuments Commission for the Battlefields of Gettysburg and Chattanooga, *Final Report on the Battlefield of Gettysburg,* 3 vols. (Albany, N.Y.: J. B. Lyon Company, 1900), Vol. 3, p. 992.

53. McLean, *Cutler's Brigade at Gettysburg,* pp. 92–95.

54. New York Monuments Commission for the Battlefields of Gettysburg and Chattanooga, *Final Report on the Battlefield of Gettysburg,* Vol. 3, p. 992.

55. McLean, *Cutler's Brigade at Gettysburg,* p. 95.

56. Abner Doubleday, *Chancellorsville and Gettysburg* (New York: Charles Scribner's Sons, 1882), pp. 131–132.

57. Rufus R. Dawes, *Service with the Sixth Wisconsin Volunteers* (Marietta, Ohio: E. R. Alderman & Sons, 1890; reprint edition, Dayton, Ohio: Morningside Bookshop, 1984), pp. 167–168.

58. Lance J. Herdegen and William J. K. Beaudot, *In the Bloody Railroad Cut at Gettysburg* (Dayton, Ohio: Morningside, 1990), p. 193.

59. Dawes, *Service with the Sixth Wisconsin Volunteers,* pp. 46, 168; Herdegen and Beaudot, *In the Bloody Railroad Cut at Gettysburg,* p. 192; Busey, *These Honored Dead,* pp. 348–349.

60. Barnes, *The Medical and Surgical History of the Civil War,* Vol. 11, p. 241.

61. Dawes, *Service with the Sixth Wisconsin Volunteers,* p. 169.

62. D. Scott Hartwig, "The Defense of McPherson's Ridge," *The Gettysburg Magazine,* No. 1 (July 1989), pp. 15–16.

63. *OR,* Vol. 27, Part 1, p. 246.

64. Dr. George New to John Bachelder,

September 8, 1865, in Ladd and Ladd, *The Bachelder Papers,* Vol. 1, pp. 197–198.

65. George Worthington Adams, *Doctors in Blue: The Medical History of the Union Army in the Civil War* (Baton Rouge: Louisiana State University Press, 1952), pp. 60–61, 66, 68; Gregory A. Coco, *A Strange and Blighted Land, Gettysburg: The Aftermath of a Battle* (Gettysburg: Thomas Publications, 1995), pp. 154–157, 189; Louis Duncan, *The Medical Department of the United States Army in the Civil War* (Washington, D.C.: U.S. Government Printing Office, 1910), pp. 236, 271.

66. Barnes, *The Medical and Surgical History of the Civil War,* Vol. 11, p. 74.

67. Coco, *A Vast Sea of Misery,* p. 9.

68. Chamberlin, *History of the One Hundred and Fiftieth Regiment Pennsylvania Volunteers,* p. 118; Doubleday, *Chancellorsville and Gettysburg,* p. 136.

69. Harry M. Kieffer, *The Recollections of a Drummer Boy* (New York: Houghton, Mifflin and Co., 1883; reprint edition, Mifflinburg, Pa.: Bucktail Books, 2000), pp. 111–112. The corps ambulance train reported to the Seminary upon its arrival near noon. Duncan, *The Medical Department of the United States Army in the Civil War,* p. 237.

70. Dreese, *Like Ripe Apples in a Storm,* p. 34.

71. *Ibid.,* pp. 38–39.

72. Hartwig, "The Defense of McPherson's Ridge," p. 19.

73. *OR,* Vol. 27, Part 3, p. 488.

74. Hartwig, "The Defense of McPherson's Ridge," pp. 20–23.

75. Chamberlin, *History of the One Hundred and Fiftieth Regiment Pennsylvania Volunteers,* p. 120.

76. Allan Nevins, ed., *A Diary of Battle: The Personal Journals of Colonel Charles S. Wainwright, 1861–1865* (New York: Harcourt, Brace, & World, 1962), p. 235.

77. Richard Meade Bache, "Penned up in Gettysburg: A Surgeon's Experience During the Three Days' Battle," Gettysburg Newspaper Clippings, Vol. 6, Part 2, Gettysburg National Military Park Library.

78. Coco, *A Vast Sea of Misery,* p. 20.

79. Dreese, *Like Ripe Apples in a Storm,* p. 42.

80. *OR,* Vol. 27, Part 1, p. 323.

81. Pension Records of Abram Swart, National Archives, Washington, D.C.; Osborne, *Holding the Left at Gettysburg,* pp. 12–14; John D. S. Cook, "Personal Reminiscences of Gettysburg," in James L. and Judy W. McLean, *Gettysburg Sources,* 3 vols. (Baltimore, Md.: Butternut and Blue, 1986–1990), Vol. 2, p. 129.

82. Lieutenant Edward Ross to Colonel

Theodore Gates, July 6, 1863, Seward Osborne Collection.

83. Dreese, "The Saga of Andrew Gregg Tucker," p. 21.

84. Dreese, *Like Ripe Apples in a Storm,* p. 43.

85. *Ibid.,* pp. 43–44.

86. Horatio Warren, *Two Reunions of the 142d Regiment, Pa. Vols.* (Buffalo, N.Y.: The Courier Company, 1890), pp. 9–10.

87. Dreese, *Like Ripe Apples in a Storm,* pp. 45–46.

88. *Ibid.,* p. 48.

89. Kieffer, *The Recollections of a Drummer Boy,* p. 113.

90. Pension Records of Thomas Chamberlin, National Archives, Washington, D.C.; William Ramsey to John Bachelder, April 16, 1883, in Ladd and Ladd, *The Bachelder Papers,* Vol. 2, pp. 948–949.

91. Chamberlin, *History of the One Hundred and Fiftieth Regiment Pennsylvania Volunteers,* p. 130.

92. "Hon. T. A. Appleby Writes on Annals of Common People," *Huntingdon Daily News,* February 4, 1929.

93. "Report of Lt. Col. John Callis," in Ladd and Ladd, *The Bachelder Papers,* Vol. 1, pp. 141–142.

94. Barnes, *The Medical and Surgical History of the Civil War,* Vol. 8, pp. 326, 364; Roy Frampton, "Civil War Profiles: Sergeant Francis Jefferson Coates," *The Battlefield Dispatch: The Newsletter of the Association of Licensed Battlefield Guides, Inc.,* Vol. 27, no. 4 (April 1998), p. 2.

95. Hartwig, "The Defense of McPherson's Ridge," p. 24.

96. *OR,* Vol. 27, Part 2, pp. 656–657.

97. Brown, *A Colonel at Gettysburg and Spotsylvania,* p. 79.

98. Dawes, *Service with the Sixth Wisconsin Volunteers,* p. 175.

99. Robert K. Beecham, *Gettysburg: The Pivotal Battle of the Civil War* (Chicago: A. C. McClure & Co., 1911), pp. 80–81.

100. J. Michael Miller, "Perrin's Brigade on July 1, 1863," *The Gettysburg Magazine,* no. 13 (July 1995), pp. 25, 27.

101. *OR,* Vol. 27, Part 2, p. 661.

102. Brown, *A Colonel at Gettysburg and Spotsylvania,* p. 79.

103. *OR,* Vol. 27, Part 2, p. 662.

104. Gates, *The Ulster Guard,* p. 444.

105. "Final Story of Mr. Nowlan on Gettysburg Reunion," July 11, 1938, *The Greenville Advocate,* Greenville, Illinois.

106. John D. S. Cook, "Personal Reminiscences of Gettysburg," in James L. and Judy W. McLean, *Gettysburg Sources,* Vol. 2, p. 130.

107. Horatio Warren, *The Declaration of Independence and War History: Bull Run to the Appomattox* (Buffalo, N.Y.: Courier, 1890), p. 30.

108. James W. Downey, *A Lethal Tour of Duty: A History of the 142d Regiment Pennsylvania Volunteer Infantry, 1862–65* (Masters thesis, Indiana University of Pennsylvania, 1995), p. 31.

109. Michael A. Dreese, "The Saga of Andrew Gregg Tucker," p. 21.

110. "Hon. T. A. Appleby Writes on Annals of Common People," *Huntingdon Daily News,* February 4, 1929.

111. Lieutenant Edward Ross to Colonel Theodore Gates, July 6, 1863, Seward Osborne Collection.

112. Dreese, *Like Ripe Apples in a Storm,* pp. 58–59.

113. *Ibid.,* p. 63; Sheldon A. Munn, *Freemasons at Gettysburg* (Gettysburg: Thomas Publications, 1993) p. 30.

114. O. B. Curtis, *History of the Twenty-Fourth Michigan of the Iron Brigade, Known as the Detroit and Wayne County Regiment* (Detroit: Winn & Hammond, 1891), p. 189; Busey, *These Honored Dead,* p. 95.

115. Isaac Trimble, in R. A. Brock, ed., *Southern Historical Society Papers,* Vol. 26, p. 123.

116. Freeman, *Lee's Lieutenants,* Vol. 3, pp. 90–92.

117. Douglas, *I Rode with Stonewall,* pp. 238–239.

118. Isaac Trimble, in R. A. Brock, ed., *Southern Historical Society Papers,* Vol. 26, p. 123.

119. *OR,* Vol. 27, Part 2, p. 318.

120. William M. Grace, *Isaac Ridgeway Trimble, The Indefatigable and Courageous,* pp. 126–127.

121. Isaac Trimble to John Bachelder, February, 8, 1883, in Ladd and Ladd, *The Bachelder Papers,* Vol. 2, p. 930.

122. Tagg, *The Generals of Gettysburg,* pp. 270–271.

123. For additional reading on this controversial subject, see Martin, *Gettysburg July 1,* pp. 498–523 and Coddington, *The Gettysburg Campaign,* pp. 315–322.

124. Douglas, *I Rode with Stonewall,* pp. 239–240.

125. David A. Murdoch, ed., "Catherine Mary White Foster's Eyewitness Account of the Battle of Gettysburg," *Adams County History,* Vol. 1 (1995), p. 49.

126. Martin Luther Culler, "Interesting Incidents Connected with the Battle of Gettysburg," Gettysburg *Compiler,* July 19, 1911. Culler does not identify his companion in his account, but the available evidence suggests that the individual was Mahlon Horine, a

24-year-old Maryland native. Horine graduated from Pennsylvania College in 1861 and then entered the Seminary. Wentz, *Gettysburg Lutheran Theological Seminary*, Vol. 2, p. 58.

127. Hugh M. Ziegler, "Lincoln's Gettysburg Address," May 13, 1933, Civilian Files, ACHS; Hugh M. Ziegler, "Reminiscence of Hugh M. Ziegler of the Battle of Gettysburg Which Occurred on the First, Second, and Third Days of July, 1863," Civilian Files, ACHS; Lydia Ziegler Clare, "A Gettysburg Girl's Story of the Great Battle," Civilian Files, ACHS. There are several discrepancies in these memoirs. Most notably, Lydia wrote that her father, Emanuel, was with the family at the Seminary during the July 1st fighting and that he accompanied them on their journey. However, Hugh asserted, "My father was not home at the time." According to his recollection, Emanuel served as a civilian volunteer with the Union signal corps throughout the battle. Generally, there is a correlation between the accuracy of an account and the length of time that has elapsed since the event. Lydia's account was written near the turn of the century, while Hugh set down his recollections in 1933, 70 years after the battle. Thus, I have placed more reliance on Lydia's account whenever a major disagreement crops up.

128. Lydia Ziegler Clare, "A Gettysburg Girl's Story of the Great Battle," Civilian Files, ACHS.

129. Hugh M. Ziegler, "Reminiscence of Hugh M. Ziegler of the Battle of Gettysburg Which Occurred on the First, Second, and Third Days of July, 1863," Civilian Files, ACHS.

130. Lydia Ziegler Clare, "A Gettysburg Girl's Story of the Great Battle," Civilian Files, ACHS.

131. "Local Woman Fled with Mother to Seminary Here," *The Gettysburg Times,* 75th anniversary edition, July 1938.

132. Abdel R. Wentz, "Beautiful Silver Tea Service Stolen From Doctor Krauth's Residence on Seminary Campus by Confederate Soldiers During Battle of Gettysburg Rests in Church Home Here," *Gettysburg Times,* September 30, 1970; "The Great Battle of Gettysburg," *Lutheran and Missionary,* Philadelphia, Pa., July 16, 1863.

133. Charles P. Krauth to "Dear Aunt Jane," July 9, 1863, Civilian Files, ACHS; Elizabeth McClean, "The Rebels Are Coming!" Gettysburg *Compiler,* July 8, 1908. The Hankeys fed and housed nearly three dozen neighbors during the battle and their farm was utilized as a hospital for as many as 1,000 soldiers of Rodes' division. Coco, *A Vast Sea of Misery,* p. 130.

134. Eugene Blackford Manuscript, United States Army Military History Institute, Carlisle Barracks, Pa.

135. *Ibid.* Unfortunately, Blackford did not explain why the Union soldier was threatening the ladies, nor did he reveal the first names of the Schmucker women. Caroline Blackford, the wife of Dr. Thomas Blackford, was a sister of Samuel Schmucker's first wife, Mary Catherine Steenbergen. Since Mary had died in 1848, the female occupants of the house during the battle were undoubtedly her daughters. The most probable candidates were the two youngest — Alice, who was single at the time and living at home, and Catherine, the wife of William Duncan, a lawyer who resided near the square in Gettysburg. It seems likely that the ladies whom Blackford met were the same ones that passed out cool drinks of water to the arriving First Corps infantrymen on the morning of July 1st. It remains unclear why these women remained in such an exposed position for so long. Abdel Ross Wentz maintained that Alice and Esther Schmucker, Samuel's third wife, sought refuge with Catherine and William Duncan after being ordered out of the residence by Confederate soldiers on the afternoon of July 1st. Wentz, *Pioneer in Christian Unity,* pp. 329–330.

136. *Ibid.*

137. Broadhead, *The Diary of a Lady,* pp. 12–13.

Chapter 6

1. Duncan, *The Medical Department of the United States Army in the Civil War,* pp. 228, 237.

2. George McFarland, "An Hour in the Hospital," George McFarland Papers, J. Horace McFarland Collection, PSA.

3. *OR,* Vol. 27, Part 1, pp. 256, 263.

4. Dreese, "Ordeal in the Lutheran Theological Seminary," p. 106. On June 19, 1862, Union General George B. McClellan sent General Robert E. Lee a copy of General Orders No. 60, dated June 6, 1862, which stipulated that medical officers should not be held as prisoners of war and would be "immediately and unconditionally discharged." Almost immediately, the Confederate government reciprocated with a similar order. Horace H. Cunningham, *Doctors in Gray: The Confederate Medical Service* (Baton Rouge: Louisiana State University Press, 1958), pp. 130–131.

5. Alan D. Gaff, "The Indiana Relief Effort at Gettysburg," *The Gettysburg Magazine,* no. 3 (July 1990), p. 113.

6. Adams, *Doctors in Blue,* pp. 49–50, 65.

7. Dreese, *Like Ripe Apples in a Storm,* pp. 87–88.

8. Busey and Martin, *Regimental Strengths and Losses at Gettysburg,* p. 266.

9. Adams, *Doctors in Blue,* pp. 50–51, 118; Susan Provost Beller, *Medical Practices in the Civil War* (Charlotte, Vt.: Susan Provost Beller, 1992), pp. 19, 21.

10. Adams, *Doctors in Blue,* pp. 125–127; Beller, *Medical Practices in the Civil War,* p. 21.

11. For example, the 151st Pennsylvania and the 26th North Carolina exchanged devastating musketry volleys "at a distance not greater than 20 paces." *OR,* Vol. 27, Part 2, p. 643.

12. Adams, *Doctors in Blue,* pp. 114–115.

13. *Ibid.,* pp. 113, 115, 131–132.

14. *Ibid.,* pp. 117, 134; Beller, *Medical Practices in the Civil War,* p. 67.

15. Dreese, "Ordeal in the Lutheran Theological Seminary," p. 106.

16. Wilbur S. Nye, ed., *Thomas Francis Galwey: The Valiant Hours, Narrative of "Captain Brevet," an Irish-American in the Army of the Potomac* (Harrisburg, Pa.: Stackpole, 1961), pp. 101–102; Charles Carleton Coffin, *Marching to Victory: The Second Period of the War of the Rebellion, Including the Year 1863* (New York: Harper & Brothers, 1889), p. 231.

17. Dreese, "Ordeal in the Lutheran Theological Seminary," pp. 106–109; George McFarland, "An Hour in the Hospital," George McFarland Papers, J. Horace McFarland Collection, PSA; Samuel Simon Schmucker, Report of the Chairman of the Faculty, August 11, 1863, Abdel Ross Wentz Library, LTSG.

18. Dreese, "Ordeal in the Lutheran Theological Seminary," pp. 107–108.

19. *Ibid.,* p. 107.

20. *Ibid.,* p. 107.

21. Dreese, *An Imperishable Fame,* p. 143.

22. George McFarland, "An Hour in the Hospital," George McFarland Papers, J. Horace McFarland Collection, PSA. Since they were combat soldiers, men detailed from the ranks to serve on the nursing staff of a hospital were subject to capture by the enemy. Adams, *Doctors in Blue,* p. 68.

23. Lieutenant Edward Ross to Colonel Theodore Gates, July 6, 1863, Seward Osborne Collection.

24. Coco, *A Strange and Blighted Land,* p. 259.

25. *Ibid.,* pp. 257–258. Early on the morning of July 4, Lee sent a message to Meade in which he proposed an immediate exchange of prisoners "to promote the comfort and convenience of the officers and men captured by the opposing armies in the recent engagements." Two hours later, Meade responded that it was not in his power "to accede to the proposed arrangement." *OR,* Vol. 27, Part 3, p. 514. This exchange clearly illustrates the confusing state of the parole and exchange system at Gettysburg. Numerous Union soldiers who dutifully turned down the parole offer later regretted their decision as they languished in Southern prisons for many months.

26. Chamberlin, *History of the One Hundred and Fiftieth Regiment Pennsylvania Volunteers,* p. 311; Pension Records of Thomas Chamberlin, National Archives, Washington, D.C.

27. Surgeon Robert Loughran to Andrew J. Ward, Surgeon in Chief, First Army Corps Hospitals, August 16, 1863, Seward Osborne Collection.

28. George S. Bisbee to Mr. Babcock, September 23, 1863, Pension File of George S. Bisbee, National Archives, Washington, D.C.

29. Dreese, "Ordeal in the Lutheran Theological Seminary," p. 109.

30. "Thirteenth Regiment of South Carolina Volunteers of the Confederate States of America," http://hometown.aol.com/adj61/page3.html.

31. Dreese, "Ordeal in the Lutheran Theological Seminary," p. 107.

32. Cunningham, *Doctors in Gray,* p. 234; Adams, *Doctors in Blue,* p. 129.

33. Barnes, *Medical and Surgical History of the Civil War,* Vol. 8, p. 364; Vol. 11, p. 74.

34. Coco, *A Strange and Blighted Land,* pp. 164–166; Barnes, *Medical and Surgical History of the Civil War,* Vol. 11, p. 241.

35. Adams, *Doctors in Blue,* p. 135.

36. Dreese, "The Saga of Andrew Gregg Tucker," p. 21.

37. Barnes, *Medical and Surgical History of the Civil War,* Vol. 9, p. 88.

38. Adams, *Doctors in Blue,* p. 136.

39. Dreese, *Like Ripe Apples in a Storm,* p. 93.

40. *Ibid.,* p. 145.

41. D. Scott Hartwig, "The 11th Army Corps on July 1, 1863," *The Gettysburg Magazine,* no. 2 (January 1990), p. 48.

42. Barnes, *Medical and Surgical History of the Civil War,* Vol. 8, p. 316.

43. Adams, *Doctors in Blue,* p. 113.

44. Barnes, *Medical and Surgical History of the Civil War,* Vol. 7, p. 6.

45. *Ibid.,* Vol. 7, p. 2.

46. Busey and Martin, *Regimental Strengths and Losses at Gettysburg,* p. 292.

47. Duncan, *The Medical Department of the United States Army in the Civil War,* p. 259.

48. Barnes, *Medical and Surgical History of the Civil War,* Vol. 9, pp. 307, 312, 324.

49. *Ibid.,* Vol. 7, p. 85; Vol. 10, p. 671.

50. Cunningham, *Doctors in Gray*, pp. 134–139.

51. Duncan, *The Medical Department of the United States Army in the Civil War*, pp. 231–232.

52. Jennie Croll, "Days of Dread: A Woman's Story of Her Life on a Battlefield," ACHS.

53. Wentz, *Gettysburg Lutheran Theological Seminary*, Vol. 1, pp. 218–219.

54. George McFarland, "An Hour in the Hospital," George McFarland Papers, J. Horace McFarland Collection, PSA.

55. Harry W. Pfanz, *Gettysburg: The Second Day* (Chapel Hill: The University of North Carolina Press, 1987), pp. 429, 431.

56. Barnes, *Medical and Surgical History of the Civil War*, Vol. 9, p. 165.

57. Frederick W. Hawthorne, *Gettysburg: Stories of Men and Monuments* (Gettysburg: The Association of Licensed Battlefield Guides, 1988), p. 65.

58. Barnes, *Medical and Surgical History of the Civil War*, Vol. 7, p. 188.

59. *Ibid.*, Vol. 7, p. 105.

60. Adams, *Doctors in Blue*, p. 115.

61. Barnes, *Medical and Surgical History of the Civil War*, Vol. 7, p. 217.

62. Pfanz, *Gettysburg: The Second Day*, pp. 410–411, 414.

63. Barnes, *Medical and Surgical History of the Civil War*, Vol. 7, p. 221.

64. Pfanz, *Gettysburg: The Second Day*, p. 301.

65. *Ibid.*, p. 301; Barnes, *Medical and Surgical History of the Civil War*, Vol. 11, p. 179.

66. Barnes, *Medical and Surgical History of the Civil War*, Vol. 9, p. 92.

67. Harry W. Pfanz, *Gettysburg: Culp's Hill & Cemetery Hill* (Chapel Hill: The University of North Carolina Press, 1993), p. 151.

68. Pfanz, *Gettysburg: The Second Day*, pp. 387–389; Busey and Martin, *Regimental Strengths and Losses at Gettysburg*, p. 294.

69. Barnes, *Medical and Surgical History of the Civil War*, Vol. 8, p. 402.

70. *Ibid.*, Vol. 9, p. 312.

71. *Ibid.*, Vol. 7, p. 76.

72. *Ibid.*, Vol.9, pp. 81, 105, 406.

73. Broadhead, *The Diary of a Lady*, p. 14.

74. *Ibid.*, pp. 14–15.

75. Coddington, *The Gettysburg Campaign*, p. 443.

76. Douglas, *I Rode with Stonewall*, p. 240.

77. Hawthorne, *Gettysburg: Stories of Men and Monuments* p. 91; Barnes, *Medical and Surgical History of the Civil War*, Vol. 7, p. 219. Allen recovered and was transferred to the Veteran Reserve Corps on February 15, 1864.

78. Douglas, *I Rode with Stonewall*, pp. 240–241.

79. *Ibid.*, pp. 241–244; Henry Kyd Douglas to Miss Tippie Boteler, August 5, 1863, Rare Book, Manuscript, and Special Collections Library, Duke University.

80. Harold R. Woodward, Jr., *Major General James Lawson Kemper, C. S. A.: The Confederacy's Forgotten Son* (Natural Bridge Station, Va.: Rockbridge Publishing Company, 1993), pp. 6–29, 36.

81. Boatner, *The Civil War Dictionary*, p. 452.

82. Woodward, *Major General James Lawson Kemper, C. S. A.*, pp. 51, 53, 66–67.

83. Boatner, *The Civil War Dictionary*, p. 452.

84. Grace, *Isaac Ridgeway Trimble*, pp. 129–130.

85. Broadhead, *The Diary of a Lady*, p. 15.

86. Barnes, *Medical and Surgical History of the Civil War*, Vol. 9, p. 418.

87. Woodward, *Major General James Lawson Kemper, C. S. A.*, pp. 96–97.

88. *Ibid.*, pp. 97–99; Wayne E. Motts, *"Trust in God and Fear Nothing": Gen. Lewis A. Armistead, CSA* (Gettysburg: Farnsworth House, 1994), p. 45.

89. Grace, *Isaac Ridgeway Trimble*, pp. 132–133.

90. *Ibid.*, p. 133.

91. *Ibid.*, pp. 134–135; Myers, "The Civil War Diary of General Isaac Ridgeway Trimble," p. 12.

92. Grace, *Isaac Ridgeway Trimble*, pp. 136–137.

93. Woodward, *Major General James Lawson Kemper, C. S. A.*, pp. 100–101.

94. Joseph W. Muffly, *The Story of Our Regiment: A History of the 148th Pennsylvania Vols.* (Des Moines, Iowa: Kenyon Printing, 1904), p. 541.

95. Barnes, *Medical and Surgical History of the Civil War*, Vol. 9, p. 372.

96. *Ibid.*, Vol. 9, p. 99. Dowdy was exchanged in March of 1864. He died on December 9, 1905, in the Richmond Soldiers' Home. Frank E. Fields, *28th Virginia Infantry* (Lynchburg, Va.: H. E. Howard, 1985), p. 57.

97. Barnes, *Medical and Surgical History of the Civil War*, Vol. 8, p. 298.

98. Horn, *Memoirs of Henry Eyster Jacobs*, Vol. 1, p. 59.

99. Broadhead, *The Diary of a Lady*, pp. 15–16.

100. Horn, *Memoirs of Henry Eyster Jacobs*, Vol. 1, p. 60.

101. Martin Luther Culler, "Interesting Incidents Connected with the Battle of Gettysburg," Gettysburg *Compiler*, July 19, 1911.

102. Chamberlin, *History of the One Hundred and Fiftieth Regiment Pennsylvania Volunteers*, p. 152.

103. "Notes Regarding the 24th Michigan Vols. and its Commander Col. Henry A. Morrow," in Ladd and Ladd, *The Bachelder Papers*, Vol. 1, pp. 333–335; Curtis, *History of the Twenty-Fourth Michigan*, pp. 187–191.

104. Duncan, *The Medical Department of the United States Army in the Civil War*, pp. 238–239.

105. J. Howard Wert, "Little Stories of Gettysburg," Gettysburg *Compiler*, December 24, 1907, J. Howard Wert File, ACHS.

106. Dreese, *Like Ripe Apples in a Storm*, pp. 90–91.

107. *Ibid.*, pp. 91–92.

108. Chamberlin, *History of the One Hundred and Fiftieth Regiment Pennsylvania Volunteers*, pp. 152–153.

109. Barnes, *Medical and Surgical History of the Civil War*, Vol. 7, p. 215. Cunningham recovered and returned to duty on January 15, 1864.

110. Dreese, "Ordeal in the Lutheran Theological Seminary," p. 107.

111. *Ibid.*, p. 108.

112. *Ibid.*, p. 109.

113. *Ibid.*, p. 109.

114. Horn, *Memoirs of Henry Eyster Jacobs*, Vol. 1, p. 59.

115. Duncan, *The Medical Department of the United States Army in the Civil War*, p. 233; Coco, *A Strange and Blighted Land*, p. 153.

116. Broadhead, *The Diary of a Lady*, p. 16.

117. Frank Moore, *Women of the War* (Hartford, Conn.: S. S. Scranton & Co., 1867), pp. 176, 201.

118. Dreese, *Like Ripe Apples in a Storm*, p. 92.

119. Moore, *Women of the War*, p. 201.

Chapter 7

1. Dreese, "The Saga of Andrew Gregg Tucker," p. 21.

2. Dreese, "Ordeal in the Lutheran Theological Seminary," p. 107.

3. J. Howard Wert, "In the Hospitals of Gettysburg, July 1863," no. 11, *Harrisburg Telegraph*, September 30, 1907, Robert L. Brake Collection, United States Army Military History Institute, Carlisle Barracks, Pa. (hereafter referred to as USAMHI). This piece was part of a 12-article series printed between July 2 and October 7, 1907.

4. Frampton, "Civil War Profiles: Sergeant Francis Jefferson Coates," p. 2.

5. Barnes, *Medical and Surgical History of the Civil War*, Vol. 8, p. 326.

6. Dreese, *Like Ripe Apples in a Storm*, pp. 92–93.

7. Broadhead, *The Diary of a Lady*, pp. 16–17.

8. Horn, *Memoirs of Henry Eyster Jacobs*, Vol. 1, p. 61.

9. "The Great Battle at Gettysburg," *Lutheran and Missionary*, July 16, 1863.

10. J. Howard Wert, "In the Hospitals of Gettysburg, July 1863," *Harrisburg Telegraph*, July 2, 1907, USAMHI.

11. Henry W. Bellows, "The Field of Gettysburg," *New York Times*, July 16, 1863.

12. "The Battlefield," *Lutheran Observer*, July 31, 1863.

13. *OR*, Volume 27, Part 1, p. 28.

14. Adams, *Doctors in Blue*, pp. 4–5.

15. *Ibid.*, pp. 24–26.

16. *Ibid.*, pp. 31–38, 88, 92.

17. *Ibid.*, p. 91.

18. Duncan, *The Medical Department of the United States Army in the Civil War*, pp. 231–232; *OR*, Volume 27, Part 1, pp. 195–196.

19. Patterson, *Debris of Battle*, pp. 10–11.

20. Coco, *A Strange and Blighted Land*, pp. 152–153; Duncan, *The Medical Department of the United States Army in the Civil War*, p. 233.

21. Henry W. Bellows, "The Field of Gettysburg," *New York Times*, July 16, 1863.

22. Coco, *A Vast Sea of Misery*, pp. 148–149; Coco, *A Strange and Blighted Land*, pp. 216–217; Woodward, *Major General James Lawson Kemper, C. S. A.*, pp. 101–102.

23. David E. Johnston, *Four Years a Soldier* (Princeton, W.V.: David E. Johnston, 1887), p. 273.

24. "Not Killed," Gettysburg *Compiler*, July 27, 1863.

25. Myers, "The Civil War Diary of General Isaac Ridgeway Trimble," p. 12; Grace, *Isaac Ridgeway Trimble*, p. 137.

26. Charles M. McCurdy, *Gettysburg, A Memoir* (Pittsburgh, Pa.: Reed & Witting, 1929), p. 9.

27. Henry Kyd Douglas to Miss Tippie Boteler, August 5, 1863, Rare Book, Manuscript, and Special Collections Library, Duke University.

28. Douglas, *I Rode with Stonewall*, pp. 243–244.

29. *OR*, Volume 27, Part 1, p. 79.

30. *Ibid.*, pp. 195–199.

31. *Ibid.*, p. 197; Duncan, *The Medical Department of the United States Army in the Civil War*, pp. 234–235.

32. Patterson, *Debris of Battle*, p. 211.

33. Charles J. Stille, *History of the United States Sanitary Commission* (Philadelphia: J.B. Lippincott, 1866), pp. 388–389.

34. *OR*, Vol. 27, Part 1, p. 28.

35. Patterson, *Debris of Battle*, pp. 39–41;

Adams, *Doctors in Blue,* pp. 5–9. Initially, official Washington considered the agency to be superfluous and intrusive, but bowed to public pressure in approving it. Lincoln compared the new commission to "a fifth wheel on the coach." However, by the end of the war, even the organization's biggest critics had been won over. The group supplemented its limited funds by holding huge sanitary fairs in cities across the North. All told, these efforts pulled in over four million dollars. See Donald Dale Jackson, *Twenty Million Yankees: The Northern Home Front* (Alexandria, Va.: Time-Life Books, 1985), pp. 116–135. Sarah Broadhead donated 75 copies of the first edition of her published diary to the Great Central Fair in Philadelphia "to aid the Sanitary Commission in its holy work of succoring the wounded soldiers of the Union army." Broadhead, *The Diary of a Lady,* pp. 3–4.

36. Stille, *History of the United States Sanitary Commission,* pp. 376–381; Henry W. Bellows, "The Field of Gettysburg," *New York Times,* July 16, 1863; Frassanito, *Early Photography at Gettysburg,* pp. 98–99.

37. Frassanito, *Early Photography at Gettysburg,* p. 96.

38. Patterson, *Debris of Battle,* pp. 87–88.

39. "Delegates Wanted," *Lutheran and Missionary,* July 9, 1863.

40. "Telegraph from the Battlefield to the United States Christian Commission," July 7, 1863, *Philadelphia Inquirer,* July 10, 1863. The pressing need for shirts and drawers was due to the fact that the clothing of the wounded almost always had to be cut to facilitate treatment. Besides, it was obviously not desirable for the men to remain in dirty, blood-stained clothing. Cunningham, *Doctors in Gray,* p. 113.

41. Andrew B. Cross, *Battle of Gettysburg and the Christian Commission* (Baltimore, Md.: United States Christian Commission, 1865), pp. 17–18.

42. United States Christian Commission, *Second Report of the Committee of Maryland* (Baltimore, Md.: Sherwood & Co., 1863), pp. 90–91.

43. Hon. T. A. Appleby Writes on Annals of Common People," *Huntingdon Daily News,* February 4, 1929.

44. Biographical Sketch of Henry Chancellor, Jr., George McFarland Papers, J. Horace McFarland Collection, PSA.

45. *Ibid.*

46. Henry W. Bellows, "The Field of Gettysburg," *New York Times,* July 16, 1863.

47. "The Great Battle of Gettysburg," *Lutheran and Missionary,* July 16, 1863.

48. Cross, *Battle of Gettysburg and the Christian Commission,* p. 18.

49. United States Christian Commission, *Second Report of the Committee of Maryland,* pp. 32–33.

50. *OR,* Vol. 27, Part 1, p. 25.

51. United States Christian Commission, *Second Annual Report* (Philadelphia: United States Christian Commission, 1864), pp. 82–83.

52. Broadhead, *The Diary of a Lady,* p. 21.

53. *OR,* Vol. 27, Part 1, p. 28.

54. Broadhead, *The Diary of a Lady,* pp. 18–19.

55. Lydia Catherine Ziegler Clare, "A Gettysburg Girl's Story of the Great Battle," ACHS.

56. *Ibid.*

57. Hugh M. Ziegler, "Reminiscence of Hugh M. Ziegler of the Battle of Gettysburg Which Occurred on the First, Second, and Third Days of July, 1863," ACHS.

58. Martin Luther Culler, "Interesting Incidents Connected with the Battle of Gettysburg," Gettysburg *Compiler,* July 19, 1911.

59. Wentz, *Gettysburg Lutheran Theological Seminary,* Vol. 1, p. 213. Not everyone was as fortunate as Holloway. One report declared that "the private property of students, such as furniture, clothing, and books, was either stolen or destroyed, or rendered utterly useless, by the rebels." Proceedings of the 22nd Annual Convention of the Evangelical Lutheran Synod of East Pennsylvania, Lutheran Theological Seminary File, ACHS. During their August 11, 1863, meeting, the Board of Directors of the Lutheran Theological Seminary passed a resolution "to seek funds to compensate students for losses they suffered during the battle." Abstract of Meeting Minutes of the Board of Directors, Lutheran Theological Seminary, Gettysburg, Pa., August 11, 1863, Abdel Ross Wentz Library, LTSG.

60. "Gettysburg During the Battle," *Lutheran and Missionary,* July 16, 1863.

61. Elizabeth McClean, "The Rebels Are Coming!" Gettysburg *Compiler,* July 8, 1908; Abdel R. Wentz, "Beautiful Silver Tea Service Stolen From Doctor Krauth's Residence on Seminary Campus by Confederate Soldiers During Battle of Gettysburg Rests in Church Home Here," *Gettysburg Times,* September 30, 1970.

62. Charles Krauth, letter of July 13, 1863, printed in *Lutheran and Missionary,* July 23, 1863; Charles Krauth to "Dear Aunt Jane," July 9, 1863, Civilian Files, ACHS; Elizabeth McClean, "The Rebels Are Coming!" Gettysburg *Compiler,* July 8, 1908.

63. Charles Krauth to "Dear Aunt Jane," July 9, 1863, Civilian Files, ACHS.

64. Charles Krauth, letter of July 13, 1863, printed in *Lutheran and Missionary,* July 23, 1863.

65. Samuel Schmucker, Report of the Chairman of the Faculty, August 11, 1863, Abdel Ross Wentz Library, LTSG. One of these shells is still embedded in the south wall of the Schmucker house. Historian Timothy Smith identified the projectile as a shell from a 10-pounder Parrot Rifle. Smith believes it was fired from a Union gun positioned on Cemetery Hill. Timothy Smith, "A Tour of Gettysburg's Visual Battle Damage," *Adams County History*, Vol. 2 (1996), p. 55.

66. Samuel Schmucker, Report of the Chairman of the Faculty, August 11, 1863, Abdel Ross Wentz Library, LTSG.

67. Wentz, "A Biography of the Schmucker House," p. 12.

68. Damage Claim of Samuel S. Schmucker, Quartermaster Claim 214–719, box 608, National Archives, Washington, D.C. This file was located by Gettysburg Licensed Battlefield Guide Jim Clouse. The Federal Claims Act of July 4, 1864, only allowed reimbursement for damages caused by Union soldiers before and after the battle. Thus, the claim was rejected.

69. Gobbel, Matthews, and Matthews, *On the Glorious Hill*, p. 29. The Bible is on display in the Abdel Ross Wentz Library at the Lutheran Theological Seminary, in Gettysburg. The exact identity of the Confederate soldier remains elusive. A search by Gettysburg Licensed Battlefield Guide Jim Clouse revealed only one name that matches the signature. First Lieutenant John G. Bearden served in Company F, 2nd Mississippi Infantry, which fought near the Seminary campus on July 1st. However, as Clouse points out, the poor grammar and spelling which appear on the Bible are inconsistent with that of a commissioned officer. Jim Clouse, "Samuel Simon Schmucker," *The Battlefield Dispatch: The Newsletter of the Association of Licensed Battlefield Guides, Inc.*, Vol. 28, no. 7 (July 1999), p. 10.

70. John T. Slentz to Edward McPherson, August 10, 1863, Edward McPherson Papers, Library of Congress, Washington, D.C.

71. Coco, *A Vast Sea of Misery*, pp. 20–21; Jennie Croll, "Days of Dread: A Woman's Story of Her Life on a Battlefield," ACHS. One of the doctors at Christ Lutheran was Assistant Surgeon William F. Osborn of the 11th Pennsylvania. Osborn remained at the Seminary Hospital on July 1st until the First Corps fell back. He then made his way to the church, which had been previously selected as the Second Division hospital. William F. Osborn, "Letter of Union Surgeon," Gettysburg Newspaper Clippings, Vol. 6, Gettysburg National Military Park Library.

72. "The Great Battle at Gettysburg," *Lutheran and Missionary,* July 16, 1863.

73. Colver, "Reminiscences of the Battle of Gettysburg," p. 180.

74. Henry W. Bellows, "The Field of Gettysburg," *New York Times,* July 16, 1863.

75. Broadhead, *The Diary of a Lady*, pp. 19–20. During a meeting of the Board of Directors later in the summer, Dr. Schmucker reported that "the joists on the first floor of the seminary edifice were rotten, because [of] the pavements being too high around the building." The lack of adequate drainage away from the building, combined with the heavy rain storms following the battle, apparently caused the flooding in the basement. Abstract of Meeting Minutes of the Board of Directors, Lutheran Theological Seminary, August 11, 1863, Abdel Ross Wentz Library, LTSG.

76. List of Female Nurses at the Seminary Hospital, Medical Registers 558 and 562, Seminary Hospital: Gettysburg, Pa., National Archives, Washington, D.C.; Patterson, *The Debris of Battle*, pp. 100–105; Ruth W. Davis, "Behind the Battle of Gettysburg: American Nursing Is Born," *Pennsylvania Heritage*, Vol. 13 (Fall 1987), pp. 11–15.

77. Dreese, *An Imperishable Fame*, p. 147.

78. Eileen F. Conklin, *Women at Gettysburg 1863* (Gettysburg: Thomas Publications, 1993), p. 212.

79. Virginia Walcott Beauchamp, "The Sisters and the Soldiers," *Maryland Historical Magazine*, Vol. 81, no. 2 (Summer 1986), p. 118.

80. Conklin, *Women at Gettysburg 1863*, p. 401. As per an agreement with Federal authorities, the Government provided the Sisters with lodging, food, clothing, and travel expenses. They were also allowed complete freedom at the hospitals and did not wish to work with other female volunteers since they "would be rather an encumbrance than a help." Beauchamp, "The Sisters and the Soldiers," pp. 131–132.

A medical register lists four Sisters of Charity as being on duty at the Seminary Hospital: Sister Gabriella [Rigney], Sister Melia (possibly Ameliana Schroeder), Sister Annie [McShane or Ewers], and Sister Mary Ellen [Farrell or Shaw]. List of Female Nurses, Medical Registers 558 and 562, Seminary Hospital: Gettysburg, Pa., National Archives, Washington, D.C.

81. Conklin, *Women at Gettysburg 1863*, p. 210.

82. J. R. Balsley, "A Gettysburg Reminiscence," *National Tribune*, May 19, 1898.

83. Martha Ehler, *Hospital Scenes After the Battle of Gettysburg, July 1863* (Philadelphia: Henry B. Ashmead, 1864; Reprint, Gettysburg: G. Craig Caba, 1993), pp. 21–22.

84. Broadhead, *The Diary of a Lady*, pp. 21–22.

85. Patterson, *Debris of Battle,* pp. 50, 52.

86. Adams, *Doctors in Blue,* p. 88.

87. Biographical Sketch of Andrew J. Ward, George McFarland Papers, J. Horace McFarland Collection, PSA.

88. Biographical Sketch of Henry Leaman, Archives Collection, Franklin & Marshall College, Lancaster, Pa.

89. Robert Loughran to Gettysburg Cemetery Association, August 17, 1869, Gettysburg Cemetery Association Files, Gettysburg College Archives, Gettysburg, Pa.; Biographical Sketch of Robert Loughran, George McFarland Papers, J. Horace McFarland Collection, PSA.

90. *OR,* Vol. 27, Part 1, p. 329; W. C. Storrick, *Gettysburg: The Place, The Battles, The Outcome* (Harrisburg, Pa.: J. Horace McFarland Company, 1932), p. 146.

91. Jeffrey B. Roth, "Civil War Medicine at Gettysburg," *The Gettysburg Hospital Quarterly,* Vol. 1, no. 1 (Spring 1985), p. 3.

92. Hugh M. Ziegler, "Reminiscence of Hugh M. Ziegler of the Battle of Gettysburg Which Occurred on the First, Second, and Third Days of July, 1863," ACHS.

93. Pension Records of Daniel McMahon, National Archives, Washington, D.C.

94. Pension Records of Abram Swart, National Archives, Washington, D.C.

95. Busey, *These Honored Dead,* p. 283.

96. Beller, *Medical Practices in the Civil War,* p. 69; Busey, *These Honored Dead,* p. 205.

97. Henry W. Bellows, "The Field of Gettysburg," *New York Times,* July 16, 1863; Elizabeth McClean, "The Rebels Are Coming!" Gettysburg *Compiler,* July 8, 1908; Broadhead, *The Diary of a Lady,* p. 22.

98. *Union County Star and Lewisburg Chronicle,* July 10, 1863.

99. J. Howard Wert, "In the Hospitals of Gettysburg," *Harrisburg Telegraph,* July 25, 1907, USAMHI.

100. Broadhead, *The Diary of a Lady,* pp. 22–23.

101. Lydia Catherine Ziegler Clare, "A Gettysburg Girl's Story of the Great Battle," ACHS.

102. Dreese, "The Saga of Andrew Gregg Tucker," p. 21.

103. Dreese, *An Imperishable Fame,* pp. 143–144.

104. Dreese, *Like Ripe Apples in a Storm,* p. 94.

105. *Ibid.,* pp. 94–95.

106. Broadhead, *The Diary of a Lady,* pp. 23–24; Mr. Clair P. Lyons to Author, December 4 & December 10, 2000. Mr. Lyons is in possession of Sarah Broadhead's handwritten diary from which she fashioned her published account. Apparently, Sarah took the liberty of condensing some later events from her original diary into the entries for July 13th and 14th in the published version. Two of the wounded soldiers remained in her home until July 22nd and the other departed on the following day.

107. *OR,* Vol. 27, Part 1, pp. 24–28; List of Wounded Sent to Baltimore, Medical Registers 558 and 562, Seminary Hospital: Gettysburg, Pa., National Archives, Washington, D.C.; Duncan, *The Medical Department of the United States Army in the Civil War,* pp. 262–264.

108. Dreese, "Ordeal in the Lutheran Theological Seminary," p. 109.

109. Barnes, *Medical and Surgical History of the Civil War,* Vol. 8, p. 326.

110. Dreese, *Like Ripe Apples in a Storm,* p. 138.

111. Barnes, *Medical and Surgical History of the Civil War,* Vol. 7. p. 92.

112. *Ibid.,* Vol. 8, p. 364.

113. *Ibid.,* Vol. 11, p. 74.

114. *Ibid.,* Vol. 8, p. 350.

115. Sarah Sites Rodgers, *The Ties of the Past: The Gettysburg Diaries of Salome Myers Stewart, 1854–1922* (Gettysburg: Thomas Publications, 1996), pp. 162–164; Busey, *These Honored Dead,* p. 278.

116. This tally was obtained from the following sources: List of Deaths in Seminary Hospital, July 9 to August 7, 1863, Medical Registers 558 and 562, Seminary Hospital: Gettysburg, Pa., National Archives, Washington, D. C.; Busey, *These Honored Dead;* Weymouth T. Jordan, Jr., and Louis H. Manarin, eds., *North Carolina Troops, 1861–1865, A Roster,* 12 vols. (Raleigh, N.C.: Division of Archives and History, 1971–1996), Vol. 9, p. 176; and the case histories from Barnes, *Medical and Surgical History of the Civil War.*

117. Adams, *Doctors in Blue,* p. 122.

118. Barnes, *Medical and Surgical History of the Civil War,* Vol. 8, p. 350.

119. Adams, *Doctors in Blue,* pp. 138–145; Cunningham, *Doctors in Gray,* pp. 236–241.

120. Busey, *These Honored Dead,* pp. 204–208.

121. *Ibid.,* pp. 296–299.

122. Dreese, *Like Ripe Apples in a Storm,* p. 96.

123. Gregory A. Coco, *Killed in Action* (Gettysburg: Thomas Publications, 1992), p. 16.

124. Dreese, *An Imperishable Fame,* p. 144.

125. Biographical Sketch of Henry Chancellor, George McFarland Papers, J. Horace McFarland Collection, PSA.

126. Dreese, *Like Ripe Apples in a Storm,* p. 96.

127. Chamberlin, *History of the One Hun-*

dred and Fiftieth Regiment Pennsylvania Volunteers, p. 130.

128. Biographical Sketch of Henry Chancellor, George McFarland Papers, J. Horace McFarland Collection, PSA.

129. Adams, *Doctors in Blue,* pp. 136–137; Barnes, *Medical and Surgical History of the Civil War,* Vol. 8, p. 504. The two fatalities were Sergeant Alexander Ross, Company E, 140th New York and Private John Contoil, Company G, 6th United States Infantry.

130. Adams, *Doctors in Blue,* pp. 120–121.

131. Barnes, *Medical and Surgical History of the Civil War,* Vol. 12, p. 895.

132. Coco, *A Vast Sea of Misery,* p. 7; Ehler, *Hospital Scenes After the Battle of Gettysburg,* p. 47; Samuel Simon Schmucker, Report of the Chairman of the Faculty, August 11, 1863, Abdel Ross Wentz Library, LTSG.

133. Timothy Smith, *John Burns, "The Hero of Gettysburg"* (Gettysburg: Thomas Publications, 2000), pp. 163–164. Lehman is listed as a non-graduate in the college records for the class of 1867 and eventually became an attorney in Washington, D.C. Frassanito, *Early Photography at Gettysburg,* p. 87. Frederick's father was Colonel Theodore F. Lehman, the commander of the 103rd Pennsylvania. This unit was stationed in coastal North Carolina throughout much of its service. Charles P. Potts, "A First Defender in Rebel Prison Pens," *Publications of the Historical Society of Schuylkill County,* Vol. 4 (1914), p. 344.

134. Wentz, *Gettysburg Lutheran Theological Seminary,* Vol. 1, p. 214; Frassanito, *Early Photography at Gettysburg,* pp. 87–88; Proceedings of the Sixty-Fourth Annual Convention of the Hartwick Synod of the Evangelical Lutheran Church, in the State of New York, Abdel Ross Wentz Library, LTSG.

135. Fred Hawthorne, "John Chase of the 5th Maine Battery," *The Battlefield Dispatch: The Newsletter of the Association of Licensed Battlefield Guides, Inc.,* Vol. 28, no. 7 (July 1999), pp. 3–5.

136. Mr. Clair P. Lyons to Author, December 4, 2000; Broadhead, *The Diary of a Lady,* p. 24.

137. Muffly, *The Story of Our Regiment,* p. 927. Sergeant Leitzel recovered from a severe wound to his right knee. He was transferred to the Veteran Reserve Corps on March 17, 1864, and discharged on July 6, 1865. *Ibid.,* pp. 538, 927.

138. Shay, "Recollections of Visitations at Gettysburg After the Great Battle in July, 1863," pp. 293, 295.

139. *Ibid.,* pp. 297–298.

140. Dreese, *An Imperishable Fame,* pp. 146–147. The 179th Pennsylvania was a nine months unit of drafted militia organized in the fall of 1862. The regiment spent much of its service performing garrison duty at Yorktown, Virginia. The 179th was mustered out on July 27, 1863, at Harrisburg, Pennsylvania. The next day, Dr. Reily was hired as a contract surgeon at the Seminary Hospital. Although Schantz recorded the drinking incident as taking place on the 26th, it is possible he was off by a week in his recollections, which he wrote in 1890. Bates, *History of the Pennsylvania Volunteers,* Vol. 8, pp. 1285–1286; List of the Medical Contract Physicians in Seminary Hospital at Gettysburg, Pa., August 1, 1863, Medical Registers 558 and 562, National Archives, Washington, D.C.

141. Shay, "Recollections of Visitations at Gettysburg After the Great Battle in July, 1863," p. 298.

142. Robert M. Powell, "With Hood at Gettysburg," *Philadelphia Weekly Times,* December 13, 1884.

143. Douglas, *I Rode with Stonewall,* p. 247.

144. Henry Kyd Douglas to Miss Tippie Boteler, August 5, 1863, Rare Book, Manuscript, and Special Collections Library, Duke University.

145. *Ibid.*

146. Douglas, *I Rode with Stonewall,* p. 246. Philip Schaff (1819–1893) was the preeminent church historian and ecumenist of late 19th century America. In 1863, he was well-known for his leadership at the Mercersburg Seminary and within the German Reformed church. He moved to New York in 1870 to accept a professorship at Union Theological Seminary. Schaff authored a number of scholarly volumes, was a leader in Bible translation, and was one of the founders of the American Society of Church History. His influence surpassed even that of Samuel Schmucker. Frederick K. Wentz to Author, March 17, 2001.

147. Henry Kyd Douglas to Miss Tippie Boteler, August 5, 1863, Rare Book, Manuscript, and Special Collections Library, Duke University.

148. Douglas, *I Rode with Stonewall,* p. 247.

149. *Ibid.,* p. 248; Henry Kyd Douglas to Miss Tippie Boteler, August 5, 1863, Rare Book, Manuscript, and Special Collections Library, Duke University.

150. Douglas, *I Rode with Stonewall,* p. 248.

151. Robert M. Powell, "With Hood at Gettysburg," *Philadelphia Weekly Times,* December 13, 1884; Gregory A. Coco, ed., *Recollections of a Texas Colonel at Gettysburg* (Gettysburg: Thomas Publications, 1990), p. 3.

152. Robert M. Powell, "With Hood at Gettysburg," *Philadelphia Weekly Times,* December 13, 1884.

153. Donald E. Everett, ed., *Chaplain Davis and Hood's Texas Brigade* (Baton Rouge: Louisiana State University Press, 1999), p. 172.

154. Robert M. Powell, "With Hood at Gettysburg," *Philadelphia Weekly Times,* December 13, 1884.

155. *Ibid.*

156. *Ibid.*

157. Henry Kyd Douglas to Miss Tippie Boteler, August 5, 1863, Rare Book, Manuscript, and Special Collections Library, Duke University; Douglas, *I Rode with Stonewall,* pp. 248–249.

158. McCurdy, *Gettysburg, A Memoir,* p. 9. Trimble later sent Mrs. McCurdy a silver soup ladle with the inscription, "General Trimble to Mrs. McCurdy. The tribute of a grateful heart."

159. *OR,* Vol. 27, Part 3, p. 646. Cameron's reference to the McCurdy family as "Rebel sympathizers" is unfair. The family also cared for a wounded Union lieutenant in their home. Unfortunately, the officer died after refusing to allow a surgeon to amputate his arm. McCurdy, *Gettysburg, A Memoir,* p. 9.

160. McCurdy, *Gettysburg, A Memoir,* p. 9; Report of Wounded Received in Seminary Hospital at Gettysburg, Pa., Medical Registers 558 and 562, Seminary Hospital: Gettysburg, Pa., National Archives, Washington, D.C.

161. Myers, "The Civil War Diary of General Isaac Ridgeway Trimble," p. 13.

162. Emily Souder, *Leaves from the Battlefield of Gettysburg* (Philadelphia: Caxton Press of C. Sherman, Son & Co., 1864), p. 59.

163. Ehler, *Hospital Scenes After the Battle of Gettysburg,* pp. 49–50.

164. Myers, "The Civil War Diary of General Isaac Ridgeway Trimble," p. 13; Ehler, *Hospital Scenes After the Battle of Gettysburg,* pp. 50–51.

165. *Lutheran and Missionary,* August 6, 1863.

166. Ehler, *Hospital Scenes After the Battle of Gettysburg,* pp. 48–49, 51.

167. Fannie J. Buehler, *Recollections of the Rebel Invasion and One Woman's Experience During the Battle of Gettysburg* (Gettysburg: Star and Sentinel, 1896), p. 28.

168. United States Christian Commission, *Second Report of the Committee of Maryland,* p. 33.

169. Dreese, *An Imperishable Fame,* p. 145.

170. All three were employed by the Government starting on July 23, 1863. List of the Medical Contract Physicians in Seminary Hospital at Gettysburg, Pa., August 1, 1863, Medical Registers 558 and 562, National Archives, Washington, D.C.

171. *OR,* Vol. 27, Part 1, p. 25.

172. *Ibid.,* p. 197.

173. Dreese, *An Imperishable Fame,* p. 146.

174. United States Christian Commission, *Second Report of the Committee of Maryland,* p. 28.

175. Barnes, *Medical and Surgical History of the Civil War,* Vol. 11, p. 241. Crawford was discharged from the service on May 3, 1864.

176. Dreese, *An Imperishable Fame,* p. 145.

177. Samuel Simon Schmucker, Report of the Chairman of the Faculty, August 11, 1863, Abdel Ross Wentz Library, LTSG. Schmucker directed a letter, dated August 13, 1863, to Quartermaster General Montgomery Meigs asking for his assistance in clearing out the hospital. On the 18th, Meigs replied that he had no authority in the matter, and he advised Schmucker to apply to the surgeon in charge or to the surgeon general. Montgomery Meigs to Samuel Schmucker, August 18, 1863, Abdel Ross Wentz Library, LTSG.

178. Abstract of Meeting Minutes of the Board of Directors, Lutheran Theological Seminary, August 11, 1863, Abdel Ross Wentz Library, LTSG.

179. *Ibid.*

180. Henry Janes to James R. Smith, August 28, 1863, Gettysburg National Military Park Library. General Orders No. 2 from Colonel Henry C. Alleman, the commander of the post at Gettysburg, stated: "During the months of August and September 1863, no corpses will be allowed to be disinterred from any parts of the burial grounds, cemeteries, or battlegrounds of Gettysburg. The health of the wounded soldiers and citizens of this community requires the stringent enforcement of this order, and any violation of it reported to these headquarters will meet summary and severe punishment." This order was printed in the *Lutheran and Missionary,* August 6, 1863.

181. Henry Janes to James R. Smith, August 28, 1863, Gettysburg National Military Park Library; Daily Hospital Records, Seminary Hospital: Gettysburg, Pa., August 14 to August 28, 1863, Medical Registers 558 and 562, National Archives, Washington, D.C.

182. "Found Union Soldier's Remains," Gettysburg *Compiler,* June 30, 1909.

183. E. M. Hays to John B. Bachelder, in Ladd and Ladd, *The Bachelder Papers,* Vol. 3, p. 1777. According to hospital records, the remains of 16 Confederates buried near the Seminary were exhumed and later interred in the Hollywood Cemetery, Richmond, Virginia. Interestingly, there was one recorded burial with no record of removal. Edward G. J. Richter, "The Removal of the Confederate Dead from Gettysburg," *The Gettysburg Magazine,* no. 2 (January 1990), p. 116.

184. Myers, "The Civil War Diary of General Isaac Ridgeway Trimble," p. 13.

185. Woodward, *Major General James Lawson Kemper, C. S. A.,* p. 103.

186. Dreese, *An Imperishable Fame,* p. 146.

187. Barnes, *Medical and Surgical History of the Civil War,* Vol. 11, p. 241.

188. *Ibid.,* Vol. 11, p. 148. McGeehen was discharged from the military on April 23, 1864. Nearly two years later, he entered a Philadelphia hospital, and after a careful examination, it was determined to remove his deformed limb at the hip joint. He died of a secondary hemorrhage on May 2nd. *Ibid.,* Vol. 11, pp. 148–149.

189. Hawthorne, "John Chase of the 5th Maine Battery," p. 5.

190. Busey, *These Honored Dead,* p. 173.

191. Dreese, *An Imperishable Fame,* p. 147.

192. *Ibid.,* p. 161.

193. *Ibid.,* p. 147.

194. Broadhead, *The Diary of a Lady,* p. 24.

Epilogue

1. *Lutheran and Missionary,* September 17, 1863.

2. Samuel Simon Schmucker, Report of the Chairman of the Faculty, August 8, 1864, Abdel Ross Wentz Library, LTSG.

3. Abstract of Meeting Minutes of the Board of Directors, Lutheran Theological Seminary, August 9, 1864, Abdel Ross Wentz Library, LTSG.

4. Samuel Simon Schmucker, Report of the Chairman of the Faculty, August 8, 1864, Abdel Ross Wentz Library, LTSG; Wentz, *Gettysburg Lutheran Theological Seminary,* Vol. 1, pp. 220–221.

5. Hugh M. Ziegler, "Lincoln's Gettysburg Address," May 13, 1933, Civilian Files, ACHS; Robert McClean, "A Boy in Gettysburg—1863," Gettysburg *Compiler,* June 30, 1909.

6. Daniel Skelly, *A Boy's Experiences During the Battle of Gettysburg,* p. 27.

7. Samuel Simon Schmucker, Report of the Chairman of the Faculty, August 8, 1864, Abdel Ross Wentz Library, LTSG.

8. Wentz, *Gettysburg Lutheran Theological Seminary,* Vol. 1, p. 223.

9. Samuel Schmucker, Resignation Letter to Board of Directors, August 9, 1864, Abdel Ross Wentz Library, LTSG.

10. Wentz, *Gettysburg Lutheran Theological Seminary,* Vol. 1, p. 128.

11. Samuel Schmucker, Resignation Letter to Board of Directors, August 9, 1964, Abdel Ross Wentz Library, LTSG.

12. Quotes from undated newspaper clippings in the personal scrapbook of Samuel S. Schmucker, Abdel Ross Wentz Library, LTSG.

13. Wentz, *Pioneer in Christian Unity,* pp. 348–352; Brian A. Kennell, *Beyond the Gatehouse: Gettysburg's Evergreen Cemetery* (Gettysburg: Evergreen Cemetery Association, 2000), p. 19.

14. Wentz, *Gettysburg Lutheran Theological Seminary,* Vol. 1, pp. 392–393.

15. *Star and Sentinel,* Gettysburg, Pa., September 23, 1874.

16. Samuel Simon Schmucker, Report of the Chairman of the Faculty, August 8, 1864, Abdel Ross Wentz Library, LTSG.

17. Hugh M. Ziegler, "Reminiscence of Hugh M. Ziegler of the Battle of Gettysburg Which Occurred on the First, Second, and Third Days of July, 1863," ACHS.

18. Donald Clare, "A Seminary Saga: The Clare Family," *Seminary Views* (Summer 1998), p. 1.

19. Mr. Clair P. Lyons to Adams County Historical Society, May 12, 1992.

20. Horn, *Memoirs of Henry Eyster Jacobs,* Vol. 1, p. 66.

21. Wentz, *Gettysburg Lutheran Theological Seminary,* Vol. 2, p. 62.

22. *Ibid.,* p. 59.

23. Obituary of Martin L. Culler, in Proceedings of the Eighty-Fifth Annual Convention of the Evangelical Lutheran Synod of East Pennsylvania, pp. 77–79, Abdel Ross Wentz Library, LTSG.

24. Shay, "Recollections of Visitations at Gettysburg After the Great Battle in July, 1863," pp. 276–277.

25. Biographical Sketch of Henry Leaman, Archives Collection, Franklin & Marshall College, Lancaster, Pa.

26. Douglas, *I Rode with Stonewall,* p. 251.

27. *Ibid.,* 335–340; Ranck, *Franklin and Marshall College Obituary Record,* Vol. 2, pp. 114–119; Roger Long, "The Confederate Prisoners of Gettysburg," *The Gettysburg Magazine,* no. 2 (January 1990), p. 99.

28. Coco, *Recollections of a Texas Colonel at Gettysburg,* p. 36.

29. Roger Long, "General Isaac R. Trimble in Captivity," *The Gettysburg Magazine,* no. 1 (July 1989), p. 127.

30. *Ibid.,* pp. 127–128.

31. Grace, *Isaac Ridgeway Trimble,* pp. 179–182.

32. Woodward, *Major General James Lawson Kemper, C. S. A.,* pp. 105–107, 110, 131–132, 139, 149, 152–153, 166–168.

33. *Ibid.,* p. 116.

34. *Ibid.,* pp. 186, 194.

35. *Ibid.,* p. 190.

36. Dreese, *Like Ripe Apples in a Storm*, pp. 132–133.

37. Dreese, *An Imperishable Fame*, p. 15.

38. Obituary of Captain Brice Blair, *Huntingdon Monitor*, March 27, 1890.

39. Pension Records of Daniel McMahon, National Archives, Washington, D.C.; Officer Biographical Information: 20th New York State Militia, Seward Osborne Collection.

40. Frampton, "Civil War Profiles: Sergeant Francis Jefferson Coates," pp. 2–3; Dreese, *Like Ripe Apples in a Storm*, p. 138.

41. Frampton, "Civil War Profiles: Sergeant Francis Jefferson Coates," p. 3.

42. *Ibid.*, p. 3.

43. Dreese, *Like Ripe Apples in a Storm*, p. 139.

44. Hawthorne, "John Chase of the 5th Maine Battery," pp. 5–6.

45. Dreese, "Ordeal in the Lutheran Theological Seminary," p. 110.

46. Martin B. Sloat, "Springs Hotel," *The Gettysburg Times*, October 20, 1984.

47. J. Howard Wert, *A Complete Hand-Book of the Monuments and Indications and Guide to the Positions on the Gettysburg Battle-Field* (Harrisburg, Pa.: R. M. Sturgeon & Co., 1886), p. 148.

48. Wentz, *Gettysburg Lutheran Theological Seminary*, Vol. 1, pp. 223–224.

49. Lewis E. Beitler, ed., *Fiftieth Anniversary of the Battle of Gettysburg: Report of the Pennsylvania Commission* (Harrisburg, Pa.: Wm. Stanley Ray, State Printer, 1914), pp. 49–50, 60, 134, 173–174, 227–228; Wentz, *Gettysburg Lutheran Theological Seminary*, Vol. 1, pp. 224–225.

50. Wentz, *Gettysburg Lutheran Theological Seminary*, Vol. 1, pp. 225–226. Unfortunately, only the concrete base of the structure remains today. The ornate wooden roof and columns were torn down after falling into a state of disrepair.

51. Gettysburg *Compiler*, August 20, 1913.

52. Gettysburg *Compiler*, August 27, 1913.

53. Wentz, *Gettysburg Lutheran Theological Seminary*, Vol. 1, p. 254.

54. *Ibid.*, Vol. 1, pp. 255–261.

55. *Ibid.*, Vol. 1, pp. 273, 316–319, 321–322.

56. *Ibid.*, Vol. 1, pp. 325–326; Charles H. Glatfelter, "The Historical Society and the Seminary Old Dorm," December 16, 1993, copy in, Lutheran Theological Seminary File, ACHS.

57. Charles H. Glatfelter, "The Historical Society and the Seminary Old Dorm," December 16, 1993.

58. *Ibid.*

59. *Ibid.*

60. Letter to the Editor, *The Gettysburg Times*, October 31, 1957.

61. "Seminary President Says Board Does Not Have Funds to Preserve its Old Dorm," *The Gettysburg Times*, November 1, 1957.

62. "Razing of Old Dorm Is Up to Seminary Board, *The Gettysburg Times*, November 15, 1957; Charles H. Glatfelter, "The Historical Society and the Seminary Old Dorm," December 16, 1993.

63. Charles H. Glatfelter, "The Historical Society and the Seminary Old Dorm," December 16, 1993.

64. Interview with the Reverend John R. Spangler, Director of Communications, Lutheran Theological Seminary at Gettysburg; Facts and Figures Brochure, Lutheran Theological Seminary at Gettysburg.

65. "Preserving Civil War Legacies of Seminary Ridge," Informational Brochure, Seminary Ridge Historic Preservation Foundation. The web site of the group is: www.seminaryridge.org.

66. Statement by State Treasurer Barbara Hafer Regarding the Seminary Ridge Historic Preservation Foundation, May 23, 2000.

67. "Seminary Ridge Foundation Receives Grant," News Release, Seminary Ridge Historic Preservation Foundation, May 22, 2000.

Bibliography

Manuscript Collections and Official Documents

Adams County Historical Society, Gettysburg, Pa.

Clare, Lydia Ziegler. "A Gettysburg Girl's Story of the Great Battle," circa 1900.

Croll, Jennie. "Days of Dread: A Woman's Story of Her Life on a Battlefield."

Glatfelter, Charles H. "The Historical Society and the Seminary Old Dorm," December 16, 1993.

Charles Krauth File

Lutheran Theological Seminary File

Richards, Henry M. M. *Pennsylvania's Emergency Men at Gettysburg,* February 1895.

Skelly, Daniel. *A Boy's Experiences During the Battle of Gettysburg,* 1932.

Ziegler, Hugh M. "Reminiscence of Hugh M. Ziegler of the Battle of Gettysburg Which Occurred on the First, Second, and Third Days of July, 1863," May 1933.

_____. "Lincoln's Gettysburg Address," May 1933.

Duke University, Rare Book, Manuscript, and Special Collections Library, Durham, N.C.

Henry Kyd Douglas to Miss Tippie Boteler, August 5, 1863.

Franklin and Marshall College, Shadek-Fackenthal Library, Lancaster, Pa.

Henry Kyd Douglas Papers

Henry Leaman Sketch

Obituary Records

Gettysburg College, Musselman Library, Gettysburg, Pa.

Gettysburg Cemetery Association Files

Samuel S. Schmucker Manuscript Collection

Gettysburg National Military Park Library, Gettysburg, Pa.

Field Hospital Files

Gettysburg Newspaper Clippings

Library of Congress, Washington, D.C.

Edward McPherson Papers

Lutheran Theological Seminary at Gettysburg, Abdel Ross Wentz Library, Gettysburg, Pa.

Abstract of Meeting Minutes of the Board of Directors

Benjamin Oehrle Letters

Samuel S. Schmucker Papers

Samuel S. Schmucker, Personal Scrapbook

Samuel S. Schmucker, Reports to Board of Directors

National Archives, Washington, D.C.

Medical Registers 558 and 562, Seminary Hospital: Gettysburg, Pa.

Pension Records and Military Service Records

Pennsylvania State Archives, Harrisburg, Pa.

George McFarland Papers, J. Horace McFarland Collection

Private Collections

Dr. Charles L. Eater, Jr., Collection

Seward R. Osborne Collection

United States Army Military History Institute, Carlisle Barracks, Pa.

Eugene Blackford Manuscript

Robert L. Brake Collection

Newspapers

Gettysburg *Compiler*

The *Gettysburg Times*

The *Greenville Advocate,* Greenville, Illinois.

Harrisburg Telegraph, Harrisburg, Pa.

Huntingdon Daily News, Huntingdon, Pa.

The *Huntingdon Monitor,* Huntingdon, Pa.

Lutheran and Missionary, Philadelphia, Pa.
Lutheran Observer
The *National Tribune*
New York Times
Philadelphia Inquirer
Philadelphia Weekly Times
Union County Star and Lewisburg Chronicle,
    Lewisburg, Pa.

Published Works

Adams, George Worthington. *Doctors in Blue:
    The Medical History of the Union Army in
    the Civil War.* Baton Rouge: Louisiana
    State University Press, 1952.
Alleman, Tillie Pierce. *At Gettysburg or What a
    Girl Saw and Heard of the Battle.* New
    York: W. Lake Borland, 1889. Reprint, Bal-
    timore, Md.: Butternut and Blue, 1987.
Anstadt, P. *Life and Times of Reverend S. S.
    Schmucker.* York, Pa.: P. Anstadt and Sons,
    1896.
Appelbaum, Stanley, ed. *Great Speeches: Abra-
    ham Lincoln, with Historical Notes by John
    Grafton.* Mineola, N.Y.: Dover Publica-
    tions, 1991.
Barnes, Joseph K., ed. *The Medical and Surgi-
    cal History of the Civil War.* 12 vols. Wash-
    ington, D.C.: Government Printing Office,
    1870. Reprint, Wilmington, N.C.: Broad-
    foot Publishing Company, 1990–1991.
Bates, Samuel P. *History of the Pennsylvania Vol-
    unteers: 1861–1865.* 5 vols. Harrisburg, Pa.:
    B. Singerly, 1869–1871.
Beauchamp, Virginia Walcott. "The Sisters and
    the Soldiers." *Maryland Historical Maga-
    zine,* Vol. 81, no. 2 (Summer 1986): 117–
    133.
Beitler, Lewis, ed. *Fiftieth Anniversary of the
    Battle of Gettysburg: Report of the Pennsyl-
    vania Commission.* Harrisburg, Pa.: Wm.
    Stanley Ray, State Printer, 1914.
Beller, Susan Provost. *Medical Practices in the
    Civil War.* Charlotte, Vt.: Susan Provost
    Beller, 1992.
Bloom, Robert. "We Never Expected a Battle:
    The Civilians at Gettysburg, 1863." *Penn-
    sylvania History,* no. 55 (October 1988):
    161–200.
Boatner, Mark M. III. *The Civil War Dictionary.*
    New York: David McKay, 1988.
Breidenbaugh, E. S., ed. *The Pennsylvania Col-
    lege Book, 1832–1882.* Philadelphia: Luthe-
    ran Publication Society, 1882.
Broadhead, Sarah. *The Diary of a Lady of Get-
    tysburg, Pennsylvania, From June 15 to July
    15, 1863.* Gettysburg: Privately printed,
    1864.

Brock, R. A., ed. *Southern Historical Society Pa-
    pers.* 52 vols. Richmond, Va.: Southern
    Historical Society, 1876–1952.
Brown, Varina D. *A Colonel at Gettysburg and
    Spotsylvania.* Columbia, S.C.: The State
    Company, 1931.
Buehler, Fannie J. *Recollections of the Rebel In-
    vasion and One Woman's Experience Dur-
    ing the Battle of Gettysburg.* Gettysburg:
    Star and Sentinel, 1896.
Busey, John W. *These Honored Dead: The Union
    Casualties at Gettysburg.* Hightstown, N.J.:
    Longstreet House, 1996.
_____, and David G. Martin. *Regimental
    Strengths and Losses at Gettysburg.* Hight-
    stown, N.J.: Longstreet House, 1994.
Cameron, Bill. "The Signal Corps at Gettys-
    burg." *The Gettysburg Magazine,* no. 3
    (July 1990): 9–15.
Campbell, Eric A. "The Aftermath and Recov-
    ery of Gettysburg," Part 1. *The Gettysburg
    Magazine,* no. 11 (July 1994): 102–118.
Chamberlin, Thomas. *History of the One Hun-
    dred and Fiftieth Regiment Pennsylvania
    Volunteers.* Philadelphia: F. McManus, Jr.
    & Co., Printers, 1905. Reprint, Baltimore,
    Md.: Butternut and Blue, 1986.
Coco, Gregory A. *A Vast Sea of Misery: A His-
    tory and Guide to the Union and Confeder-
    ate Field Hospitals at Gettysburg, July
    1–November 20, 1863.* Gettysburg: Thomas
    Publications, 1988.
_____. *A Strange and Blighted Land, Gettysburg:
    The Aftermath of a Battle.* Gettysburg:
    Thomas Publications, 1995.
_____. *Recollections of a Texas Colonel at Get-
    tysburg.* Gettysburg: Thomas Publica-
    tions, 1990.
Coddington, Edwin B. *The Gettysburg Cam-
    paign: A Study in Command.* New York:
    Charles Scribner's Sons, 1968.
Colver, Michael. "Reminiscences of the Battle
    of Gettysburg." *The Spectrum* (Pennsylva-
    nia College Yearbook, 1902).
Conklin, Eileen F. *Women at Gettysburg 1863.*
    Gettysburg: Thomas Publications, 1993.
Cross, Andrew B. *Battle of Gettysburg and the
    Christian Commission.* Baltimore, Md.:
    United States Christian Commission, 1865.
Cunningham, Horace H. *Doctors in Gray: The
    Confederate Medical Service.* Baton Rouge:
    Louisiana State University Press, 1958.
Curtis, O. B. *History of the Twenty-Fourth
    Michigan of the Iron Brigade, Known as the
    Detroit and Wayne County Regiment.* De-
    troit: Winn & Hammond, 1891.
Dawes, Rufus R. *Service with the Sixth Wiscon-
    sin Volunteers.* Marietta, Ohio: E. R. Al-
    derman & Sons, 1890. Reprint, Dayton,
    Ohio: Morningside Bookshop, 1984.

Doubleday, Abner. *Chancellorsville and Gettysburg.* New York: Charles Scribner's Sons, 1882.

Douglas, Henry Kyd. *I Rode with Stonewall.* Chapel Hill: The University of North Carolina Press, 1940. Reprint, Atlanta, Ga.: Mockingbird Books, 1976.

Dreese, Michael A. *An Imperishable Fame: The Civil War Experience of George Fisher McFarland.* Mifflintown, Pa.: Juniata County Historical Society, 1997.

_____. *The 151st Pennsylvania at Gettysburg: Like Ripe Apples in a Storm.* Jefferson, N.C.: McFarland & Company, 2000.

_____. "Ordeal in the Lutheran Theological Seminary: The Recollections of First Lt. Jeremiah Hoffman, 142nd Pennsylvania Volunteers." *The Gettysburg Magazine,* no. 23 (July 2000): 100–110.

_____. "The Saga of Andrew Gregg Tucker." *Bucknell World,* Vol. 26, no. 6 (November 1998): 20–21.

Duncan, Louis. *The Medical Department of the United States Army in the Civil War.* Washington, D.C.: U.S. Government Printing Office, 1910.

Ehler, Martha. *Hospital Scenes After the Battle of Gettysburg, July 1863.* Philadelphia: Henry B. Ashmead, 1864. Reprint, Gettysburg: G. Craig Caba, 1993.

Frampton, Roy. "Civil War Profiles: Sergeant Francis Jefferson Coates." *The Battlefield Dispatch: The Newsletter of the Association of Licensed Battlefield Guides, Inc,* Vol. 27, no. 4 (April 1998): 2–3.

Frassanito, William A. *Early Photography at Gettysburg.* Gettysburg: Thomas Publications, 1995.

Freeman, Douglas Southall. *Lee's Lieutenants.* 3 vols. New York: Charles Scribner's Sons, 1944.

Gaff, Alan D. "The Indiana Relief Effort at Gettysburg." *The Gettysburg Magazine,* no. 3 (July 1990): 109–114.

Gates, Theodore B. *The Ulster Guard and the War of the Rebellion.* New York: Benjamin H. Tyrrel, Printer, 1879.

Gobbel, A. Roger and Donald N. and Elaine C. Matthews. *On the Glorious Hill: A Short History in Word and Picture of the Lutheran Theological Seminary at Gettysburg.* Lancaster, Pa.: Pridemark Press/Copy Print, 1990.

Grace, William M. *Isaac Ridgeway Trimble, The Indefatigable and Courageous.* Masters thesis, Virginia Polytechnic Institute, 1984.

Haines, Douglas Craig. "Lee's Advance Along the Cashtown Road." *The Gettysburg Magazine,* no. 23 (July 2000): 6–29.

Hartwig, D. Scott. "The Defense of McPherson's Ridge." *The Gettysburg Magazine,* no. 1 (July 1989): 15–24.

Hawthorne, Frederick W. *Gettysburg: Stories of Men and Monuments.* Gettysburg: The Association of Licensed Battlefield Guides, 1988.

_____. "John Chase of the 5th Maine Battery." *The Battlefield Dispatch: The Newsletter of the Association of Licensed Battlefield Guides, Inc.,* Vol. 28, no. 7 (July 1999): 3–6.

Hefelbower, Samuel G. *History of Gettysburg College, 1832–1932.* Gettysburg: Gettysburg College, 1932.

Herdegen, Lance J. and William J. K. Beaudot. *In the Bloody Railroad Cut at Gettysburg.* Dayton, Ohio: Morningside, 1990.

Horn, Henry E., ed. *Memoirs of Henry Eyster Jacobs.* 3 vols. Huntingdon, Pa.: Church Management Service, Inc., 1974.

Jacobs, Michael. *Notes on the Rebel Invasion of Maryland and Pennsylvania and the Battle of Gettysburg.* Philadelphia: J. B. Lippincott, Co., 1864.

Kennell, Brian A. *Beyond the Gatehouse: Gettysburg's Evergreen Cemetery.* Gettysburg: Evergreen Cemetery Association, 2000.

Kieffer, Harry M. *The Recollections of a Drummer Boy.* New York: Houghton, Mifflin and Co., 1883. Reprint, Mifflinburg, Pa.: Bucktail Books, 2000.

Krolick, Marshall D. "Gettysburg: The First Day, July 1, 1863." *Blue & Gray Magazine,* Vol. 5, issue 2 (November 1987): 10–57.

Kross, Gary. "Fight Like the Devil to Hold Your Own." *Blue and Gray Magazine,* Vol. 7, issue 3 (February 1995): 9–22.

Ladd, David L. and Audrey J., eds. *The Bachelder Papers: Gettysburg in Their Own Words.* 3 vols. Dayton, Ohio: Morningside, 1994–1995.

Long, Roger. "The Confederate Prisoners of Gettysburg." *The Gettysburg Magazine,* no. 2 (January 1990): 91–112.

_____. "General Isaac R. Trimble in Captivity," *The Gettysburg Magazine,* no. 1 (July 1989): 125–128.

Martin, David G. *Gettysburg July 1.* Conshohocken, Pa.: Combined Books, 1995.

Matthews, Richard E. *The 149th Pennsylvania Volunteer Infantry Unit in the Civil War.* Jefferson, N.C.: McFarland & Company, 1994.

McCurdy, Charles M. *Gettysburg, A Memoir.* Pittsburgh, Pa.: Reed & Witting, 1929.

McLean, James L. *Cutler's Brigade at Gettysburg.* Baltimore, Md.: Butternut and Blue, 1994.

_____, and Judy W. McLean. *Gettysburg Sources.* 3 vols. Baltimore, Md.: Butternut and Blue, 1986–1990.

Miller, John C. *The Wolf by the Ears: Thomas Jefferson and Slavery.* New York: The Free Press, 1974.

Motts, Wayne E. *"Trust in God and Fear Nothing": Gen. Lewis A. Armistead, CSA.* Gettysburg: Farnsworth House, 1994.

Muffly, Joseph W. *The Story of Our Regiment: A History of the 148th Pennsylvania Vols.* Des Moines, Iowa: Kenyon Printing, 1904.

Munn, Sheldon A. *Freemasons at Gettysburg.* Gettysburg: Thomas Publications, 1993.

Murray, R. L. *First on the Field: Cortland's 76th and Oswego's 147th New York State Volunteer Regiments at Gettysburg.* Wolcott, N.Y.: Benedum Books, 1998.

Myers, Frank M. *The Comanches: A History of White's Battalion, Virginia Cavalry, Laurel Brigade, Hampton's Division, A. N. V., C. S. A.* Baltimore, Md.: Kelly, Pieta & Co., 1871. Reprint, Gaithersburg, Md.: Butternut, 1987.

Myers, William S., ed. "The Civil War Diary of General Isaac Ridgeway Trimble." *Maryland Historical Magazine,* Vol. XVII, no. 1 (March 1922): 1–20.

New York Monuments Commission for the Battlefields of Gettysburg. *Final Report on the Battlefield of Gettysburg.* 3 vols. Albany, N.Y.: J. B. Lyon Company, 1900.

Nicholson, John P., ed. *Pennsylvania at Gettysburg: Ceremonies at the Dedication of the Monuments Erected by the Commonwealth of Pennsylvania to Mark the Positions of the Pennsylvania Commands Engaged in the Battle.* 3 vols. Harrisburg, Pa.: William Stanley Ray, 1914.

Nye, Wilbur S. "The First Battle of Gettysburg." *Civil War Times Illustrated,* Vol. 4, no. 5 (August 1965): 12–19.

_____. *Here Come the Rebels!* Baton Rouge: Louisiana State University Press, 1965.

Oldenburg, Mark. "Happy Birthday, Samuel!: College Founder Samuel Simon Schmucker Celebrates His 200th Birthday." *Gettysburg,* Vol. 90, no. 3 (Summer 1999): 11–15.

Osborne, Seward. *Holding the Left at Gettysburg: The 20th New York State Militia on July 1, 1863.* Hightstown, N.J.: Longstreet House, 1990.

Patterson, Gerald A. *Debris of Battle: The Wounded of Gettysburg.* Mechanicsburg, Pa.: Stackpole Books, 1997.

Pfanz, Harry W. *Gettysburg: The Second Day.* Chapel Hill: The University of North Carolina Press, 1987.

Ranck, Samuel H., ed. *Franklin and Marshall College Obituary Record.* 3 vols. Lancaster, Pa.: The Franklin and Marshall College Alumni Association, 1904.

Riley, Michael A. *"For God's Sake, Forward!,"* *Gen. John F. Reynolds, USA.* Gettysburg: Farnsworth House, 1995.

Roth, Jeffrey B. "Civil War Medicine at Gettysburg." *The Gettysburg Hospital Quarterly,* Vol. 1, no. 1 (Spring 1985): 2–4.

Shay, Ralph S., ed. "Recollections of Visitations at Gettysburg After the Great Battle in July, 1863, by the Reverend F. J. F. Schantz." *Reflections on the Battle of Gettysburg* (The Lebanon County Historical Society, 1963), Vol. 13: 275–300.

Shue, Richard S. *Morning at Willoughby Run.* Gettysburg: Thomas Publications, 1998.

Sifakis, Stewart. *Who Was Who in the Civil War.* 2 vols. New York: Facts on File, 1988.

Smith, Timothy H. *The Story of Lee's Headquarters, Gettysburg, Pennsylvania.* Gettysburg: Thomas Publications, 1995.

Souder, Emily. *Leaves from the Battlefield of Gettysburg.* Philadelphia: Caxton Press of C. Sherman, Son & Co., 1864.

Stille, Charles J. *History of the United States Sanitary Commission.* Philadelphia: J.B. Lippincott, 1866.

Storrick, W. C. *Gettysburg: The Place, The Battles, The Outcome.* Harrisburg, Pa.: J. Horace McFarland Company, 1932.

Tagg, Larry. *The Generals of Gettysburg.* Campbell, Ca.: Savas Publishing Company, 1998.

United States Christian Commission, *Second Annual Report.* Philadelphia: United States Christian Commission, 1864.

_____. *Second Report of the Committee of Maryland.* Baltimore, Md.: Sherwood & Co., 1863.

The War of the Rebellion: A Compilation of the Official Records of the Union and Confederate Armies, 79 vols. in 128 parts. Washington, D.C.: Government Printing Office, 1880–1901.

Warner, Ezra J. *Generals in Gray.* Baton Rouge: Louisiana State University Press, 1959.

Warren, Horatio. *The Declaration of Independence and War History: Bull Run to the Appomattox.* Buffalo, N.Y.: Courier, 1890.

Wentz, Frederick K. "A Biography of the Schmucker House." *Lutheran Theological Seminary Bulletin: Gettysburg, Pennsylvania,* Vol. XXXVI, no. 2 (April 1956): 10–15.

_____. *Gettysburg Lutheran Theological Seminary, 1826–1965.* 2 vols. Harrisburg, Pa.: The Evangelical Press, 1965.

_____. *Pioneer in Christian Unity: Samuel Simon Schmucker.* Philadelphia: Fortress Press, 1967.

Woodward, Harold R., Jr. *Major General James Lawson Kemper, C. S. A.: The Confederacy's Forgotten Son.* Natural Bridge Station, Va.: Rockbridge Publishing Company, 1993.

Index

197